Classics in Child Development

BABIES AND THEIR MOTHERS
By D. W. Winnicott
Introduction by Benjamin Spock, M.D.

THE CHILD, THE FAMILY, AND THE OUTSIDE WORLD
By D. W. Winnicott
Introduction by Marshall H. Klaus, M.D.

TALKING TO PARENTS
By. D. W. Winnicott
Introduction by T. Berry Brazelton, M.D.

BIOGRAPHY OF A BABY
By Milicent Washburn Shinn
Introduction by T. Berry Brazelton, M.D.

THE LIVES OF CHILDREN
By George Dennison
Introduction by John Holt

CHILDREN'S SECRETS
By Thomas J. Cottle

THE CONTINUUM CONCEPT
By Jean Liedloff

THE SELF-RESPECTING CHILD
By Alison Stallibrass
Introduction by John Holt

HOW CHILDREN FAIL
By John Holt

HOW CHILDREN LEARN
By John Holt

BOOKS BY JOHN HOLT

□How Children □Learn

REVISED EDITION

JOHN HOLT

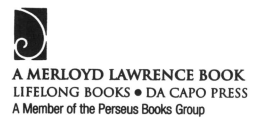

A MERLOYD LAWRENCE BOOK
LIFELONG BOOKS • DA CAPO PRESS
A Member of the Perseus Books Group

Many of the designations used by manufacturers and sellers to distinguish their products are claimed as trademarks. Where those designations appear in this book and Da Capo Press was aware of a trademark claim, the designations have been printed in initial capital letters (i.e., Cuisenaire).

Copyright © 1967, 1983 by John Holt

Cataloging-in-Publication data for this book is available from the Library of Congress.

Originally published in 1964 by Pitman Publishing Company, New York
Revised edition first published in 1982 by Merloyd Lawrence, Delta/Seymour Lawrence, New York.
ISBN 0–201–48404–8

Published by Da Capo Press
A Member of the Perseus Books Group
http://www.dacapopress.com

Da Capo Press books are available at special discounts for bulk purchases in the U.S. by corporations, institutions, and other organizations. For more information, please contact the Special Markets Department at the Perseus Books Group, 11 Cambridge Center, Cambridge, MA 02142, or call (800) 255-1514 or (617) 252-5298, or e-mail j.mccrary@perseusbooks.com.

☐ How
Children
☐ Learn

REVISED
EDITION

CONTENTS

PREFACE

How Children Fail described children using their minds
badly. This book tries to describe children—in a few
cases, adults—using their minds well, learning boldly and
effectively. Some of the children described are in school;
most are not yet old enough. It is before they get to school
that children are likely to do their best learning. Many experts agree that this is so, though they differ about the
reason. I believe, and try to show here, that in most situations our minds work best when we use them in a certain
way, and that young children tend to learn better than
grownups (and better than they themselves will when
they are older) because they use their minds in a special
way. In short, children have a style of learning that fits
their condition, and which they use naturally and well
until we train them out of it. We like to say that we send
children to school to teach them to think. What we do, all
too often, is to teach them to think badly, to give up a natural and powerful way of thinking in favor of a method
that does not work well for them and that we rarely use
ourselves.

Worse than that, we convince most of them that, at
least in a school setting, or any situation where
words or symbols or abstract thought are concerned,
they can't think at all. They think of themselves as

"stupid" and incapable of learning or understanding anything that is complicated, or hard, or simply new.

What are the results? Only a few children in school ever become good at learning in the way we try to make them learn. Most of them get humiliated, frightened, and discouraged. They use their minds, not to learn, but to get out of doing the things we tell them to do—to make them learn. In the short run, these strategies seem to work. They make it possible for many children to get through their schooling even though they learn very little. But in the long run, these strategies are self-limiting and self-defeating, and destroy both character and intelligence. The children who use such strategies are prevented by them from growing into more than limited versions of the human beings they might have become. This is the real failure that takes place in school; hardly any children escape.

When we better understand the ways, conditions, and spirit in which children do their best learning, and are able to make school into a place where they can use and improve the style of thinking and learning natural to them, we may be able to prevent much of this failure. School may then become a place in which *all* children grow, not just in size, not even in knowledge, but in curiosity, courage, confidence, independence, resourcefulness, resilience, patience, competence, and understanding. To find how best to do this will take us a long time. We may find, in fifty or a hundred years, that all of what we think of as our most up-to-date notions about schools, teaching, and learning are either completely inadequate or outright mistaken. But we will make a big step forward if, by understanding children better, we can undo some of the harm we are now doing.

All I am saying in this book can be summed up in two words—Trust Children. Nothing could be more simple—or more difficult. Difficult, because to trust children we must trust ourselves—and most of us were taught as children that we could not be trusted. And so we go on treating children as we ourselves were treated, calling this "reality," or saying bitterly, "If I could put up with it, they can too."

What we have to do is break this long downward cycle of fear and distrust, and trust children as we ourselves were not trusted. To do this will take a long leap of faith—but great rewards await any of us who will take that leap.

Since I wrote this book our schools have with few exceptions moved steadily and often rapidly in the wrong direction. Schools are on the whole bigger than they used to be, more depersonalized, more threatening, more dangerous. What they try to teach is even more fragmented than it was, what Professor Seymour Papert in *Mindstorms* calls "dissociated," i.e., not connected with anything else, and hence meaningless. Teachers have even less to say than they used to about what they teach and how they teach and test it. The schools cling more and more stubbornly to their mistaken idea that education and teaching are industrial processes, to be designed and planned from above in the minutest detail and then imposed on passive teachers and their even more passive students.

I recall something that at the time seemed less significant than it does now. During the late sixties, at the height of the so-called revolution in education (which in fact never took place), a prominent educator, after spending a few days at a big top-level conference on the future of education, said to me, "Those people weren't the least bit interested in alternative schools or open classrooms or any of that stuff. You know what they were *really* excited about? Something called behavior modification and behavioral objectives." It proved to be so. Fragmented learning became even more so, the weekly test became the daily or hourly or even the fifteen-minute test.

The Back to Basics era is now seven or eight years old, with, so far, mostly bad results. But this only leads the schools to say, "Now we're *really* going back to basics," as if that particular wheel had been invented only the day before yesterday.

In any case, I no longer believe we can make schools into places in which all children grow in the ways described above. An exception might be a few very specific kinds of schools, like schools of the dance, or computer programming, or flying. But on the whole I don't think children with any range of real choices in the world are going to want to spend much time in places where nothing but learning happens, and where the only adults they meet are child specialists whose job it is to watch them and make them do things.

This book is more concerned with describing effective learning than explaining it, or giving a theory about it. In many places people are busy trying to find out what goes on in the brain, electrically, chemically, and otherwise, when we think and learn. Such research is interesting and may prove to be useful, but it has nothing to do with the aims of this book. We do not need to learn more about the brain, as an organ, in order to make schools better. We could make them a great deal better, knowing no more about the brain than most people know right now. Thus it is interesting that people should be finding evidence that experiences are stored in the brain, in the shape of complicated molecules, like file cards stored in a file. What teachers and learners need to know is what we have known for some time: first, that vivid, vital, pleasurable experiences are the easiest to remember, and secondly, that memory works best when unforced, that it is not a mule that can be made to walk by beating it. It is interesting to read Wolfgang Köhler's theory, perhaps now held by many others, that electrical fields are set up in the brain when we perceive, think, and feel. This would certainly account for the fact that we think badly, and even perceive badly, or not at all, when we are anxious and afraid. But we don't need the explanation to know that the fact is a fact, and to learn from it that when we make children afraid we stop their learning dead in its tracks.

This book is more about children than about child psychology. I hope those who read it will come to feel, or feel more than when they opened it, that children are interesting and worth looking at. I hope that when they look they will notice many things they never noticed before, and in these find much food for thought. I want to whet their curiosity and sharpen their vision, even more than to add to their understanding; to make them skeptical of old dogmas, rather than give them new ones.

A friend said to me after reading this book, "I always was very fond of little children, especially my own. But until now I could never have imagined that they might be *interesting.*"

They interest me now even more than when I wrote this book. Watching babies and children explore and make sense of the world around them is for me one of the most exciting things in the world. I have watched them and been with them at many times and places, and I find not just more pleasure but much more food for serious thought in what they say and do than in the sayings and doings of a great many older people. Not to like little children, or find them interesting and enjoy their company, is no crime. But it is surely a great misfortune and a great loss, like having no legs or being deaf or blind.

The human mind, after all, is a mystery, and, in large part, will probably always be so. It takes even the most thoughtful, honest, and introspective person many years to learn even a small part of what goes on in his own mind. How, then, can we be sure about what goes on in the mind of another? Yet many people talk as if we could measure and list the contents of another person's mind as easily, accurately, and fully as the contents of a suitcase. This is not to say that we ought not to try to understand more about other people's minds and thoughts, but only that we must be very modest and tentative about what we think we have found out.

There's an old story about two men on a train. One of them, seeing some naked-looking sheep in a field, said, "Those sheep have just been sheared." The other looked a moment longer, and then said, "They seem to be—on this side." It is in such a cautious spirit that we should say whatever we have to say about the workings of the mind, and it is in this spirit that I have tried to write, and in which I hope others will read, this book.

☐ LEARNING ABOUT CHILDREN

In the early sixties, when I wrote much of the original *How Children Learn,* few psychologists were paying close attention to the learning of very young children. As a field of research it was not important or well known—or in some places even respectable—precisely the reason why a friend of mine at a major university, who wanted to do a Ph.D. thesis on the work of Piaget, was told by his thesis adviser that he could not do so. And even Piaget himself, except perhaps for his own children, did most of his work with children four or five years old and older. Babies were still seen mostly as blobs, waiting for time to begin to turn them into people worthy of serious attention.

Now all this is changed. The study of very young children, their view of the world, their powers and abilities, and their learning, has become a very important field in psychology. Everyone agrees that we should know much more than we do about young children, and how they perceive the world, and live, grow, and learn within it. The question is, how to do so.

Many think the best way to do this is by doing direct research on the brain itself. Some of this was going on when I wrote the Foreword to this book; much more is going on now. So far, it has still had little effect on schools. Thus, one theory now much in fashion is the right-brain left-brain theory, which holds that for some kinds of thinking we use one side of our brain, while for other kinds we use the other. People who want to change schools try to use the theory as an argument. So far, they have not had much success. Thus, people who, because they liked or believed in art, have tried for years to get more of it in the schools, now say that we need it in order to develop the right side of children's brains. But the people who always wanted art out of the schools are no more impressed by the right-brain argument in its favor than they were by any other. They still want it out. It seems unlikely that in any near future schools will be much changed because of this or any other new theories about the workings of the brain.

For one thing, the theories themselves change faster than we can keep up with them. In a recent issue of *Omni* magazine an article called "Brainstorms" tells us that the still new right-left brain theory has already been disproved and that different kinds of mental activities cannot be precisely located in either one side or the other. The article says, in part:

Alan Gevins, director of the EEG Systems Laboratory at Langley Porter Neuropsychiatric Institute at the University of California School of Medicine, in San Francisco, says, "What we're doing now is to try to develop a new way of imaging the functional electrical activity of the brain, to see things that couldn't be seen before." Electrical patterns never before seen in such detail have suddenly become coherent schematic designs. . . . The people at the EEG Systems Lab are now working to perfect their 64-channel EEG scalp recording helmet, which will allow them to carry out even more advanced types of computerized signal processing of the brain's functional electricity.... The long-term results of their line of research could virtual-ly open a door into the brain, admitting its user for the first time to look in on his own "wiring.".....

But a few days at the EEG Systems Lab made it obvious to me that, *as in so much of science,* [em-phasis added] the lab's new research ... was con-cerned with a subtle and complex series of experiments that would appear almost as incom-prehensible to most of us as a tablet of ancient Su-merian trade regulations.

What happened to the old idea that a central task of science was to make the world *more* comprehensi-ble? Back to the lab:

By careful design of their test conditions, and by using mathematical pattern-recognition analysis, they have charted rapidly changing, complex cor-relations of electrical patterns, involving many areas of the brain.... This suggests to them that different types of information are not processed in only a few specialized areas of the brain, as has been a theory for decades. Rather, many regions of the brain are involved, even in the most elemen-tary cognitive functions.

In a study of 23 persons, the lab initially con-firmed the hypothesis that writing sentences [etc.] ... did indeed seem to be more associated with ei-ther the right or the left side of the brain. But by looking closer with the mathematical pattern rec-ognizer, they failed to see any significant differ-ences in electrical activity between the tests in which the participants were writing paragraphs or those in which they were just scribbling.... So they went back and wired up 32 more willing par-ticipants.... The researchers saw that hemispheric differences between tasks in the EEG "spectra" disappeared entirely. Instead, they witnessed rather uniform patterns involving many areas of both hemispheres. "This suggested," Gevins states, "that different types of tasks are not processed in a few specialized areas but that many widely dispersed areas of the brain are involved. So it is not correct to say that arithmetic, for example, is located in one place just because damage there results in an inability to add numbers. All you can say is that the damaged area is critical for doing arithmetic."

If I am doubtful of the value of this kind of research, as indeed I am, it is not because in this case I don't agree with its findings. I agree with them very strongly, and would be happy to see them confirmed by later research. From the first the right-left brain theory seemed to make far too simple what my own experience as a mind user told me was not simple at all. There is of course no doubt that we do indeed use our minds in different ways, sometimes a very conscious, directed, linear, analytical, verbal way—as when the car won't start and we try to figure out why—at other times (and perhaps even sometimes at the same time) much more randomly, inclusively (many things at once), intuitively, often sub- or unconsciously. We "hear" sounds, "see" images, experience directly our mental models of reality rather than any verbal or mathematical descriptions of them. We let our minds roam freely, keeping ourselves open to whatever they may tell us.

So far I have no quarrel with the brain theorists. It is even possible that some kinds of mental activity may be largely centered in some parts of the brain, and other kinds in others. But it would be simpleminded and silly to say that all the complicated varieties of thought, of mental experience, can be neatly separated into two kinds and that one of these can be exclusively assigned to the left side of the brain, the other to the right. When I say that I am sometimes surprised by what my mind tells me, I am talking about a very common experience. But where in my brain is the "my mind" who does the telling, where the "me" who is surprised?

The idea used to be that the "me," the conscious observer, was in a kind of upstairs, in the living room maybe, while "the mind" was down somewhere in the (often dark and dirty) basement. Has right-left brain theory merely shifted the old upstairs "me" over to the left brain and the old basement "mind" over to the right? How then do I account for this experience, well known to us all, that a name which I have been consciously and unsuccessfully struggling to remember will suddenly pop into consciousness, the awareness of the "me," while that "me" is thinking about something else? In right-left brain theory, it is the left brain that is supposed to be the maker, keeper, and rememberer of lists. What of the fact that often, while thinking of something else, I will find that "my mind" has suddenly presented "me" with a complete sentence, sometimes even two or three, which "I" like so much that I rush to write them down before I forget them? "I" have certainly not produced those sentences in the way I am now producing these sentences on the typewriter, thinking about what words to use or where to put them. On which side of my brain is the producer of these sentences, on which side the observer, critic, editor who judges them to be good?

The right-left brain theorists, at least the more modest of them (some are far from modest), might say, "We're not trying to say that every kind of thinking can be clearly assigned to either the left or the right brain, but only that certain kinds of thoughts can. So we give our subjects simple tasks and see where the electrical squiggles turn up." The problem—as I've said for years—is that it is hardly ever possible to separate what we think about something from how we feel about it. It is dangerously simple-minded for any brain researcher (or other psychologist) to suppose that when as part of his experiment he gives us some "simple" task to do we are not thinking about anything except that task. Chances are we are thinking about many other things—why does he want me to do this, am I doing it right, am I being a good subject in this experiment, will he ask me back, what will happen if I do it wrong, will I mess up his data, what is this for, anyway? and so on.

The problem with all such research and researchers is that, even with sixty-four-channel helmets, the data is so crude compared to the activity. The living mind probably processes (to use their way of talking) many hundreds of thousands, perhaps millions of bits of information every second. Making judgments about how the mind or the brain (they're not the same) works on the basis of a few (or even sixty-four) squiggles on a chart is like deciding what lives in the ocean by lowering and then pulling up a five-gallon bucket and seeing what you can find in it. Nor is the situation much improved by using bigger buckets. You won't find out that way. Learning about the mind is a lot more like learning about the ocean than figuring out how to start a car. The only way we will ever learn much about it—and even this will be highly incomplete and uncertain—will be to dive, swim about, and see what we can see in the deep waters of our own thoughts.

There is another very profoundly mistaken assumption in all this research: that from what we can learn about people in a very limited, unusual, and often very anxious situation we can make reliable judgments about what they do in very different and more usual situations.

During the sixties a famous educational psychologist decided to do some research into how children look at things, in what kinds of patterns they scan unfamiliar objects. One of his team designed what they called an "eye camera." While the subjects looked at pictures put before them, the eye camera, only a few inches away, shone a fine beam of light at their eyeballs and took a series of photographs of its reflection. The idea was that these photographs of tiny dots of light would tell the researchers which way the eyes had been pointing from instant to instant. From this the researchers were supposed to be able to figure out the patterns in which the eyes moved as the subjects looked at the test pictures.

Since it was essential that the subjects not move their heads while these photos were being taken, the researchers attached to the subjects' chairs U-shaped bars of flat metal, into which the subjects were supposed to push their heads until the bar clamped them very firmly at the temples. Since they might still move their heads a little up and down, another piece of metal was put before them, the "bite bar." As the subjects pushed their heads as far as they could into the U-shaped clamp, they were also supposed to open their mouths, let the bite bar (covered with cardboard) go in, and then bite down hard on it, so that their heads could not move in any direction.

But, as anyone who knew anything about children could have predicted, more than half of those who were to be the subjects in these experiments were so frightened by the strange look of the apparatus that they would not go near it. Some bolder ones would go so far as to put their heads into the U-shaped clamp, but about half of these could not put the bite bar into their mouths and bite down on it without gagging. Only a small fraction of the children who were brought in to do the experiment could in fact go through with it. The question which naturally follows—and one cannot but wonder about the competence of the researchers who failed to ask it—is, What in the world could one possibly expect to learn about how children normally look at real objects in the real world from an experiment done under such artificial and threatening circumstances?"

The Scottish psychiatrist R. D. Laing has for years written angrily and eloquently about these kinds of distortions and perversions of the "scientific method," as he has seen them in his own lifetime of training and work in medicine and psychiatry. In a recent book, *The Facts Of Life,* in a chapter called "The Scientific Method and Us," he writes:

> The scientific method is based on tampering with what would be happening if we were doing nothing to it.
>
> *Scientific* interference is the most destructive interference. Only a scientist knows *how* to interfere most destructively.
>
> Love reveals *facts* which, without it, remain undisclosed.
>
> A heartless intellect can do no other than investigate the hell of its own hellish constructions by its own hellish instruments and methods, and to describe, in the language of hell, its own hellish conclusions.

These strong words are well justified by what Laing tell us in this book and others about what modern doctors and psychiatrists actually write, say, and do. He later quotes a leading American psychologist as writing, in what was generally judged an extremely important book:

> Everything we learn of organisms leads us to conclude not merely that they are analogous to machines but that they are machines. Man-made machines are not brains, but brains are a very ill-understood variety of computing machines.

I disagree flatly with that sentence on the face of it. Everything *I* learn of organisms, *including what these people tell me,* leads me to conclude that they are not like machines at all. One famous experiment with rats showed that their behavior changed markedly for the worse in almost every respect when they were crowded into a small space. Other experiments with rats showed that their performance on tasks could be strongly affected by how their human handlers felt about them; rats who had been described to their handlers as smart performed better than *identical* rats described to their handlers as dumb. Do machines get nervous and break down when we put a lot of them in one room? Do they work better if we talk nicely to them? Some might say that we could someday design computers that would do that. I doubt it very much. But even if we could, the fact that we might make certain machines a little more like animals does not prove in the least that organisms are, or even are like, machines.

This notion, now very popular in leading universities, that organisms, including human beings, are nothing but machines, is for me one of the most mistaken, foolish, harmful, and dangerous of all the many bad ideas at large in the world today. If an idea can be evil, this one surely is.

Enough of this corrupted view of science and of human beings. Let us look instead at some good science, specifically the work of the American biologist Millicent Washburn Shinn, whose book *The Biography of a Baby* was published by Houghton Mifflin in 1900, and very briefly put back into print by Arno Press a few years ago. The baby was her niece Ruth, who comes to life so vividly in the book that it is hard to believe that she is not a baby or little child somewhere right now, instead of, if she still lives, a woman in her eighties. About how and why she wrote her book, Millicent Shinn said:

Most studies of children deal with later childhood, the school years, and these are almost always statistical in their method, taking the individual child very little into account. My own study has been of babyhood, and its method has been biographical, that of watching one baby's development, day by day, and recording it.

I am often asked if the results one gets in this way are not misleading, since each child might differ greatly from others. One must, of course, use great caution in drawing general conclusions from a single child, but in many things all babies are alike, and one learns to perceive pretty well which are the things. Babyhood is mainly taken up with the development of the large, general racial powers; individual differences are less important than in later childhood. And the biographical method of child study has the inestimable advantage of showing the process of evolution going on, the actual unfolding of one stage out of another, and the steps by which the changes come about. No amount of comparative statistics could give this. If I should find out that a thousand babies learned to stand at an average age of forty-six weeks and two days, I should not know as much that is important about standing, as a stage in human progress, as I should after watching a single baby carefully through the whole process of achieving balance on his little soles.

Perhaps I should say a word here as to the way in which I came to make a baby biography, for I am often asked how one should go to work at it. It was not done in my case for any scientific purpose, for I did not feel competent to make observations of scientific value. But I had for years desired an opportunity to see the wonderful unfolding of human powers out of the limp helplessness of the newborn baby; to watch this fascinating drama of evolution daily, minutely, and with an effort to understand as far as I could, for my own pleasure and information. . . .

There is one question that I have been asked a hundred times about baby biography: "Doesn't it do the children some harm? Doesn't it make them nervous? Doesn't it make them self-conscious?" At first this seemed to me an odd misapprehension— as if people supposed observing children meant doing something to them. But I have no doubt it could be so foolishly managed as to harm the child. There are thousands of parents who tell anecdotes about children before their faces every day in the year, and if such a parent turns child student it is hard to say what he may not do in the way of dissecting a child's mind openly, questioning the little one about himself, and experimenting with his thoughts and feelings. *But such observing is as worthless scientifically as it is bad for the child: the whole value of an observation is gone as soon as the phenomena observed lose simplicity and spontaneity* [emphasis added]. It should be unnecessary to say that no competent observer tampers with the child in any way.... If I sit by the window and catch with my pencil my niece's prattle as she plays about below—and if [she] afterward turns out spoiled, the mischief must be credited to some other agency than the silent notebook.

In 1980 there was published a book which Millicent Shinn would have rejoiced to read, as I have— *Gnys at Wrk,* by Glenda Bissex (Cambridge: Harvard University Press, 1980). At the start of the Preface, she writes:

This is an account of one child learning to read and write, from the beginning of literacy at age five up to age eleven.

When I began taking notes about my infant son's development, I did not know I was gathering "data" for "research"; I was a mother with a propensity for writing things down. Because of my experience in Courtney Casden's Child Language course at Harvard, I was particularly interested in my son's language development; and as an English teacher just retrained in reading, I wanted to observe his learning to read. When Paul started spelling, I was amazed and fascinated. Only somewhat later did I learn of Charles Read's research on children's invented spelling. Excited by his work, I started seeing my notes as "data." ...

What I hope this study offers, rather than generalizations to be "applied" to other children, is encouragement to look at individuals in the act of learning. And I do mean *act,* with all that implies of drama and action....

At the beginning, Paul was an unconscious subject, unaware of the significance of my tape recorder and notebook. When he first became aware, at about age six, he was pleased by my interest and attention. By seven, he had become an observer of his own progress. When I worked on my initial analysis of the first year's data (5:1–6:1) and had Paul's early writings spread out on my desk, he loved to look at them with me and try to read them. They offered the challenge of breaking what then appeared to him a code, and their visible evidence of his progress since he had written them gave him a sense of achievement. "I notice I didn't know about silent *e*'s then," he once observed (7:8). About this same time Paul had observed me writing down a question he had asked about spelling, and I inquired how he felt about my writing it down. "Then I know that when I'm older I can see the stuff I asked when I was little," he commented.

At eight he was self-conscious enough to object to obvious observation and note taking, which I then stopped. One day when I was making informal observations of his laterality, he looked at my notebook to see what I was putting down, and said, "I don't like to be charted in everything I do." (8:0) Paul still brought his writings (except personal ones) to me, sharing my sense of their importance. At nine he became a participant in the research, interested in thinking about *why* he had written or read things as he once had. When I speculated aloud that his early oral reading had been aimed at receiving adult feedback and correction, he argued instead that *he* needed to hear the sounds in order to know if they were right.

The study has become a special bond between us, an interest we share in each other's work, a mutual enjoyment of Paul's early childhood and of his growing up. I have come to appreciate certain qualities in my son that I might not have seen except through the eyes of this study.

In 1960, when I first began writing notes about Lisa, I did not think of myself as collecting data, or doing research, or getting ready to write a book. I was a charmed and delighted adult with (like Mrs. Bissex) "a propensity for writing things down," in the form of letters to friends or notes to myself, of which I sometimes later sent copies to friends. I had no thought at first of making these letters and notes into a book, and indeed when my friend Peggy Hughes first suggested to me that I could and should do so, the idea seemed impossible and absurd.

As a result of my experience as a teacher of teen-agers and ten-year-olds, and as a friend of the many children of my sisters and of many of my other friends, I had come to feel and to hope that from very young children I might learn some interesting and important things about children's learning. In the spring of that same year, in the school where I taught fifth grade, I had spent as much time as I could, in the early morning before school officially began, with the nursery school group of three-year-olds. But Lisa was even younger, only one and a half, and I had never before had a chance to spend so much time with a child so young. So I was enormously interested in everything she did, and every day more astonished and delighted by her skill, patience, industry, intelligence, and seriousness. If I looked at her closely, it was not with the eye and feelings of someone looking at a specimen through a microscope, but more in the spirit in which I looked every day that summer at the snow-covered Colorado mountains across the valley—a mixture of interest, pleasure, excitement, awe, and wonder. I was watching, and in some small way taking part in, a miracle.

But let me return again to the world of modern, big-money, "value-free" (as they say) science—in this case, the brain research lab described before. In my mind's ear is the humane and sensible voice of Millicent Shinn saying, as if it were so obvious that it hardly even needed to be said, " ... as if people supposed that observing children meant doing something to them." Or "The whole value of an observation is gone as soon as the phenomena observed lose simplicity and spontaneity." Or, most bitterly ironical of all, "It should be unnecessary to say that no competent observer tampers with the child in any way."

The article describing the brain research goes on:

> While the participant, wired to the gills, is pressing the pressure-sensitive transducer at numbers and arrows, the EEG polygraph is recording conventionally; the oscilloscope is oscillating conventionally; the brainwave information is being fed into the computer, where the average evoked potential is being averaged conventionally, narrowing down the range of scrutiny.... The focus is on "time windows," defined by the average evoked potential's components, and then the scientists zero in on the wave pattern interrelationships all over the brain during each single task trial. At the heart of this analysis is the advanced mathematical pattern-recognition they call SAM. This program compares the similarity of wave shapes between the different areas and extracts the tiny task-related signals from the obscuring noise.

And so on. This is indeed, as Laing says, the language of hell, of intellect without heart, run wild. To be sure, these researchers are not hurting or harming their subjects, who so far, at least, seem to be adult middle-class volunteers. But this may very well change if someone decides one day that it will be useful and important, or perhaps only interesting, to find out what happens to these patterns when the subject is experiencing pain. After all, more than a few scientists in this country have done dangerous research on human beings, often prisoners, or poor nonwhites, without getting their informed consent—one such very extensive program was the subject of a recent book. In the fields of nuclear power and genetic research, where reputations, Nobel prizes, and now large fortunes are at stake, we hear much talk about "acceptable risks," as if it were morally acceptable to bring sickness or death to considerable numbers of people as long as you couldn't be sure which ones they were—like standing blindfolded in the middle of a crowded stadium and firing a machine gun at random into the crowd.

In *The New Yorker* (December 14, 1981) a physicist, Jeremy Bernstein, wrote a long profile of Professor Marvin Minsky, one of the leading researchers into what they call "artificial intelligence." Here he quotes approvingly some of Minsky's observations on free will:

> Our everyday intuitive models of higher human activity are quite incomplete, and many notions in our informal explanations do not tolerate close examination. Free will or volition is one such notion; people are incapable of explaining how it differs from stochastic caprice but feel strongly that it does. I conjecture that this idea has its genesis in a strong primitive defense mechanism. Briefly, in childhood we learn to recognize various forms of aggression and compulsion and to dislike them, whether we submit or resist. Older, when told that our behavior is "controlled" by such-and-such a set of laws, we insert this fact in our model (inappropriately) along with other recognizers of compulsion. . . . Although resistance is logically futile, the

resentment persists and is rationalized by defective explanations, since the alternative is emotionally unacceptable.

This slippery little paragraph demonstrates clearly and often the logical fallacy known as "begging the question," i.e., taking as already proven the thing you are trying to prove. Thus, who says our behavior is in fact "controlled"? Who says these "laws" are laws at all, let alone what they are? Who says it's a "fact"? It's not a fact at all, but an inference, a hypothesis, in this case little more than a wild guess. And so on, and so on. Minsky goes on in the same vein: "When intelligent machines are constructed," he says, again begging the important question of whether intelligence, as we understand it in people, *can* be ascribed to a machine,

we should not be surprised to find them as confused and stubborn as men in their convictions about mind-matter, consciousness, free will, and the like. For all such questions are pointed at explaining the complicated interactions between parts of the self-model. A man's or a machine's strength of conviction about such things tells us nothing about the man or about the machine except what it tells us about his model of himself.

What is most terrible and terrifying about this cool, detached, witty voice—for Minsky is clearly not only brilliant but interesting and amusing—is the contempt it expresses for the deepest feelings we humans have about ourselves. His argument is a perfect example of what Laing, in *The Politics of Experience,* called "the invalidation of experience." In the words quoted above Minsky tells us that our strongest and most vivid experiences of ourselves are not real and not true, and tell us nothing about ourselves and others except our own delusions, and that in any case he and his colleagues will soon make machines that will "feel about themselves" exactly as we do. His message could be summed up, You cannot learn anything about yourself from your own experience, but must believe whatever we experts tell you.

In *The Facts of Life* Laing quotes a distraught woman as asking the head of her philosophy department, "If I do not feel I exist, why should I not kill myself?" By "exist" she meant, of course, exist as something *other and more than* a machine. Her question was dismissed as trivial. But it is the farthest thing in the world from trivial. If we do not feel that we exist and that our existence is somehow important, why indeed should we not kill ourselves—and everyone else, and all unborn generations as well—which we seem to be getting ready to do.

To return for the last time to the article about brain research, there is a photograph in it of one of the subjects, a seated woman, wearing a scalp recording helmet; behind her, adjusting it, a white-coated scientist; in the foreground, another scientist, taking notes. The subject is bathed in a red light, the note-taking scientist in a blue one. The effect is frightening, like a scene from a horror science-fiction movie. To this the lab people might protest, "Oh, come on, now, we don't actually work under those red and blue lights. The magazine just threw them in to make an exciting picture." Sure, fine. But why did the magazine want such a picture? And since it is false, a lie, why did the lab people allow it? Because it makes science look like a powerful and forbidding mystery, not for the likes of you and me. Because it tells us that only people with expensive and incomprehensible machines can discover the truth, about human beings or anything else, and that we must believe whatever they tell us. Because it turns science from an activity to be done into a commodity to be bought. Because it prevents ordinary human beings from being the scientists, the askers of questions and seekers and makers of answers that we naturally and rightfully are, and makes us instead into science consumers and science worshipers.

This may not seem to have much to do with children and how they learn, and how we may learn how they learn. But in fact it has everything in the world to do with it. It is only in the presence of loving, respectful, trusting adults like Millicent Shinn or Glenda Bissex that children will learn all they are capable of learning, or reveal to us what they are learning. The tinkerers, dissectors, and manipulators will only drive children into artificial behavior, if not actual deception, evasion, and retreat. It is not so much a matter of technique as of spirit. The difference between fond and delighted parents playing "This Little Piggy Went to Market" with their laughing baby's toes and two anxious home-based would-be clinicians giving "tactile stimulation" to those same toes, so that the child will one day be smarter than other children and thus get into the best colleges, may not on the face of it seem to be very much. But in fact it is the difference between night and day. Of two ways of looking at children now growing in fashion—seeing them as monsters of evil who must be beaten into submission, or as little two-legged walking computers whom we can program into genuises, it is hard to know which is worse, and will do more harm. I write this book to oppose them both.

□GAMES &
EXPERIMENTS

I am sitting on a friend's terrace. Close by is Lisa, sixteen months old, a bright and bold child. She has invented a very varied pseudo-speech which she uses all the time. Some sounds she says over and over again, as if she meant something by them. She likes to touch and handle things, and is surprisingly dexterous; she can fit screws and similar small objects into the holes meant for them. Can it be that little children are less clumsy than we have always supposed?

One of Lisa's favorite games is to take my ball point pen out of my pocket, take the top off, and then put it on again. This takes some skill. She never tires of the game; if she sees me with the pen in my pocket, she lets me know right away that she wants it. There is no putting her off. She is stubborn, and if I pretend—which is a lie— not to know what she wants, she makes a scene. The trick, when I know I will need to use my pen, is to have an extra one hidden in a pocket.

The other day she was playing on the piano, hitting out more or less at random with both hands, pleased to be working the machine, and making such an interesting noise. Curious to see whether she would imitate me, I bounced up and down the keyboard with my index finger. She watched, then did the same.

☐ August 11, 1960

Yesterday I had the portable electric typewriter on the terrace. The older children were looking at it and using it. Lisa was busy eating an ice cream cone and, for a while at least, was not interested. When the cone was gone, however, she came to see what the others were doing, and soon asked, by sounds and signs, to be picked up and given a chance. So I sat her on my lap in front of the machine. Having seen me poke at the keys, one finger at a time, she did the same, and seemed pleased by what happened—something flew through the air and made a sharp click, and there was a general impression of activity and motion, and mysterious things going on inside the machine, things that she was making happen.

Now and then she would hit more than one key at a time, and keys would get stuck. I would then turn off the machine and straighten them out. After seeing me turn the rotary On-Off switch a few times, she tried to turn it herself, but her fingers weren't strong enough. When this happened, she reached down, took my right hand, brought it up to the switch, and made me work it. Soon we had a good game going. I would turn off the typewriter; she would try for a while to turn it back on; then she would take my hand and make me do it.

She also liked the carriage-return lever. Each time I returned the carriage for a new line, she would take hold of the lever and give it one more push. Only rarely did she get excited and begin to slam and bang on the keys. Once she showed me that she wanted me to put the typewriter on the ground. I did so, but soon saw that this was a mistake; she wanted to climb on and even into it, to see what was really going on inside. After a bit of an argument and tussle I got it back up on the table. We were busy with all this for about forty minutes. Perhaps the attention span of infants is not as short as we think.

Today, with her elder brother more or less in charge,

Lisa was in more of a banging mood, and often slapped the keyboard with her hands. Each time she did this, we turned the machine off and carefully unscrambled the stuck keys. Since this slowed up the action, I thought it might in time show her that it was not a good idea to slap the keyboard. But it was also interesting for her to watch us unstick the keys. After this had happened a number of times, I suggested to her brother that next time she piled the keys up we turn off the machine and just wait to see what she would do. We did so. She poked a key or two, but nothing happened. Then, seeming to notice that the machine was not making its usual busy hum, she reached up herself and pulled back the stuck keys.

> Something else happened here that I forgot to write about at the time. I spoke of turning off the machine when Lisa jammed the keys. In order to do this I had to stand close to the typewriter, to be able to reach the On-Off switch. But Lisa did not like me hovering over her as she worked, and I did not like it either—I wanted her to be free to give all her attention to the machine. I solved this particular problem by plugging the typewriter into a long extension cord that had an On-Off switch in it. With this I could stand well behind Lisa, completely out of her sight, yet still turn off the machine instantly whenever the keys jammed. Then I would come forward, free up the keys, and then turn the machine back on.
>
> But Lisa was not fooled by this arrangement for very long. For a while she may have been willing to take it as a mysterious coincidence that when the keys jammed the machine went off. But it didn't take her very long to figure out that *I* must have something to do with the machine stopping when the keys jammed, and going on again when they were free. Before very long, every time I turned off the machine—I should add that my On–Off switch was very

quiet—she would turn around and look at me with a puzzled expression. I kept up the illusion that I had nothing to do with the machine going off; that is, I did not show her the extension cord switch. If I had it to do again I think I would have shown her the switch, though that too had its risks—she was a very fierce and stubborn little child, and might have become angry with me for turning the machine on and off. As I have since learned very well, little children strongly dislike being given more help than they ask for.

It amuses me now to read how astonished I was then to realize how intelligent small children were, how patient, skillful, and resourceful, how thoroughly capable of doing many things that experts assured us they could not do. It is not news any more that babies are smart; sometimes it seems as if half the psychologists in the country are bending over babies' cribs and "discovering" there what loving and observant mothers have always known. But in 1960 this was private knowledge, not public.

□ July 24, 1961

This morning Lisa bent down to pick up a balloon, and as she did a puff of wind coming through the door blew the balloon across the floor. She watched it go. When it stopped, she moved close to it, and blew at it, as if to make it go farther. This surprised me. Can such young children make a connection between the ability of the wind to move objects, and their own ability to move them by blowing on them? Apparently they can.

> This seems to me a good example of the kind of abstract thinking that many people tell us children cannot do until they are at least nine or ten.

One game almost all babies seem to like is to have you blow across their hands or fingers, moving your head from side to side so that the airstream moves back and forth. They smile; then after a while they begin to investigate where this mysterious stuff is coming from, and try to poke a finger into your mouth. They find it interesting that you can get a similar effect by fanning them with a fan, or piece of cardboard.

Later, Lisa walked round and round the balloon, singing, more or less, her own version of "Ring-around-a-rosie." As she sang it, she began to change it, until before long it had become an entirely different song. Much of what she says, sings, and does is like this; it starts out as one thing and gradually turns into another. A musician might call it variations on a theme.

Many other little children I have known love to tell endless stories and sing endless songs. Sometimes the song is about what they did or would like to do. A mother told me that her four-year-old boy, whose seven-year-old sister was in school, began one day, alone in his room, to chant a song about, "I wish I had a sister, who didn't have to go to school, and would do everything I say...." Often the song is nonsensical, words and nonsense syllables; sometimes sense and nonsense are mixed. Many children like to play a game with a grownup in which each takes turns adding something to the song. It is not as easy as it sounds. Trying to make up words and music at the same time is a strain on the imagination, and what comes out is usually no better than what the child does, and, as a rule, very much like it.

These are good games, and we might do well to encourage them, pay attention to them, take part in them, both at home and in school.

Children first going to school do a lot of singing, to be sure; but they all sing the same songs, taught and led by the teacher, and the aim is to get them "right," not to make up something new. Some children like this and get good at it; for others, it just becomes one more of those things that you have to do in school—compulsory fun, as so much of early school is. Many of these children become non-singers, a needless waste. The work of Carl Orff and others who have used his method of instruction suggests that when children are given many opportunities to improvise, to make up their own chants, rhythms, and tunes, their musical and verbal growth can be very rapid.

> I have since come to feel very strongly, partly from my experience in music and my own work on the cello (about which I wrote in *Never Too Late*), partly from the little I know of music history, that improvisation lies at the very heart of all music making and should be a central part of every kind of music instruction. Much of my own time on the cello I spend improvising in different ways, and if I were teaching cello or any kind of instrument to children or adults, I would urge them to spend some of their time doing the same: either trying to play by ear tunes they know, or thinking up tunes in their mind and trying to play them, or simply moving their hands around the fingerboards or keyboards, with no conscious plan, just hearing whatever notes come out.
>
> In other words, there can be varying amounts of conscious control in improvising. At one extreme, we try to make our muscles play the tunes, other people's or our own, that we hear in our minds. At the other, we let our hands move on their own, and listen to and think about what they bring to us. It is when our muscles, hands, and fingers can improvise with the least conscious control that we are most truly improvising and have the most natural and effortless control of our instruments.
>
> Little children do this when they are singing their charming endless made-up songs. They are not first

hearing a tune in their minds and then trying to sing
it. They are simply singing, and letting whatever
comes out, come out. We ought to encourage them in
this, and do more of it ourselves.

☐ July 25, 1961

Cries from the living room announce a new collision between Lisa and the institution of private property. She is
interested in everything she sees, wants to examine it,
handle it, test it, take it apart if she can. Naturally, she
has no sense of what is valuable, or fragile, or dangerous.
Having seen me plug in the electric typewriter, she was
eager to plug it in herself, and fiercely resented being told
that she was not to fool around with electric sockets. The
other day she managed to turn on all the burners on top of
the stove, fortunately far enough so that the pilot light
was able to light them. She did not like being told to leave
the stove alone. It's impossible for her to see why she
should not be allowed to touch what everyone else touches. When she takes things, she never thinks to put them
back where she got them—even if she could remember
where she got them.

There is no very good or easy answer to this problem.
Every day we find ourselves saying, "No, no, don't touch
that, it's too hot, it's too sharp, it will hurt you, it will
break, it belongs to me, I need it." Each time she feels,
naturally, that we are attacking her right and need to investigate every part of the world around her so that she
may make some sense out of it. Everyone else touches
this; why can't I? It is easy to see how too much of such
treatment could destroy a child's curiosity, and make him
or her feel that the world, instead of being full of interesting things to explore and think about, is full of hidden
dangers and ways of getting into trouble.

We try to solve the problem by giving Lisa toys of her

own, and telling her to leave other things alone. This doesn't work very well. For one thing, the toys aren't interesting enough. For another, she can't remember, even if she wants to, what she is free to touch, and what not. Most important, it is the fact that older and bigger people use various objects around the house that makes these objects so interesting. Like all little children, Lisa wants to be like the big people, and do what they do. When dishes are being washed, she demands to be allowed to help. When cooking is going on, she wants to cook; when lemonade is being made, she wants to help make it. And she will not be put off by obviously phony substitutes.

It is hard not to feel that there must be something very wrong with much of what we do in school, if we feel the need to worry so much about what many people call "motivation." A child has no stronger desire than to make sense of the world, to move freely in it, to do the things that he sees bigger people doing. Why can't we make more use of this great drive for understanding and competence? Surely we can find more ways to let children see people using some of the skills we want them to acquire—though this will be difficult when in fact those skills, like many of the "essential" skills of arithmetic, are not really *used* to do anything. Who, in real life, divides one fraction by another?

Meanwhile, at home, we should try to keep out of reach, and even out of sight, valuable or dangerous objects that we don't want children to touch. At the same time, we should keep on hand a good many objects cheap and durable enough so that a child can touch them and use them; we shouldn't have to worry if they get broken. Maybe certain ordinary household objects would be good presents for small children: an eggbeater, a saucepan, a flashlight. After all, it doesn't make much sense, in a family that will later spend tens of thousands of dollars on the child's education, to get upset, and to upset him because he or she may ruin something worth twenty-five cents. I have so often seen people in drugstores and supermarkets, where there is very little that children could spoil or break, and where anything the children did break would hardly cost over a dollar, get all upset because the children are touching, feeling, picking up the various things they see. Why not? This is how they learn about them. If they move things out of their proper places, it's easy enough to put them back.

It is probably a mistake, anyway, to assume that whatever little children touch they will destroy, and that we must therefore keep them from touching anything that is not theirs. This dampens their curiosity and confidence. More than that, it probably makes them too fiercely possessive of what is their own. We should try instead, I think, to teach that respecting property does not mean never touching what is not yours, but means treating objects carefully, using them as they are meant to be used, and putting them back where they belong. Children are perfectly able to learn these things; they are less clumsy and destructive than we suppose. And it is only by handling and using objects that children can learn the right way to handle them. One of Maria Montessori's many valuable contributions to education was that she showed that very little children could easily be taught to move, not just exuberantly, but also deftly, precisely, gently.

□ **July 30, 1961**

Little children love games, and can make them out of anything. This morning Lisa was in bed with her older sister, Nell. First Nell would turn out the light over the bed; then Lisa would turn it back on, saying, "Don't turn it off." The older girl would move her hand slowly, slowly toward the light. Every time the hand moved, Lisa would say, "Don't turn it off." This could be dragged out a long time. Finally, off would go the light. Lisa would then turn it on and the game would start again.

A lot of the games little children play begin as if by accident. One day I took a magazine across the room, put it on a table, and went to do something else. Lisa went to the table, took the magazine off, put it on the floor, and then looked meaningfully at me. I went back and put it on the table. She took it off. Soon we had a fine game going, which lasted for some time.

The spirit behind such games should be a spirit of joy, foolishness, exuberance, like the spirit behind all good games, including the game of trying to find out how the world works, which we call education.

> I'm afraid this is not what most people understand by the word "education." They understand it as being made to go to a place called school, and there being made to learn something they don't much want to learn, under the threat that bad things will be done to them if they don't. Needless to say, most people don't much like this game, and stop playing as soon as they can.

But even in a more narrow sense games like those I played with Lisa are educational. They give a child a stronger feeling of cause and effect, of one thing leading to another. Also, they help a child to feel that he makes a difference, that he can have some effect on the world around him. How exciting it must be for a child, playing a game with an adult, to feel that by doing a certain thing, he can make that omnipotent giant do something, and that he can keep this up as long as he likes.

Once, visiting friends in Chicago, I was left for a while one morning in charge of the children—Alice, three and a half, and Patrick, just over two. They were used to playing on the sidewalk of the rather quiet street where they live, so I told them they could do this as long as they stayed in sight. But they soon strayed out of sight, and I had to fetch them back, protesting and wailing. They were furious. They told me that I was bad, and that they were going to tell their mommy on me. I told them to go ahead. Patrick then said that his mommy would spank me—"Like this." I pretended to cry. This is an absolutely foolproof game to play with little children; they all love it. Soon we had a game going. The little children would "spank" me—slap me on the back —and I would pretend to cry. When I stopped, Patrick would say, "I'm still spanking you," and I would have to start again. Now and then I would say, "I'm a good boy." He would say, very firmly, "You bad boy." And so we went on for some time, until they found something else to do. Later we showed the game to the children's parents.

☐ August 1, 1961

Recently Lisa has started to play fierce games. She bares her teeth, growls, roars, rushes at me. I pretend to be afraid, and cower behind a chair. It can go on for some time. From this and many other things she does, it seems as if she feels a *Me* inside her, growing stronger, doing things, demanding things. Any game that makes *Me* seem more powerful must be a good game. Most of the time she knows all too well how powerless that *Me* is.

Sometimes she takes a stick and hits the seat of a chair with it, making the sound of an explosion with her mouth. As she hits the chair she blinks, as if the great force of her own blow scared her a little. It reminds me of a nine-year-old boy I knew who, when he first began to play soccer, and I think without knowing that he did it, made this same kind of explosive noise with his mouth every time he kicked the ball. It may be worth noting that he was not very big or athletic, and could not kick the ball very hard; had he been able to, he would not have needed the explosion-noise.

For all her fierceness, pride, and stubborn independence, Lisa is at heart kind and obliging. One game she likes to play is the "you-can't" game. Sometimes it begins with me outside the screen door, she inside. She says, "Can't come in." I begin to pull gently on the door. She pulls as hard as she can from the other side. After a while, as if exhausted, I let go, and the door shuts with a small bang. She gives me a triumphant look, and again says, "You can't come in." Again I try the door, again she resists, until I let the door shut again. This may happen five or six times. But always, at the end, she lets me in, saying very sweetly, "Come in, John."

The other morning, hearing her talking to her sister, I went into their room. She gave me a flirty look and said, "Go away." "Why?" I asked. She said, "Because." "Because what?" She said, "You have to." "But I don't want to." She said, "You need to," this being even more emphatic than having to. I said again that I didn't want to. Then an odd thing happened. She said, "You can't." She had slipped into a pattern of answers that she ordinarily uses in different circumstances. At about this time I left the room. A moment later I came back, and the game began again. This time, after we had played a few times, she said, "Don't go way." Children don't mind letting us adults win the game, as long as we let them score a few points. But so many of us, like some football coaches, seem never to be content with merely winning; we have to run up the big score.

☐ August 2, 1961

The other day we went to Carlsbad Caverns, a strange and beautiful place. To get there, we rode many hours in the car. On the way, we played games. The radio was on, and with Lisa watching, I began to clap my hands in time to the music. She did the same. Then I began to clap one palm against the other fist. She watched a while, then made both her hands into fists, clapped together a bit,

looked again, saw this wasn't right, and soon did what I
was doing. From this grew a whole series of games. I
clapped hand against head; so did she. I clapped hand
against stomach; so did she. I made my games more complicated. I clapped head with one hand and stomach with
another; or clapped head with one hand while holding
that elbow with the other, and so on. It was most interesting to see how she copied what I was doing. Each time
she began by doing something fairly quickly. As she did
it, she checked what she was doing against what I was doing. Then she made a change in what she was doing,
checked again, and so went on until she was satisfied that
what we were both doing was the same. Watching her do
this, I was struck by two things. First, she did not feel that
she had to get everything right before she started to do
anything. She was willing—no, more than willing, eager—to begin by doing *something*, and then think about
fixing it up. Secondly, she was not satisfied with incorrect
imitations, but kept on looking and comparing until she
was satisfied that she was correct—which she almost always was.

An older child, playing this game, might well play it
differently, and in doing so, get his imitation right the
first time. He could do his imitating in his mind, checking to see whether he had it right before doing it with his
body. Or, he could put my action into words, and then suit
his action to the words. But very small children, at least
this one, do not seem to work that way, can't carry out an
act in their imagination and correct it there. They have to
imitate, compare, and correct, all at the concrete or physical level, and continue until they get it right.

In one way—one of many, in fact—Lisa is strikingly different from the unsuccessful ten-year-olds I have known
in school. She wants to get things right, and will stick at
them until she does; they just want to get things over with
and out of the way. Very young children seem to have
what could be called an Instinct of Workmanship. We

tend not to see it, because they are unskillful and their materials crude. But watch the loving care with which a little child smooths off a sand cake, or pats and shapes a mud pie. They want to make it as well as they can, not to please someone else but to satisfy themselves.

☐ August 3, 1961

Watching Lisa, I am reminded often of Bill Hull's story about the first-grader who burst into tears upon hearing that the word "once" was spelled O-N-C-E. What puzzles me is why six-year-olds should be so much more bothered by this kind of confusion and paradox than this baby. She hears things all day long that make no sense, but she doesn't appear to mind. She lives and moves in uncertainty as naturally and easily as a fish moves in water. When, and why, do children begin to crave certainty?

Children don't seem to be born fearful. Oh, there are a few things they seem to fear instinctively—loud noises and loss of support—though there are many babies who love to be tossed into the air and caught, or otherwise tumbled about. It looks very much as if children catch most of their fears from their elders.

Lisa, for example, never used to be afraid of bugs. When she saw any kind of crawling or flying thing, she wanted to pick it up and look at it. One day a twelve-year-old friend of her older sister came to visit. Lisa was in the room with the two older girls, when the visitor saw a spider in a corner. She began to scream hysterically, and kept on until they got her out of the room and killed the spider. Since then, Lisa has been afraid of all bugs—flies, moths, worms, anything. She has learned her lesson. She doesn't scream or carry on, only draws away from them and doesn't want to have anything to do with them. A part of her curiosity about the world and her trust in it has been shut off. Who can tell when it will turn on again?

Most of the fear that children catch is of a more subtle kind. They catch it bit by bit, in very small doses. The other day Lisa was playing with the electric portable typewriter. She can turn it on and off, and can work the carriage return. While typing away, she suddenly got the urge to bring both hands down on the keys. A bunch of keys flew up and stuck. She leaned over the keyboard to pull them back. I feared that as she tried to get the keys back she might touch a key on the keyboard, which would make another key come up and give her fingers a sharp rap. Also, I feared that in tugging back the keys she might bend some of them out of line. So I showed her again how to turn the machine off, and then carefully untangled the stuck keys.

> By now we have portable electric typewriters with ball-type elements. With these there is no danger of stuck keys, though an exploring child might damage the ball if she tugged at it too hard, or get a painful rap if she got a finger under the ball and then touched a key. Such typewriters are fairly expensive, but several families might pool their money to buy one, sharing it among themselves. Typewriters with what are called daisy-wheel printers would be even better—but these are even more expensive. Best of all, as Seymour Papert points out in *Mindstorms,* are the word processors on which people can actually edit their own writing (as I am doing now), but these are the most expensive of all—though here, as in many things having to do with electronics, prices seem to be coming down. Anyway, better to save up or pool money and spend it on a few good tools than waste it on closets full of junky toys.

Lisa did an interesting bit of exploration. On each side of the keyboard there is a shift key, and on the left side a shift lock. She saw that when you push the shift key down, it comes back up, but when you push the shift lock down, it stays down, and the shift key with it. Then the problem is how to get them back up. Tugging does no good. After a while she found that if she pushed the shift key down it unlocked the shift lock, and both keys came up. Then she looked for a key on the right side that would do the same thing. The margin release did nothing that she could observe, and the tabulator key, much to her surprise, made the whole carriage slide over, and rang the bell into the bargain. After some more experimenting, she soon had the whole shift key and lock system figured out.

All this time I was standing to one side, about ten feet away. I wanted to see what she was doing; also I wanted to be able to shut the machine off if she should bang on all the keys again, or do anything else that might hurt her or the machine. I felt that I was watchful rather than anxious, but she must have sensed some quality of anxiety in my watchfulness, for as she worked with the machine she kept doing something she had never done when she was younger—looking up at me with an expression on her face that clearly seemed to ask, "Is this all right?"

Children, particularly little ones, are very sensitive to emotion. They not only catch everything we feel, they blow it up to larger-than-life size. Lisa begins to cry if any of her older brothers or sisters seem to be having a serious argument or fight. Even when they roughhouse in fun, she tries to pull them apart, pleading, "Stop! Stop!" Often, in other families, I have seen children unhappy for a long time because of an argument between their parents, which the parents had done their best to conceal. It need not even be parents. Once I was visiting some friends, whose children I knew very well and was very fond of. The mother and I got into an argument about politics. While the argument was warm, it was not unfriendly; we are generally on the same side of the fence. But even as much warmth as there was in the argument was too much for the children. They began to circle around and move in, in a conciliatory fashion, as if by giving us something else to think about they might take our minds off the quarrel, and get everything cheerful and happy again.

It is simply not true, or at least not always true, that little children have no empathy, cannot feel what others feel. They are, no doubt, often cruel to each other; but if they are near another child who is badly hurt or very unhappy, they soon become very distressed. It is a very rare child who is capable of the kind of sustained, deliberate cruelty so often shown by adults.

Often their cruelty may be experimental. Once I saw two two-year-old boys playing side by side on the floor. They were pushing cars and trucks around, and having a pleasant time. At one point one of them picked up the fairly heavy metal truck he was playing with, and looked at the other with a speculative expression. I had a faint hunch that something bad was about to happen, but I didn't feel I could say anything, because the child's father, my host, whom I did not know well, was watching with me, and said nothing. But sure enough, in a moment or so the little boy with the truck, looking very calm, picked it up and smacked the other boy in the head with it. The other little boy looked up amazed, and then burst into roars of pain and dismay. The first little boy looked at him, puzzled, and increasingly distressed (though his father for some reason made no move to punish or reprove him). All these roars and tears seemed to be more results than he had bargained for. He did not cry himself, but he was clearly frightened and unhappy.

One of my earliest recollections—actually by now I remember the telling of it rather than the event itself—was of playing in the park with a friend my own age—about three, perhaps four—who out of a clear blue sky hit me in the head with his toy shovel. We had been playing peacefully; I never understood, then or later, why he hit me. Perhaps it was this same overpowering urge to see what would happen.

☐ August 4, 1961

Lisa remembers and likes to use phrases that carry some emotional weight. Within the past few weeks I have heard her say, for the first time, "No fair!" "I'm making a mess!" "Don't make me mad!" and "Quit it!" All of these are said at times of stress and excitement. When she finds herself in such situations, such phrases come naturally.

Her talk and games are connected. The other day, as we were riding to town in the car, she in back, I in front, I turned around to look at her. She looked mischievously at me, then said, firmly, "Turn around." I had never heard her say it before. I turned around. A moment later, I looked back at her again. She said, "Turn around," and the game began. It went on for some time.

Sometimes the game is reversed. The other morning she told me to watch her, and began to walk round and round one of the living room chairs, her eye on me. I guessed that she wanted me to say something about what she was doing, so I did. Either the guess was right, or she was just as pleased with it as with whatever she might have wanted. She went on doing, first this, then that, all the while watching me and listening to what I was saying. Indeed, quite often it seems that, just as she says things to see what people will do, she does things to hear what people will say.

☐ August 6, 1961

Not long ago Lisa was patting my cheek, I forget why. I puffed the cheek full of air, and waited. It was a tempting target. She gave it a light slap, and I let the air burst forth from between my lips with a satisfactory noise. She was delighted, and asked me to do it again. Soon the whole family was playing this game with her. After a while, she invited us to play the game in reverse. She puffed out her already chubby cheek, but when we patted it there wasn't enough air pent up to make any sound. But this didn't seem to bother her; she enjoyed the game anyway.

For some time she has enjoyed games in which she imitated her elders. Now she is beginning to invent games in which we are supposed to imitate her. Like so many good games, this one began by accident. She was making a face, which she likes to do, when she caught my eye. With nothing in mind, I imitated the face. She made a different face. I imitated that one. Right away she saw that I was going to try to do whatever she did, and away we went.

Another time, her older brothers were playing, on the living room floor, a game called leg-wrestling. After watching this a while, she insisted on being allowed to play. We did some mock leg-wrestles with her, sometimes pulling her over, sometimes making it look as if she had pulled us over—accompanied by many grunts and groans. Soon she began doing various stunts, which she asked us to copy, flopping down on her knees, turning round and round on hands and knees, looking backward between her legs (a favorite with all little children), and so on. One morning she led me on a little walk through the pine woods that surround the house. Sometimes she ran, sometimes she walked, sometimes she kicked one foot in the air as she walked. All the while she watched me to see if I was imitating, and imitating properly.

Since that time much has been said and written about autistic children, children who seem to have withdrawn into a private world of their own, who don't have or want any contact with the outside world at all. Arguments rage about how best to treat them. The conventional wisdom still seems to be that for severely autistic children not much can be done; they can perhaps be trained to take physical care of themselves and meet minimal social requirements, but not much else. But there have been some astonishing "cures." Barry Kaufman, in his book *Son Rise,* describes one that he and his wife effected with their apparently hopelessly autistic little boy. The point I want to make here is that they began their cure, and first began to establish some faint communication with their terribly withdrawn child, by making a point, for hours at a time if need be, *of imitating everything he did.* This was the door or path by which they led him or persuaded him to come back into the everyday world.

No one can ever know exactly why this cure worked. But it *feels* right to me. If I felt that the world was so unpredictable and threatening and myself so powerless that I could not risk myself in that world, but had to make a tiny, safe private world of my own, that outside world might begin to seem less unpredictable and threatening and myself more powerful *if I could make things happen in it.*

All children want and strive for increased mastery and control of the world around them, and all are to some degree humiliated, threatened, and frightened by finding out (as they do all the time) that they don't have it. Perhaps autistic children need this control more and are far more frightened by not having it, and so, unlike most children, are not able to struggle patiently until they are able to get it, but instead, again unlike most children, must retreat from the big world around them into a private inner world of their own.

☐ August 9, 1961

The other day we went to a small amusement park in town. It has a tiny Ferris wheel, a train that goes round an oval track, a jeep that goes with locked wheels in a fixed circle around a post, and a ring of little metal cars that bump noisily around a circular wooden track.

From the first day, Lisa was fascinated by the cars. We put her in one, and off she went. We thought the noise and bumps might frighten her, and clearly she was on the verge of being frightened. As she went round and round, she had a set expression on her face, and only occasionally looked at us as she went by. Going round, counterclockwise, she kept turning the little steering wheel of her car. It seemed that she was always turning it to the left. Was this just a coincidence? Or had she grasped something, riding in the real car, about the relationship between the turning of the wheel and the movement of the car?

Soon the ride ended and we looked for something else to do. Some bigger children were riding around in the little train, blowing the whistle and ringing the bell. To Lisa, it looked interesting and just a bit frightening. Perhaps the train made too much noise, perhaps it was too big, too black. She kept saying, "I can't go train, I can't go train." We said that was all right, she didn't have to. The cars remained her favorites.

After a while, we left the park to go get some ice cream. As we ate it, her mental picture of the train began to be less terrifying. The more she thought about it, the smaller and safer it looked. She began to say, very boldly, "I need to ride that train *right now*!" We felt she should have this chance to conquer her fear, so back we went. But, alas, when we got there the train looked just as big and black as ever, and she said, "I can't go train, I can't go train."

It is easy to say, much of the time, why we fear the things we do. It is not so easy to say from where the drive to overcome these fears comes, particularly in a very little child. Some kinds of courage are learned, but there is surely also an instinct of courage, a wish to be brave, to overcome fear. It will grow if we do not put more strain on it than it can bear. We should give it every encouragement.

When Lisa wants to do something very much, she says, "I have to." When she does not want to do something, she says, "I can't." It is easy to see where these expressions came from. When we want her to do something, we say, "You have to." When we want her not to do something, we say, "You can't." She just turns the words back on us. She is just beginning to be aware of the conflict of will between her and the giants who run everything. Her big brother, a grownup to her, often plays a game with her. He says, "You have to." She says, very seriously, "I can't." He reverses his field, says, "You can't." Instantly she says, "I have to." And so on, for as long as he is willing to play.

To almost every question she answers "No," or the negative "Unh-unh." This does not mean that she thinks *no* is always the correct answer; she often says *no* when she knows the correct answer is *yes,* as when her older sister, whom she loves, says, "Are you my sister?" The word *no,* for a two-year-old, is the Declaration of Independence and Magna Charta rolled into one.

> Many people have by now pointed this out. A hungry two-year-old will often say no even if you ask her if she wants some of her favorite food. Of course she wants the food. But she also likes to say no. Let her say no, then give her the food. If she really doesn't want it, she will soon make that clear.

Oddly enough, most people seem alarmed by the first signs of independence in small children. Modern parents often say, "It's just a stage, they'll grow out of it," as if it were a disease from which, with care and luck, the child might recover. The more old-fashioned ones set out to show the tiny child Who Is Boss, though the child feels completely dependent and though his desire for greater independence needs all the nourishment it can get.

Lisa, like all little children, wants to do what the big people are doing. This can make problems. At dinner, she insists that her food, like everyone else's, be served from the serving dish onto a regular plate, not specially dished out in advance. A few nights ago we were having pork chops. I knew she could not possibly cut a chop and would only eat a few bites from it, so I tried to cut off some pieces of a chop for her. She protested, "I want meat! I want meat!" I said, "I'm giving you meat." No use; I knew what she wanted, and she knew I knew. An entire chop had to be put on her plate. Only after she had sawed futilely at it for a while with knife and fork ("foik"), did she allow me to cut some off for her.

She shows this independence in many ways. In the yard behind the little house are some swings, attached to the frame by chains so that their height may be adjusted. An older child had taken off one of the swings and left it on the ground. Lisa wanted to swing on it, and was fooling around with it on the ground. I said, "Do you want to swing on it?" She said no, but as she always says that, and as she looked as if she wanted to swing, I started to attach one of the chains to its hook. She said sternly, "No fix swing." She then took the other chain and, holding it by the end, began to reach toward the top bar of the frame, meanwhile making earnest jumps, which took her about an inch and a half off the ground. After a while she gave up and turned to something else. I moved toward the swing again. Right away she said, "No fix swing, John." By degrees this turned into a game. I would slowly approach the chain; she would say, "No fix swing." I would move away. A little later, we would go through it again. Her expression was playful, but she was serious. Not until later, when she had gone off on other business of her own, was I able to fix the swing.

Even a year ago she wanted very much to be included in any game that people were playing. Then it was easier to fool her. If the older children were playing checkers, or Parcheesi, or chess, they could generally appease and get rid of Lisa by giving her a few extra pieces to play with on the floor. But this didn't last for long. She soon saw that cards, or pieces, were being used in a particular way, and she wanted to use them that way—on the board itself.

This makes it hard for the chess players. When she sees a chess game going on, or hears one mentioned, she immediately wants to play. Not that she particularly cares about the game, even as she understands it—or doesn't understand it—she just doesn't want to be excluded from what the others are doing. Sometimes her brothers try to hide the game by playing on the top bunk in their room. But she soon tracks them down and begins to say "Need to play chess! Need to! Need to!" No use to give her extra pieces; she wants to play right on the board itself. We can only persuade her to let the boys finish their game by promising her a chance to play later, which she does, happily, with whomever will "play" with her, for a long time.

Her patience and concentration are astonishing. The other day she found a green ball point pen and took it apart. There were four pieces: the cartridge; the two pieces that made up the body of the pen, and that had to be screwed together; and a metal band, which had to be put on one of the plastic pieces before they were screwed together. There should have been a spring, but by the time I saw the pen, it was gone. I started to put the pieces together for her, but she told me not to. She worked clumsily but patiently with the pieces, trying all possible ways of combining them. She was not sure how the pieces ought to look when fitted together, and did not have the skill to fit them; nevertheless, she came close. She often got the parts together in the proper order, but could not engage the screw threads to get the two halves of the case together. Time and time again she would seem to have the pieces put together properly, only to have them fall apart. She did not get angry or discouraged, and worked on it for more than twenty minutes, only stopping when called to lunch.

As I watched, I thought of many four-year-olds I had seen in nursery school trying to put puzzles together, and often getting tearful or angry when they could not. Why are older children so much less able to stand the frustration of—let us call it, not failure, but—deferred success? I suspect it is because they are already, even in nursery school, in a very competitive, status-conscious situation, all struggling for the approval of the teacher, or each other. The child who cannot do the puzzle knows that older children have already done it, and that the teacher and other children expect him to do it, and will be disappointed or make fun of him, if he can't do it. But Lisa is still interested only in the pen, and whether she can get it together; she doesn't care whether other people can do it, or what they think of her efforts to do it. To many four-year-olds, doing a puzzle is often only a means to an end—gaining someone else's approval. To Lisa, putting the pen together is an end in itself.

☐ March 7, 1963

The other day Danny did something so exactly like what little children are supposed to do that it sounds made up. He has three picture puzzles, like jigsaw puzzles, only much simpler. Two are the Playskool variety, seen in many nursery schools. The other is a very pretty, and much more intricate and interesting, Dutch puzzle. Though Danny is only twenty-nine months old, he can put these puzzles together with no outside help. It is surprising that he should have such skillful fingers, or be able to keep three such complicated patterns in his head. He does not do these puzzles by trial and error, not any more. He *knows* where each piece in each of the puzzles goes. He has a rough order in which he likes to put the puzzles together, but he is not a prisoner of that order. At any one point there is probably a piece that he would rather put in than any other, but if that piece doesn't fall under his eye, he can use another, and place it correctly. It is quite something to watch.

The other day he was working on one of the Playskool puzzles, which is about boats. One of the pieces, which fits along an edge, is a cloud. He picked it up, took it to its proper place, and tried to fit it in. But he had turned it a little bit away from the proper angle, so that he couldn't get it to go right up to the edge. Also, there were no other pieces in place around it to guide it in. He struggled and pushed with it, turning it this way and that, but couldn't quite get it to fit. He grew more and more uneasy; he *knew* that it was supposed to go there, but it wouldn't. His movements became more rapid and anxious. Suddenly he turned away from the puzzle, crawled to his blanket, a few feet behind him, grabbed it, stuck his thumb in his mouth, and sat down on the floor, looking at us as if to say, "I know what to do at a time like this." We all laughed delightedly. In a moment or so he had recharged his battery enough so that he could go back to the puzzle, put in some other pieces, and soon finish it, including the piece that had caused the trouble.

> How much people can learn at any moment depends on how they feel at that moment about the task and their ability to do the task. When we feel powerful and competent, we leap at difficult tasks. The difficulty does not discourage us; we think, "Sooner or later, I'm going to get this." At other times, we can only think, "I'll never get this, it's too hard for me, I never was any good at this kind of thing, why do I have to do it," etc. Part of the art of teaching is being able to sense which of these moods learners are in. People can go from one mood to the other very quickly. In *Never Too Late* I wrote about an eight-year-old who could go from an up mood to a down and then back to up, all in a thirty-minute cello lesson. When people are down, it's useless to push them or urge them on; that just frightens and discourages them more. What we have to do is draw

back, take off the pressure, reassure them, console them, give them time to regain—as in time they will—enough energy and courage to go back to the task.

☐ March 22, 1963

I had another visit with Danny. We were walking around the Visual Arts Center at Harvard, when he looked up and saw the moon. He pointed it out to us. A moment later, after we had walked a short way up the street, he looked up and noticed it again. He seemed surprised to see it in what may have seemed to be a different place.

He talks a great deal. I notice that, when we say something to him, he will often repeat the last word or two, as if for practice.

When we got home, we invented two good games. I don't know how either of them got started. There was a small, soft cushion on the couch. For some reason, at one point, I threw it to him. He caught it, and threw it back. This was very exciting for him. I imagine that following the cushion through the air with his eyes, and timing his grab with its arrival, was a good exercise in coordination. It is also an easy game, since the cushion is soft, does not bounce away from him, and is easy to hold on to. He also has a big balloon that he likes to catch, though it behaves quite differently.

The other game was "hit-the-bed." When we were playing catch, I was sitting on a day bed. I felt that this little boy had more energy on hand than he could either contain or get rid of, and remembering how Lisa used to love to hit the cushion of a chair with a stick, making a noise that made her blink, I raised my hand over my head and brought it, palm down, hard as I could, on the bed, making a good, solid noise. Danny was delighted. I said to him, "*You* hit the bed." He came up and gave it a rather tentative slap. I said, "Oh, you can hit it harder than that," and gave it another good smack. But not until after several tries did he let go his inhibitions and hit as hard as he could.

From this beginning the game developed. During our game of catch with the pillow, every so often he would stop and say, "Hit the bed." Each time I hit it with all my might; each time he laughed. Then one time, for no reason, with no plan in mind, instead of hitting the bed hard, I gave it only a little pat. Then I said, "Shall I hit it harder?" He said, "Yes." I hit it slightly harder, then repeated my question. Another yes. A harder blow; the same question; another yes, and so four or five times, until I was hitting it as hard as I could. We went through the cycle a couple of times. The third time, after giving the bed a light tap, I waited. He looked at me a second, then said, "Harder!" I hit it harder, but not very. Again, "Harder!" I put on a little more steam. Again, and louder than before, "Harder!" And so we progressed until I hit a full-sized blow. He was delighted and excited by this game; later we played it for his parents.

The real point of the story is that the best games with little children flow easily and naturally from the situation of the moment. We are not likely to get good games by planning them far in advance, but we probably will get them if we play with children just for the fun of it. And whatever the game is, we must be ready to give it up, instantly and without regret, if the child is not enjoying it. It's tempting to think, "If I can just get him to do this for a while, he will enjoy it." But he won't—and we won't.

Danny has become so good at doing his Playskool puzzles that his parents have bought him some jigsaw puzzles. He now has two or three of these that he can put together very well. Last night he was working on one that shows a picture of a Mexican boy and two goats. It was amazing to watch him. He has some picture of the completed puzzle in his mind. It tells him that this piece goes here and that piece there. He looks at the pieces for a few seconds, then suddenly reaches out, picks a piece, and puts it where he thinks it should go. Four times out of five, he is right. And when he is wrong, he usually sees very quickly that he is, and without any fuss gives up his attempt to make the piece go where it should not.

Last night there was one exception. He tried to put a piece into a spot. It was almost the right shape, and the colors matched quite well, though not exactly. It seemed clear that he does not have a feeling for an exact color match; he doesn't do puzzles this way. The piece was just close enough to being right so that he felt it should go in. Before long he had passed the point at which he could give up the effort to make it fit. Pride, face, had become involved. You could see him getting angry, and a bit frightened, as children do when a part of the world that had been making sense suddenly stops making it. His father began trying to persuade him to consider the idea that this might be the wrong piece. He went at it very gently and tactfully. But the boy wasn't ready to admit that; he knew it was the right piece, only it just wouldn't go! After a while I had a hunch. I said, "Why don't you put it here, outside, for a minute, and put some of the other pieces in, and then try it later. Let it alone for a minute." This he was ready to do. He put in a few other pieces, and then took the difficult piece and without any hesitation put it into the place that had by this time become ready for it. It turned out to be next to the place where he had been trying to put it: he had not been very far wrong after all.

It seems to me that there is some kind of lesson in this for students and teachers alike. There are times when even the most skillful learner must admit to himself that for the time being he is trying to butt his head through a stone wall, and that there is no sense in it. At such times teachers are inclined to use students as a kind of human battering ram. I've done it too often myself. It doesn't work.

Danny, his parents, and I went next door to visit a little

girl about his age. She also had some of those Playskool puzzles, but apparently had not been able to put them together. Her way of playing with the puzzle was to take a piece, any piece at all, stick it into what was obviously an impossible place, look around, and make a kind of isn't-that-silly? giggle. Her strategy is very like that of older children and adults, a strategy of deliberate failure. If you can't play a game the way it is supposed to be played, turn it into a game that you can play. If you can't do it right, do it wrong, but so obviously wrong that everyone will see that you are not trying to do it right, and that you don't think it is worth trying to do right.

Later, back at Danny's house, he put some of his puzzles out on the floor. He had already done one, and was full of energy and confidence. Suddenly he began doing what the little girl had done earlier, putting pieces in what were clearly the wrong places, looking at me, and laughing. This was a big joke; but it was very different from the girl's self-protective, camouflage joke. He knew he could do the puzzle right, and he chose to pretend to do it wrong, just because it was funny. At first the importance of this escaped me, perhaps because we soon were doing other things. But later he was showing us one of his favorite books, about machines—construction and earth-moving machines, whose names he knew by heart, and loved to say. Then he turned to the inside cover of the book, where there were a number of Walt Disney characters. Some he knew; others he asked us. Soon he went back to the inside of the book again, but now he played a different game. At each page he would show us a machine and tell us something that the machine was *not;* thus he looked at the picture of the cement mixer and said, "Tractor," and at the picture of the steam shovel and said, "Combine," with great relish and enjoyment. To look at something and deliberately call it something else was a good joke.

This seems a very healthy, confident, and powerful attitude toward the world of symbols. They are ours to use as we wish. We can use them correctly if we want; but if we want to use them incorrectly, for a joke, we can do that too. We are in charge, not the symbols.

This feeling, that when you know how to do something right it is often fun to do it wrong, is strong in children. Adults who meet it tend to discourage it. I think this is a mistake, perhaps a serious one, and that the kind of thing I saw my little friend doing the other night should be enjoyed and encouraged. It is not always necessary to be right.

> This children's trick or game of taking something that you know how to do correctly, and doing it incorrectly, just because it seems funny, seems to me a good example of what Piagetians call "operational thought" and that they tend to say children this young cannot do. Clearly the children have two ideas in mind at the same time: the correct way, the way they are supposed to do it, and know how to do it, and the incorrect way. I used to think and say that children, though full of gaiety, merriment, and slapstick humor, didn't seem to have much sense of irony, wit, being able to see things from more than one angle, until they reached the age of about ten. But this do-it-wrong trick seems a good example of just that kind of humor. In the same way, what makes little children laugh at nonsense words is precisely that they know these words are wrong.

Children can learn some cause-and-effect games when they are very young. When I was last in France, I was visiting a young schoolteacher and his family. Their boy was less than a year and a half old. I often used to watch him in his crib, talk to him, play with him. One of his toys was a rubber ring, about the size of a deck-tennis ring, slightly bigger than a doughnut. One day, as he watched, I put it on top of my head. After a second or two I nodded my head and the ring slid down over my face and fell. Then I put the ring on his head. He did the same thing. This turned into a good game. After we each had had several turns I put the ring on my head and waited. He watched me for a few seconds; then he made an insistent ducking motion with his head. I ducked my head, and the ring fell off. He was delighted, and we did this over and over again.

Once, years before, with a still younger child, not more than seven or eight months old, I played the game of "Bump." I was carrying her around, and for some reason, I forget what, we bumped heads gently. I said, "Bump." She seemed to enjoy the incident, so I said, "Bump" again, and again bumped my forehead lightly against hers. After a few times, she understood the game, and when I said "Bump," would bump her forehead against mine—and then give me a huge smile.

> The spirit of these games is everything. The only good reason for playing games with babies is because we love them, and delight in playing these games with them and in sharing their delight in playing—not because we want someday to get them into college. It is our delight in the baby and the games that make the games fun, and worthwhile and useful for the baby. Take away the delight, and put in its place some cold-hearted calculation about future I.Q. and SAT scores, and we kill the game, for ourselves and the baby. If we go on for long in this spirit the babies will soon refuse to play—or if they do, play only in the spirit of school, i.e., because they think we'll be disappointed or angry if they don't.

☐ **May 1, 1960**

A few days ago, about forty minutes before regular classes started, I took my electric portable typewriter into the three-year-olds' classroom. When I went in, I didn't say anything, just went over to a corner of the room, set the machine up on a low table, and, very slowly, one finger at a time, began to type. For a while the children circled warily at a distance, now and then, in the middle of their play, casting quick glances at me out of the corners of their eyes. Gradually the bolder children came closer and closer. Finally, as I had hoped, one of them came up close and asked if he could do it. I said, "Sure, if you want to." Before long they all wanted a turn. While one typed, the others crowded around the machine, pushing silently and insistently, like people waiting for a train. The typewriter was almost too popular. I couldn't let any one child type for even as long as five minutes, which wasn't enough time for them to do much investigating and exploring, let alone discovering. Also, the child working with the machine was more than a little distracted by the excitement of the other children.

□ May 9, 1960

The three-year-olds continue to be fascinated with the typewriter. John is usually one of the first to come in each morning. As soon as he sees me, he asks for a turn. He also likes to plug in the machine. On about the fourth day with the machine, he said to me as I left to go to my own class, "Mr. Holt, you have to bring the typewriter over to my house." Two others then said the same thing.

On the fifth day John discovered the gadget that changes the ribbon from red to black, and noticed that it made a difference in the colors that came out on the paper. By now all the veterans know about this gadget and like to work it. They are beginning to be slightly more interested in the marks made on the paper, instead of just running the machine for the sake of making it go. They might be even more interested if the letters made by the typewriter were bigger.

Elsie (aged five and a half), sister of Charlie (four), had

a turn. She can read and spell. She wrote, without help, "DEAR DADDY, I LOVE YOU AND YOUR ROOM." This excited and aroused Matt (four). He wanted to write something to his father. I showed him what keys to hit to make DEAR DADDY. He wrote DDEAR DDADDY. But this was all he could think of to say. Perhaps the slowness of having to hunt for the letters made his thinking freeze up. He was torn between his desire to make the machine go lickety-split, and his desire to make it say something.

Charlie (just four years old), unlike most of these kids, wants to know what the letters are as he hits them. He is deliberate, hits one key at a time, and looks at the mark he has made. Perhaps, in time, he might lead the group to new discoveries. One day, looking down through the keyboard, he noticed the spinning bar inside the machine— the one that moves the keys. He was eager to find out what it was.

On about the sixth day Matt, looking at the letters and numerals on the paper, suddenly said, "There's the number five!" He was very excited to see something he recognized.

When the children first started using the machine, they would type up to the end of a line and then go on typing, not noticing that nothing was happening. After a while I started saying, when we reached the end of a line, "End of the line!" before returning the carriage. By now they all know how to use the carriage return, and when to use it; I hardly ever have to say "End of the line" anymore. Charlie likes to say it himself each time he returns the carriage.

A few of the children have become skillful and surprisingly gentle at untangling stuck keys.

Some days later Matt wanted to write FATHER. I wrote it for him on a piece of paper. He found the F and the A on the keyboard by himself; I showed him the others. Then he found a most ingenious way to satisfy his desire to make the machine go fast as well as his desire to use it to say something. He wrote: FFFFFFFAAAAAAATTTTT TTHHHHHHHHEEEEEEERRRRRRR.

Charlie can find, and likes to find, the C with which his name begins. When I asked whether he could find the other letters, he gave me an anxious look, so I quickly let the matter drop. How strongly and immediately children react to being put on this kind of spot. He likes to have me name the keys that he hits. He knows that in the top row the numeral keys are followed by a dash and then the equals sign, and he often remembers to say "dash" and "equals" even when I don't.

For much of the year, when I entered the room, John has told me that he was the sheriff and that I would have to go to jail. I thought of the success that Sylvia Ashton-Warner had had, teaching her children words that they really were excited about. So one day I wrote, in large capitals on a sheet of paper, GO TO JAIL. I showed it to John and told him what it said. I thought he might be interested in writing it on the typewriter. So much for bright ideas—he couldn't have cared less. He then asked me to write, with pencil, GO HOME; but to my surprise, he showed no interest in writing any of those letters on the typewriter. However, he still gets angry if other children write J, which he claims is *his* letter.

☐ April 2, 1961

The other afternoon Scott, who will be six in a few months, was fooling around with the electric typewriter. Like most of the five-year-olds who have used it in class this year, he has looked on it, first of all, as a machine to make go, and secondly, as a device for making many marks on a sheet of paper. He has not looked on it as an easy way of writing, that is, saying something. On the other hand, he doesn't look on any kind of writing as a way of saying something. Writing, for him and his classmates, is a way of making certain kinds of marks, which the adults seem to like, with a pencil or crayon. It has nothing to do with getting speech onto paper.

At any rate, he had the shift lock depressed and was happily making patterns of dollar signs. By mistake he released the shift lock, so that he began to get, instead of dollar signs, a row of 4's. He didn't like this, and said so. Then he went about trying to get his dollar signs back. With much audible muttering of "Let's try this," he pressed first one unmarked key and then another, getting various unexpected and unwanted results, until he finally hit the shift lock and the missing dollar sign was restored, to his great satisfaction.

His teacher later said that there was a noticeable difference between the "bright" kids in the class and the less "bright," in that the bright ones made a very deliberate use of the scientific method, the selective use of trial and error. Not only did they use this as a way of finding out what they wanted to know, but they were conscious of using it. The question is, do they use the method because they are bright, or is it the use of the method that makes them bright?

In the last year or two I have seen a good deal of Tommy, Lisa's little brother. He too is a tireless and resourceful experimenter. When he was two and a half, he liked to plug the vacuum cleaner into the electric socket, so that he could hear the motor start. Since no amount of threats and punishment seemed to keep him away from plugs, and since the house is full of them, we decided the best thing to do was concentrate on making sure that he used plugs correctly—which he did. Like most children, he is eager to learn to do things the right way.

One day, as I watched him plug in the vacuum cleaner, I brought over the end of the suction pipe, which had no attachments on it, and invited him to feel the end of the pipe. He was surprised to find his hand sucked hard against it. He liked this, and did it over and over. This added a new dimension to his experiment. Now, each time he put in the plug, he would feel the end of the pipe.

I felt, watching him do this, that for a while he was not sure each time whether his hand would be sucked or not. Just because it happened once did not necessarily mean that it would happen again. It takes children some time to learn that, in many cases, a particular event A will always be followed by some other event B, and that if B follows A once, you can count on it to do so again.

One day he was happily plugging and unplugging the vacuum cleaner and testing the suction with his hand. Suddenly he looked thoughtfully at pipe and plug. He had an idea. Very deliberately he brought the end of the pipe over to the socket, and then with his other hand felt the plug! He seemed surprised to feel no suction. He repeated the experiment a time or two, again without results. Then he went back to his original game. It is hard not to feel that the experiment he had done showed a kind of mental skill that one would not expect in a two-and-a-half-year-old.

Yet there are odd limitations to what little children can do. The following summer, at age three, he was dragging one of his favorite toys—the garden hose—around the yard. Suddenly the hose, which was looped around a small cottonwood sapling that we had planted not long before, came up taut, and he could pull no further. It seemed easy enough to see what was happening; the tree wasn't far away from him. But he just pulled harder and harder, getting frustrated and angry. Finally he asked for help, and I led him and the hose around the tree, thus freeing him. I think he would have understood the hose being caught if something heavy had been lying on it. But he could not imagine that anything as static and passive as a tree could be causing the trouble.

Tommy, too, has had his turn at the typewriter. I was typing one day in the living room when he came in and saw me. He wanted a turn, so I put him on a chair before me and he started. Right away he surprised me. He is a very bold, energetic, exuberant little boy. I thought he might begin to bang on the keys, like other three-year-olds I have known. But no—he hit them quite carefully and deliberately, one at a time. Is it too far fetched to think that, living in a family where many people understand machines and can fix them, he has a kind of respect for machines?

Like all little children, he was fascinated with the typewriter, first of all, as a machine, something to make go. He made a move; it made a move. Like other small children, he looked intently at each key he hit. Only once in a while did he look at the paper to see the mark he had made; when he did look, he did not look carefully to see *what* mark had been made, much less compare it with the letter he had hit. This might have come in time, but we never got to that point.

On the other hand, like most children, he was interested in the names of at least some of the letters he was hitting. Very soon, he asked me where O was. I showed him. I also told him the names of some other letters he hit, though not all of them, and not all the time. After a while he asked me where E was, and where A was. Had he known them before he heard me mention them? I don't know. I showed him where they were, and it was only a very short time before he knew where all three of these letters were on the keyboard. He would say, "Where O is?" I would say, "Where do you think?" He would point to it.

This game was fun. But it was not as much fun as we adults tend to think, and he quickly invented a variation of it. He would ask where O (or A or E) was; I would show him, and he would say, "That's not O (or A or E)." There was a trace of exasperation in his tone. Then he would point to some other letter—remember that he *had* been able to point to O in the first place—and say that *it* was O. I would say, "No that's U (or whatever it was)." He did not insist; but he did this many times. I was puzzled what to make of it. Remembering Lisa at the same age, I guessed that this might be his way of resisting and reacting to a situation in which I was in control and had *all* the information, *all* the right answers. He was asserting himself, and his right to make some of the rules. I don't think he liked the idea that O *had* to be where I said it was. Though I doubt if he had any such conscious and definite thought in mind, I think he felt that if I could name letters, why couldn't he? Why didn't he have as much right as I to say where O was?

He insisted on being allowed to put the paper into the machine. In this he was unusual among the small children I have worked with. It was a tricky job. Unless you get the paper all the way in to where the rollers grip it, nothing happens when you try to turn the platen (the roller against which you type). He often found himself in this jam. When he had turned a while without anything happening, he would let me push the paper down far enough for the rollers to engage it; but he had to have his chance to do it first. The next problem was that the paper would go in crooked. I could usually say, "Here, let me straighten that out a bit," and do so. Then the paper would come up in front of the type, and get caught on the bar that holds it firmly against the platen. For the first few times this happened, I would lift up the bar and push the paper under it; after that, he was able to do it for himself.

At one point he asked to see "the noise." By this he meant the electric motor, which could be heard humming away inside. I said, "Do I really have to take it all the way out of its case?" He insisted; so I did. He looked at the motor, touched it. He looked as if he would like to take it out altogether. I don't remember any other child ever asking to see the motor before—but he comes from a very mechanical family.

It was near the very end of my visit that we began working with the typewriter. In the short time we did work, he showed little or no desire to learn the names of letters other than O, A, and E. Now and then he would ask the names of other letters, but not often, and he seemed not to remember them. I had the feeling that what he wanted to find out about this machine was how to operate it, and once he felt he knew that, there was not much more of importance to learn. Perhaps, with more time, he would have become interested in what the machine was doing.

What Tommy really liked to work was the player piano. It began with watching his older sister, Lisa, work it. She plays it often for the sake of the music. He wanted to play it because she does, as he wanted to do everything she can do. He could barely reach the pedals, and had to work like a Trojan to make them go. To keep himself on the piano stool, he had to hold the edge of the piano with both hands. But then the stool, sitting on a hardwood floor, would begin to slide away from the piano. After a while, it would gradually slide him out of reach. He would have to get off, move the stool back, get back on, and begin again. Once, watching this, I said, "Here, I'll hold the stool," and did so. This worked fine, but now I had a permanent job. From then on, every time he wanted to play, I would hear his piercing voice: "John! John!" If I was doing something else, and didn't want to stop, I would lie low; but that was never much good. Eventually he would track me down and say, "Peash help me." It was impossible to resist. I would ask, knowing what he wanted, "What do you want me to do?" He would say, "Hold that tool." Off we would go.

He was mainly interested in the piano as a machine, something to make go. When he began, we thought that if he tried to put in the piano roll, he would tear it. So we told him to let one of the older people put it in. At first he didn't mind; there were many other things in and on the piano to think about. But after a while he found that this meant that he couldn't play unless he could first hunt up someone to put in a roll, which was a nuisance. Also, he saw other people putting in the roll, so why couldn't he?

> Interesting to see how much of their later selves children reveal even when they are very little. Tommy has always been interested in machines, how to fix them, use them, make things with them. He has never cared much for writing or reading. He can do them when he has to, but the path of words is not the path along which he has so far chosen to explore the world. Lisa, on the other hand, has always been interested in words, both to read and to write. When she was about ten she started to write her autobiography; after ten or twelve pages she had only gone as far as her fourth birthday. A few years later she began writing poetry and has, as far as I know, written it ever since.

In Tommy's family, when a machine breaks down, someone in the family instantly tears it apart and fixes it. His father has always been an expert mechanic, and the feeling that machines can be fixed by anyone has been absorbed by the older boys, who as a matter of routine take bikes, automobiles, or anything else apart and put them together again. So when anything is broken, the little boy expects someone to "fit it." His first instinct, faced with a machine, like the player piano, is to dive into its innards and see how everything works.

Before long he learned how to put in a piano roll, and to work all the other controls. There is a lever to adjust the side-to-side position of the roll, and another to adjust the tempo. He worked them both, though I don't know if he could gauge the results he was getting. Another lever reversed the roll, to rewind it. Still another, under the keyboard, made a change in the tone of the piano, giving it a twangier sound. He found all these levers, and used all of them. In fact, for him, playing the piano meant operating every control in sight.

After a while he asked me what the lever was for that moved the roll from side to side. I showed him the holes in the paper, and how they moved over a brass perforated rod, which in turn made the piano play. Did he understand everything I said? I don't know, or care. From then on, it was a part of his piano playing routine to climb up on the stool, inspect some of the holes in the roll, say, "Hole all right," and get down again to go on playing. I guess I had once said that the holes were all right to discourage him from examining them; if I was going to have to hold the stool for him while he played, I wanted him to play, not inspect. But it didn't work out that way. He remembered my remark, and made the hole inspection a regular part of his playing.

It makes me think how much children must have learned from watching people do real work, in the days when a child could see people doing real work. It is not so easy to manage this now. So much of the so-called work done in our society is not work at all, certainly not as a child could understand it; so much of the rest is done by machines. But there are still plenty of craftsmen, of all kinds. What a good thing it would be if a way could be found for many children to see them at their work, and to be able to ask them questions about it.

Back to the player piano. Some of the controls I have mentioned are underneath a little hinged strip of wood at the edge of the keyboard. Once, when he started to play, again with the idea of discouraging him from fooling too much with the controls, I closed this hinged cover, saying, "Let's get this out of the way." This too became part of his regular routine. Every so often, when playing, he would close this cover and say, "Get this out of the way."

Thus children learn that certain phrases go along with certain actions, fit into certain situations. Is this use of language imitative? To some extent. But it is not on that account blind or purposeless imitation. A real connection has been found, and is used. Also, the child soon joins the phrase, "Get this out of the way," to the act of getting the thing out of the way, and knows that the one means the other. The question would be, how soon can he use the same phrase in a different context? Perhaps he may have to hear it used in another context before he realizes that it can fit not just one situation, but many.

Another thing he learned to do was fold back the pedals and close the doors, thus making the piano into a regular piano. He also liked to work the sliding doors that covered the roll mechanism. At one point, watching the piano keys move up and down as he pumped the pedals, he got the idea of holding on to one of the keys, to see what would happen, to find out, perhaps, how strong was the force moving them. Fearing he might break something, I prevented this contest of strength.

He also liked to turn the crank that raises and lowers the grill on the outdoor charcoal grill. Now and then he lowered it all the way and, since he kept on turning, backed the crank out of the screw threads, so that it came loose. When this happened, he tried to screw the crank back. Some kinds of screws he can thread, but this one was too tricky for him. Usually, after trying a while, he left the handle on the ground, or carried it around awhile before leaving it. We learned to recognize it, even in odd places, and to take it back to the grill. We let the game go on, because it is a good and valuable game. To crank a handle one way, and see that something goes up, and then to crank it the other way, and see the things go down, is an interesting and important experiment for a small child. He not only learns how this particular crank works; he also learns that many actions have regular and predictable effects, and that the world is in many ways a sensible and trustworthy place.

About a year after all these experiments took place, his mother wrote me, in part:

He is the most *noticing*, thoughtful, quick little boy and he hates to be *taught*. He loves to learn things and stores up all sorts of facts for future use. He uses his tools (screwdriver, hammer, spade and rake, saw, etc.) with great skill and care. He loves to do things *with* us—he plants and waters for me—clips the grass—strains sand for cement, etc.—is busy and curious. But when we try (as we are now) to *teach* him something like ABCDEFG, which appears to be without meaning or use he just can't *bear* it—in fact he becomes furious and frustrated—almost in tears. How will he react to school this fall?

Lisa is a super serious student—she now has an all A report card and really *worries* about her grades. She *hates* to be unprepared for school and yet she really deeply dislikes it.

I have since learned that Tommy's resistance to unasked-for teaching is not uncommon in small children, but usual. Many mothers have written us at *Growing Without Schooling,* a bi-monthly magazine we publish for and about people who teach their children at home, telling (often sadly) about their own little children furiously rejecting their well-meant and loving efforts to help or teach them. Children resist, almost always angrily, all such unasked-for teaching because they hear in it the (perhaps unconscious) message, "You're not smart enough to see that this is important to learn, and even if you were, you're not smart enough to learn it." Naturally it makes them hurt and angry. "Let me do it by myself!" they shout. That's just what we should do. If they need help, they will ask for it—at least, as long as we give it when it is asked for. If, in our eagerness to teach and help them, we send them enough of these messages of doubt and distrust, we may soon destroy most of all of their confidence in their ability to learn for themselves, and convince them that they really are too lazy, incurious, and stupid to learn. We will have made our fears come true.

On one of my visits, Tommy invented the game of Gear. Having discovered that he and I were the early wakers in the family, he started coming into my room to visit first thing in the morning. Somehow or other a game developed in which I, lying on my back in bed, arms outside the covers, would raise one forearm to a vertical position and clench my fist. Tommy would then grab this fist and try to tug it this way and that, while I resisted as best I could, now and then surprising him and making him laugh by suddenly yielding. The game started as a pure contest of strength, but Tommy soon turned it into something else. My upraised forearm was transformed into a bulldozer's gearshift (or some control), which he would tug this way and that, all the while making bulldozer noises. It became a regular morning routine; he would come in, we would talk a little, and soon he would say, "Let's play Gear."

Whenever the family went up to the ski area that his father ran, Tommy's greatest joy was to climb up into the seat of a real bulldozer and push all the controls whichever way he could, all the while pretending, of course, that he was making the bulldozer work.

I feel even more strongly now than then that it is in every way useful for children to see adults doing real work and, wherever possible, to be able to help them. One of the many great advantages of home-based education is that children not shut up in school have a chance to see their parents and other adults work, and if they wish, as many do, to join in.

One summer, when Tommy was no more than four or five, the family had a riding horse. Tommy's father asked me to build a little corral for the horse behind their house, and showed me how—dig some postholes (hard work in that tight, clayed soil), put the posts in, tamp them down solid, wrap wire on them, and hang log rails from the wires. Which I did—and the corral lasted as long as the family kept the horses. For many hours during those days of digging under the hot New Mexico sun, Tommy would be out there "helping" me—moving small piles of dirt from one place to another with his shovel or tractor, and putting dirt back in the holes after the fence posts were in. I hadn't asked him to, and didn't reward him for doing it. But he saw real work being done and wanted to be part of it.

School. Lisa remained a brilliant student, and came in time to like school once she learned to get out of it what she wanted. Tommy never liked it much. At first he was deeply curious about many things not in the school curriculum, eager to learn much more than anyone there was able or willing to tell him. In his first four years or so of school, early in each school year his mother would ask him, "What are you studying in school this year?" He would reply, not complaining, just stating a fact, "Same as last year." He meant *exactly* the same, since much of any school year is spent in "reviewing" material from the year before. When he was twelve, he took a summer college course in astronomy, which he loved and learned a great deal from. But no one at school could or would follow up on this experience. After a while he became resigned to being bored in school and went only to see his many friends, and to play soccer and basketball, which he was very good at, as he was at all sports (though he did not begin to walk until he was three).

☐ October 14, 1963

The other day I brought to school an old Army bugle that I had bought secondhand for eight dollars. When the first-grade and kindergarten children went out to recess, I took the bugle out. I gave it a tentative *blat* or two (I can't play it), and about twenty children crowded around me, clamoring for a turn. I lined them up, and off we went. Quite a number of them knew, from having watched me, what to do with their lips. Others put the whole mouth-piece in their mouths, like a lollipop, before realizing that that wouldn't work. Then they tried it the right way. Some I had to show, pursing my lips and blowing through them, what had to be done. Nine out of ten children were able to get a good sound—that is, a strong sound—out of the bugle. Some could make as much noise on it as I could. They got tremendous pleasure and satisfaction from it—particularly Martin. I could hardly get it away from him. And a few, sad, defeated little children would come up, give a weak puff through the instrument, and hand it back to me with a resigned expression. Why did these few give up so easily?

After about four days of this, one of the teachers came out—from her coffee break—and said to please stop playing the bugle, it made her too nervous. So that was the end of that. But it was interesting to see, if only for a short while, how energetically and confidently most of these little children tackled the problem of getting a sound out of a difficult instrument.

□ **November 8, 1963**

On days when I have a lesson, I bring my cello to school, take it to a classroom, and give the children a turn at "playing" it. Except for the timid ones, who make a few halfhearted passes with the bow and then quit, almost all little children attack the cello in the same way. They are really doing three things at once. They are making the machine go. They are enjoying the luxury of making sounds. And they are making scientific experiments. They start off by working the bow vigorously back and forth across one of the strings. They keep this up for a long time. Just the feel and sound of it are exciting. Then they begin to vary their bowing a bit, trying different rhythms. After a while they begin to move the bow so that it touches more than one string, or they move to another string. But it is important to note that the first few times they do this, they do not seem to be doing it in the spirit of an experiment, to find out what will happen. They do it for the sake of doing it. They have been bowing one way, making one kind of noise; now they want to bow another way, and make another kind of noise. Only after some time does it seem to occur to them that there was a relation between the way they bowed and the kind of noise they got. Then there is quite a change in their way of doing things. This time they move more deliberately, watchfully, thoughtfully, from one string to another. You can almost hear them thinking, "Ah, this string makes this kind of noise, and that string makes that kind of noise." But they have to do a good deal of what seems like random bowing, activity for its own sake, before they begin to think about what they are doing. They have to pile up quite a mass of raw sensory data before they begin trying to sort it out and make sense of it.

After they have done a good deal of bowing they begin to think about using the fingers of their left hand to press the strings down on the fingerboard. This does not have much effect, for two reasons. In the first place, their fingers are not strong enough to hold the strings down tightly enough. More important, they do not at first make the slightest effort to be sure they are holding down the same string they are bowing. The bow works furiously across all the strings. The left hand goes up and down the strings, pressing them here and there, but the two activities are not connected. While this goes on, I say nothing.

By now, mostly in homes where I have been visiting, I have seen perhaps a hundred young children try out the cello. They all do what I have described above—if they have seen me play first. I always play if asked, and one of the pieces I play is the prelude to the first of the Bach cello suites. It is a very active piece—my right arm moves rapidly up and down as well as back and forth, while my left hand does a lot of moving up and down the strings. When I then ask the children (and adults) if they want a turn, the children all start out by trying, as far as they can, to do just what I was doing. They are not so much trying to figure out how to play the cello as actually *playing* it.

How do they see their own activity? Do they think to themselves, "I'm going to do just what John was doing," expecting to get the same results? Or do they think, "I know I can't play the cello like John, but I'm going to do all the things he did, and see what happens." I don't know. It may depend a little on their age. The younger ones may really think or hope at first that they can get the same sounds from the cello that I can. Perhaps not, though; young children show clearly when they are disappointed, and I have never seen a young child look disappointed by the results of what he was doing with the instrument.

I suspect that they begin simply by trying to do on the cello as much of what they have seen me do as they possibly can. Whether, as they do this, they imagine real music coming out, I don't know. The line between fantasy and reality is so unclear for children that they are perfectly able to stand comfortably with one foot on one side and one on the other. And perhaps at first they don't think much about the sound; just making the cello go is absorbing and exciting enough to take all their attention.

But then, after a while, they realize that they really are not making quite the same kinds of sounds that I made. Like Vita at the typewriter (see page

237), they begin to realize that their cello playing is only fantasy, and like her, they grow tired of doing nonsense, and begin to want to try to figure out how the cello *really* works. But the total activity comes first.

After a while, the child begins to be aware of something. What? Perhaps his left hand becomes aware, so to speak, of holding down a vibrating string some of the time, and a silent string the rest of the time. Perhaps he becomes aware that some of the time his left hand affects the sound, and some of the time it does not. At any rate, after a while he begins to make a deliberate effort to hold down the same string he is bowing on, looking from one hand to the other. This is harder than it looks, especially for a little child holding the cello in a very awkward position. When he gets the hang of it, he bows away some more, pressing down here and there on the bowed string, again in what seems like a random, undirected way, for some time, before he begins to conduct a series of new experiments, this time to see what happens when he moves his hand up and down the string.

It doesn't take a child long, by such steps, to grasp the basic idea of the cello, the relationship of the bow, the string, and the left hand. But while he has been figuring this out, he has been ceaselessly active. One could say that he is having too much fun—a weak word, really— playing the cello to want to take time to figure it out. A scientist might say that, along with his useful data, the child has collected an enormous quantity of random, useless data. A trained scientist wants to cut all irrelevant data out of his experiment. He is asking nature a question, he wants to cut down the noise, the static, the random information, to a minimum, so he can hear the answer. But a child doesn't work that way. He is used to getting his answers *out of* the noise. He has, after all, grown up in a strange world where everything is noise, where he can only understand and make sense of a tiny part of what he experiences. His way of attacking the cello problem is to produce the maximum amount of data possible, to do as many things as he can, to use his hands and the bow in as many ways as possible. Then, as he goes along, he begins to notice regularities and patterns. He begins to ask questions—that is, to make deliberate experiments. But it is vital to note that until he has a great deal of data, he has no idea what questions to ask, or what questions there are to be asked.

There is a special sense in which it may be fair to say that the child scientist is a less efficient thinker than the adult scientist. He is not as good at cutting out unnecessary and useless information, at simplifying the problem, at figuring out how to ask questions whose answers will give him the most information. Thus, a trained adult thinker, seeing a cello for the first time, would probably do in a few seconds what it takes a child much longer to do—bow each of the strings, to see what sounds they give, and then see what effect holding down a string with the left hand has on the sound made by that string. That is, if—and it is a very big if—he could bring himself to touch the cello at all. Where the young child, at least until his thinking has been spoiled by adults, has a great advantage is in situations—and many, even most real life situations are like this—where there is so much seemingly senseless data that it is impossible to tell what questions to ask. He is much better at taking in this kind of data; he is better able to tolerate its confusion; and he is much better at picking out the patterns, hearing the faint signal amid all the noise. Above all, he is much less likely than adults to make hard and fast conclusions on the basis of too little data, or having made such conclusions, to refuse to consider any new data that does not support them. And these are the vital skills of thought which, in our hurry to get him thinking the way we do, we may very well stunt or destroy in the process of "educating" him.

But the greatest difference between children and adults is that most of the children to whom I offer a turn on the cello accept it, while most adults, particularly if they have never played any other instrument, refuse it.

Sitting in his stroller in a local store the other day was a child about a year old. His mother was busy in the store, and he was absorbed in his own affairs, playing with his stroller, looking at cans of fruit and juice. I watched him. Suddenly he said to himself, "Beng-goo." After a few seconds he said it again, then again, and so perhaps ten times. Was he trying to say, "Thank you?" More probably he had hit on this sound by accident and was saying it over and over because he liked the way it sounded and the way it felt in his mouth.

A few months ago I saw quite a bit of another one-year-old. She liked to say "Leedle-leedle-leedle-leedle." It was her favorite sound, and she said it all the time; indeed, that was about all she said. Now and then she would add an emphatic "a!" (as in *cat*)—"Leedle-leedle-leedle-a!" I asked her father how she had come to make that sound. Was she imitating a sound that someone had made to her? No; apparently she had learned to stick her tongue out and bring it back in quickly, and liked the feel of it. (Babies like all tongue-waggling games.) One day, as she was doing this, she made a sound with her voice, and was amazed and delighted to hear what the movement of her tongue did to that sound. After much practice she found that she could make the sound without having to put her tongue outside her mouth. It felt good, and it sounded good, so she kept it up for a month or two before moving on to something else.

How a sound feels seems to be as important as the sound itself. Everyone who has watched babies knows how pleased they are when they first discover how to make a Bronx cheer. And they do discover it; this sound, at least, is one that their mothers would never teach them.

> Millicent Shinn, in *The Biography of a Baby,* tells this lovely little incident in the life of her then seven-week-old niece, Ruth:
>
> > A few days later the baby showed surprise more plainly. She lay making cheerful little sounds, and suddenly, by some new combination of the vocal organs, a small, high crow came out—doubtless causing a most novel sensation in the little throat, not to speak of the odd sound. The baby fell silent instantly, and a ludicrous look of astonishment overspread her face. Here was not only evidence of the germs of memory, but also the appearance of a new emotion, that of genuine surprise.
>
> > It seems reasonable to assume that very young babies, without much control over the sounds they make, make quite a few of these by accident, enjoy what they feel and hear, and then set about trying to make those same sounds again. Later, perhaps, they more consciously try to imitate sounds they hear around them.

In France some years ago I was surprised to hear an eighteen-month-old boy, while babbling away, make the sound of the French "u." Perhaps there was no reason to be surprised; everyone who talked to him called him "tu." But I had never heard a baby make that sound before, and had had a very hard time to get even a few of my French students to make it. Of course, my students were anxious and self-conscious, and this baby was not—which makes a world of difference.

Why does a baby begin to make sounds in the first place? Is it instinctive, like crying? It seems not to be. A puppy raised apart from other dogs will know how to bark when he gets old enough, but the few children we know of who grew up without human contact grew up almost wholly mute. Babies in understaffed foundling hospitals, who see very little of older people, are said, except for crying, to be almost silent. Apparently it is from hearing people speak around them that babies get the idea of "speaking." When they make their first sounds, are they imitating the sounds they hear around them? Or are they inventing, so to speak, from scratch? Perhaps at first they mostly invent, and imitate more later.

> I now feel strongly that much of the time infants are not trying to "imitate sounds" at all, but are actually trying to speak, that is, to use sounds to convey wishes, feelings, and meanings.
> In *Instead of Education* I wrote:
>
>> We cannot separate an act from the skills involved in the act. The baby does not learn to speak by learning the skills of speech and then using them to speak with.... He learns to speak by speaking.... The baby who begins to talk, long before he makes any sounds that we hear as words, has learned from sharp observation that the sounds that bigger people make with their mouths affect the other things they do. *Their talk makes things happen.* He may not know exactly what, or how. But he wants to be a part of that talking group of bigger people, wants to make things happen with *his* voice.

Millicent Shinn again describes her baby niece, Ruth:

[At four months] She made her little sounds often with an air of friendly response when we prattled to her, giving back murmurs, croaks, and gurgles for words. From the latter part of the fourth month, if we imitated to her some of these sounds, she seemed to imitate them back....

[In her fifth month] One day when she was four and a half months old, she raised a strange little clamor at the sight of her grandfather, as if on purpose to call his attention, and was satisfied when she got it. ... And in the very last days of the fifth month she made a sound of request when she wished to be taken, a whimpering, coaxing sound, leaning and looking toward her mother, instead of the mere fretting sounds of desire, addressed to nobody, which she had made for weeks....

[About a month later] Her sounds had been more various and expressive from the first days of the month. She had taken up a curious puppy-like whine of desire or complaint, and a funny little ecstatic sniffling and catching her breath, to express some shades of delight; and she had also begun to pour out long, varied successions of babbling sounds, which expressed content, interest, or complaint very clearly. She would "talk to" any interesting object (a hedge in gorgeous bloom, for instance) with this expressive babble, sometimes holding out her arms to it at the same time.

A few years ago I was visiting some friends whose little boy was not much more than a year old. The child and I became good friends; he let me carry him around his front yard, looking at and feeling things like trees and bushes. He was already making many separate sounds. But at one point, when I had been talking to his parents about my plane reservation home, the little boy, looking right at me, spoke a long string of sounds that had in them all the rhythms and tones of adult speech. Looking right at him, I replied, explaining why I thought I had better get the earlier plane home rather than the later one. He replied with another string of speechlike sounds. This exchange went on a couple of more times. His mother was astonished; she had never heard him talk in quite that way. For the first time with a child so young, it seemed clear that he was not just imitating my speech sounds, but was having a true conversation with me. What meanings he may have been trying to send me, of course I'll never know. But meanings there surely were.

In the "Fantasy" chapter I will describe a little Australian girl named Julia, who happily wrote long letters of scribbles to her grandma, telling her all kinds of things, and was heartbroken to find out one day that her grandma couldn't read her scribbles. I suspect that early infant talkers are like Julia. They mean to send messages with their voices, as the big people around them obviously do, and they think that these messages are being received. Suddenly, perhaps around the age of one and a half or two, it dawns on them that most of their messages are not being received at all, and that they really can't talk like other people, but must go to a lot of trouble to learn how. This may be one of the things that makes two-year-olds so touchy—they have just discovered that among all the other things they don't know how to do, they don't know how to talk. They are bursting with things to say, needs, and feelings, and awarenesses, but have no way to say them.

It is a remarkable business. We are so used to talking that we forget that it takes a very subtle and complicated coordination of lips, tongue, teeth, palate, jaws, cheeks, voice, and breath. Simply as a muscular skill it is by far the most complicated and difficult that most of us ever learn, at least as difficult as the skill required to master a serious musical instrument. We realize how difficult speech is only when we first try to make the sounds of a language very different from our own. Suddenly we find that our mouths and tongues won't do what we want. Yet every child learns to make the sounds of his own language. If he lives where more than one language is spoken, he makes the sounds of them all. How does he do it? His coordination is poor to start with; how does he manage to do what many adults find so difficult?

The answer seems to be by patient and persistent experiment; by trying many thousands of times to make sounds, syllables, and words; by comparing his own sounds to the sounds made by people around him; and by gradually bringing his own sounds closer to the others; above all, by being willing to do things wrong even while trying his best to do them right.

Bill Hull once said to me, "If we taught children to speak, they'd never learn." I thought at first he was joking. By now I realize that it was a very important truth. Suppose we decided that we had to "teach" children to speak. How would we go about it? First, some committee of experts would analyze speech and break it down into a number of separate "speech skills." We would probably say that, since speech is made up of sounds, a child must be taught to make all the sounds of his language before he can be taught to speak the language itself. Doubtless we would list these sounds, easiest and commonest ones first, harder and rarer ones next. Then we would begin to teach infants these sounds, working our way down the list. Perhaps, in order not to "confuse" the child—"confuse" is an evil word to many educators—we would not let the child hear much ordinary speech, but would only expose him to the sounds we were trying to teach.

Along with our sound list, we would have a syllable list and a word list.

When the child had learned to make all the sounds on the sound list, we would begin to teach him to combine the sounds into syllables. When he could say all the syllables on the syllable list, we would begin to teach him the words on our word list. At the same time, we would teach him the rules of grammar, by means of which he could combine these newly learned words into sentences. Everything would be planned, with nothing left to chance; there would be plenty of drill, review, and tests, to make sure that he had not forgotten anything.

Suppose we tried to do this; what would happen? What would happen, quite simply, is that most children, before they got very far, would become baffled, discouraged, humiliated, and fearful, and would quit trying to do what we asked them. If, outside of our classes, they lived a normal infant's life, many of them would probably ignore our "teaching" and learn to speak on their own. If not, if our control of their lives was complete (the dream of too many educators), they would take refuge in deliberate failure and silence, as so many of them do when the subject is reading.

> This is exactly what happened in the Chicago schools, for a while at least, with respect to reading. Some committee of experts decided that the activity of reading could be broken down into *five hundred* separate skills. They finally pared this list down to two hundred and eighty-three, which they then proposed to teach, one at a time and in strict order, to all the children in the schools. I hope that this absurd project has by now been abandoned.

Last summer, in a supermarket, a young mother came with her baby to the meat counter and began to discuss with him, in the most lively and natural way, what meat they should get for supper. This piece of meat looked nice, but it was too expensive—terrible what was happening to food prices. This piece might be all right, but it would take too long to cook; they had many other errands to do and would not get home before four o'clock. These chops looked good, but they had had them just two nights ago. And so on. There was nothing forced or affected in her words or her voice; she might have been talking to someone her own age.

A year or more ago, some friends and I dropped in on some people who had a six-month-old baby. She was well rested and happy, so they brought her in to see the visitors. We all admired her before going on with our talk. She was fascinated by this talk. As each person spoke, she would turn and look intently at him. From time to time she would busy herself with a toy in her lap; then after a few minutes she would begin watching and listening again. She seemed to be learning, not just that people talk, but that they talk to each other, and respond to each other's talk with smiles, and laughter, and more talk; in short, that talk is not just a kind of noise, but messages, communication.

Babies and young children like to hear adult conversation, and will often sit quietly for a long time, just to hear it. If we want to help little children as they learn to talk, one way to do it is by talking to them—provided we do it naturally and unaffectedly—and by letting them be around when we talk to other people.

For the first few years of her life, Lisa grew up on a cattle ranch. When she was about eighteen months old, she pointed at some cattle one day and said, "See cows, see cows." We were very pleased; these were about the first real words we had heard her say. We agreed that there were indeed cows out there, and said other things about them. But a few days later, going by a field with some horses in it, she said again, "See cows." Later, passing some sheep, she said the same thing. This was puzzling. Surely she didn't think they were all the same animal.

Yet if she knew the horses and sheep were different, why did she call them cows? Or if she thought all animals were called cows, why didn't she call the family dog and cats cows? Apparently, out of all the many things she saw, heard, and felt, she had isolated a group, a class, that we would call "large animals in the fields," and to this class she had given the name "cows." We did not correct her, but just went on talking about cows, horses, and sheep in a normal way. Before long she divided her class of animals in the fields into subgroups, and put the proper label on each one.

At about this time she was given a stuffed toy horse. Soon afterward, I was with her in a store full of many kinds of stuffed toy animals. To my surprise, she called them all "horse." But it was soon clear that here again she had created a class of things in her mind, in this case animal toys, and given them the name "horse" that people used to talk about her own toy. Before long, just by listening to other people talk, she realized that this class, too, was made up of subclasses, each with its own label— dogs, cats, teddy bears, and so on. Soon she had those names well in hand.

Another child, a boy, who also grew up on a ranch, was very interested in the tractor—large, red, and noisy. One of the first words he spoke was "tracker." We soon realized that he applied it to an entire class of objects that we might label "large moving machinery." Cars, buses, trucks, steam shovels, bulldozers, road graders, cranes— all were "trackers." But before long, just by listening to other people's talk, he saw that this class had subgroups, each with its own name. In time, like most small boys, he knew the name of every kind of machine in the neighborhood.

A mother wrote us at *Growing Without Schooling:*

Jessie has two words which are recognizable at the moment. I'm sure she says other things, I just haven't been able to interpret them yet. She says "hot," which means anything which is not body temperature, whether hot or cold, and also means firewood—makes sense since we heat with wood. She also says "da" which all babies say, but it means daddy, dog, cat, and sheep (we raise sheep too). A friend's baby at 10 months said "cat." She would walk around their apartment pointing at things and saying "cat." If it was a cat (and they had two adults cats and ten kittens, so it was a logical first word) she would clap her hands and laugh and if it wasn't she would shake her head no and go on to the next thing. We decided she had sorted the world into two groups, cat and not-cat.

This feat of naming things is more remarkable than it may at first seem. When I began to work in Bill Hull's fifth grade, he used to have the students play a game called "categories." He would give them a word, say "bean." Their task was then to find into what categories a bean could fit. They could say that it was an object, a plant, a living thing, a food, a vegetable, green, something to cook, and so on. Most of the children saw in time that any object, such as a bean, could be considered a member of a large number of classes of things. When we talk about a bean, we are picking out for our attention one or more of the classes of which we consider it a member. If we are gardeners, we may think of the bean as a vine that has to have something to climb on. If we are cooks, we will think about what has to be done to prepare it for cooking, how long it takes to cook, and so on. Thus, when we name an object, we put it into a class of things that are like it, at least in certain respects, and to all of which we give the same name. This is the same procedure that Lisa used when she gave the same name to all the large animals she saw out in the fields.

But babies, when they first look at the world, do not see

it this way at all. For some time they see just a mass of shifting shapes and colors, a single, ever-changing picture in front of them. The Museum of Modern Art in New York has a kind of action picture in which rotating, curved mirrors throw colored lights on a screen in continuously changing patterns. Some people find it disturbing to watch; they keep looking for some kind of system or regularity in the pattern, and cannot find any. The world must look something like this to a baby. The picture he sees before him is not made up, as it is for us, of many separate elements, each of which we can imagine and name, by itself, and all of which we can combine in our minds in other ways. When we see a chair in a room, we can easily imagine that chair in another part of the room, or in another room, or by itself. But for the baby the chair is an integral part of the room he sees. This may be the reason, or one of the reasons, why, when we hide something from a very young baby, it ceases to exist for him. And this in turn may be one of the reasons why peek-a-boo games are such fun for small babies to play, and may contribute much to their growing understanding of the world.

> One of the games I like to play with babies I see in airports is the Hat (or Glasses) game. First I put the hat (or glasses) on, and let them look at me for a while. Then I take the hat off and hold it in my hand, and let them look at me and at it for a while. Then I put the hat back on for a while, then take it off for a while, and so on. During all this I say nothing, and keep a friendly but otherwise straight face. Almost all babies of six months or so and older find this game interesting and watch it, attentively and solemnly, for as long as I play it.

A perceptive psychologist, Dr. Herman Witkin, in a book called *Psychological Differentiation,* aptly described the world of the young baby as "undifferentiated." It can't be broken down into parts. But as a baby gets older, he begins to see the room as a collection of things that are separate. Each object in the room—chair, lamp, table—has its own existence. It can be thought about by itself. When a baby makes this step, he is said to make an idea or mental model of the world that is differentiated.

Before he can start naming things, say a chair, the baby must take one more mental step. Not only must he see, first, that this chair exists by and of itself, independent of the room, that it could be somewhere else in the room, or in another room, he must also see that this chair is like certain other objects in the room and in other rooms. He must see that this chair is more like *that* chair than either of them are like a lamp, or a table, or a rug. Wendell Johnson, in *People in Quandaries,* put it neatly when he said that a similarity is a difference that doesn't make any difference. So the baby must see that, in spite of differences between one chair and another, they are in essential respects the same. In short, he sees that the chair is one of a family or class of like things. Only then is he ready to call such a thing a "chair," or to understand what other people mean when they call it that. He must create the class in his mind before he can name it. Thus, naming things is not just blind imitation; it is a creative act of the mind.

> It seems to me that this act of the mind, of grouping things into classes and naming the classes, can only be called abstract thinking.

One day, when Danny (mentioned earlier) was very small, I was watching him play. He had not really begun to talk; there were only half a dozen or so "words" that he could say. At this time he was much interested in a big alarm clock. He liked to watch it, listen to its tick, and fiddle with its knobs and levers. Seeing the clock on the mantelpiece, he began to make an insistent, one-syllable noise, which he kept on making until someone gave him the clock. It seemed clear that he was not just saying "clock," or some baby equivalent of "clock." What he was saying was, "I want that clock, I need that clock, give me that clock!"

Long before I got into teaching, I met Jackie, about two years old, who had created in his mind a class of objects that we would call "dry, crumbly things to eat"—cookies, crackers, dry toast—to which he had given the name "Zee." Neither his father nor his mother knew how he had come to pick that word. They assured me that he had not picked up the name from them—*they* never called crackers "Zee." Clearly the baby had decided for himself that it was a good name for this class of things.

When Tommy was about two, he met his first horses. One of them was named Duke, the other Blueberry. They made a great impression on him, and from their names he invented his own word for horses in general—dukeberries. His family was delighted and often (not always) used the word themselves.

Some of Tommy's first words were not names of things, but other kinds of words. When he was still little enough to be carried around a good deal of the time, he used to show where he wanted to go to whoever was carrying him by pointing his hand in the desired direction and saying, imperiously, "Way!" When he said this to me, I used to answer, "Way," and then add, using my language, "Shall we go over this way?" Another of his early words was "Down." If he was being carried, "Down" meant "Put me down." If he wasn't being carried, "Down" meant "Pick me up." His older sister, when she was very little, had invented a word "Tup-tup," which meant exactly the same thing.

It might be interesting some time to put together a collection of these first words that babies invent, and the very large classes of things to which they attach them. Along with this we could note some of the ways in which they later break down these large classes into smaller classes. If any readers of this book have infants just starting to speak and are interested in these matters, I hope they will make a note of some of these words and send them to me.

These special, non-name words that children invent remind me of something I once read or heard about the life of Victor the Wolf Boy, so called because for most of the first ten years or so of his life, as far as anyone knew, he lived isolated from all other humans. When he was found, a French doctor tried to train and teach him. He was able to domesticate him to a certain extent, to get him to wear clothes and do simple tasks, but though he tried very patiently, he was never able to teach him to speak. At one point the doctor came close to what we now call a breakthrough, and perhaps, if he had understood as much as we now think we do about the beginnings of speech, he might have been able to make better use of his opportunity.

He had been trying without success to teach Victor to make sounds stand for objects. One day Victor was hot, hungry, and thirsty. On the kitchen table was a pitcher of cold milk, all frosty on the outside. Seeing it, Victor began to make a single insistent sound which he repeated over and over. The doctor assumed that this sound meant "milk"; at any rate, he tried thereafter to make it stand for "milk." What Victor meant it to stand for, more probably, was something stronger and more complicated—the feeling of being hot and thirsty, of seeing something he knew would taste wonderful and wanting it. Perhaps, had the doctor tried to make that sound stand for "hungry and thirsty," he might have got somewhere. As it was, the wolf-boy never was able to grasp the fundamental idea and purpose of speech.

The doctor's mistake—and it was a mistake, since the wolf-boy never learned to talk—is another good example of our mistakes in "sequencing." We assume that since words are the shortest and simplest elements of language, when we learn language we learn words first. But it is far more likely that we learn words *last.* First we learn the large idea of communication by speech, that all those noises that come out of people's mouths mean something and can make things happen. Then, from the tones of people's voices and the contexts in which they speak, we get a very general idea of what they are saying, just as I can tell, in a country of whose language I do not speak a word, that a parent is scolding a child or people are joking or arguing or that someone is giving someone else an explanation or an order. Then they begin to intuit a rough outline of the grammar—i.e., the structure—of the language. *Finally* they begin to learn words, and to put those words into their proper slots in the very rough models of grammar which they have invented.

If the good doctor had only talked to Victor as a real person, instead of talking as a teacher trying to teach something, he might have had more success. But how could Victor be expected to learn words when he had not yet figured out what language was *for?* The problem wasn't that the doctor had given him more data than he could handle, but that he hadn't given him nearly enough.

One day, when Tommy was very little, he decided that he needed to find out the names for a lot of things. He suddenly began to look very intently at various objects in the room, pointing out to me each of them in turn. At first I had no idea what he wanted. I thought he was asking me to give him whatever he was looking at, or to do something with it. But he showed me that that was not what he wanted. For a while I was baffled. Then, on a hunch, I tried telling him the name of what he was showing me. Instantly he showed by his expression that I had guessed right. He began to point to many other objects. Here I thought it might help if I gave him a question that he could ask whenever he wanted to know the name of something (a very useful thing also in studying a foreign language). So when he pointed to a vase, I said, "What's that called? That's called a vase." I hoped that if I said it often enough, he would learn to say it. For a short while, at least, he did, but I don't know how long it stuck, or for that matter how long lasting was his need to be told the names of things. For after all, any observant child, in a family where people do much talking, soon learns what things are called just by listening to what people say about them.

> By now many other children have played this game with me. I think of one in particular, the two-year-old daughter of some musician friends, who was frustrated often to the point of rage by not being able to put into words all the ideas and questions she had swirling round in her mind. She would point to one object after another in her house, each time making a repeated, insistent, almost furious sound. She sounded so angry that it would have been easy to assume that she wanted to be given the things she was pointing at. But she didn't, all she wanted was their names.

I was careful, when I told Tommy the name of something, not to tell him as if it were a lesson, something he *had* to remember. Nor did I test him by saying, "What's this? What's that?" This kind of checking up is not necessary, and it puts a child in a spot where he will feel that, if he says the wrong thing, he has done wrong and is in the wrong. I have seen kindly, well-meaning parents do this to young children, hoping to help them learn. Almost every time the child soon took on the kind of tense, tricky expression we see on so many children's faces in school, and began the same sad old business of bluffing, guessing, and playing for hints. Even in the rare case when a child does not react this defensively to questions, too much quizzing is likely to make him begin to think that learning does not mean figuring out how things work, but getting and giving answers that please grownups.

We should also remember that children (like adults), and above all young children, know and understand much more than they can put into words. If we point to a lamp and say to a young child, "What's that?," we may not always get an answer. If we get none, or the wrong one, does it mean that the child doesn't know the name for lamp, or doesn't know what the word "lamp" refers to? Not necessarily. In other contexts, he might know the word perfectly well. His reason for not answering the question "What's that?" may be only that the question itself confuses him, that he doesn't know what we want him to say or do.

Jerome Bruner once said, very aptly, that much of what we do and say in school only makes children feel that they do not know things that, in fact, they knew perfectly well before we began to talk about them. I have often seen this in mathematics, where fifth-graders, confused and frightened by rules and magic recipes, are unable to use either rules or common sense to do problems that they could easily have done a few years before. And what is true of school, is often true of home. A child's understanding of the world is uncertain and tentative. If we question him too much or too sharply, we are more likely to weaken that understanding than strengthen it. His understanding will grow faster if we can make ourselves have faith in it and leave it alone.

> This is particularly true of children just learning to read. They have a lot of very tentative hunches about the connections between the look of printed

letters and the sounds of spoken words. If we give them enough time, they will gradually, as they read *for pleasure,* test and confirm and strengthen these hunches, and make them a part of what they really know. But if we put too much pressure on these hunches, by continually asking children questions about what this or that letter says, we are liable to jar these hunches loose altogether and convince the children that they don't know anything, can't figure out anything, and must depend on us for all their information.

One good way to help children learn the names of things is by talking about anything we do together. Many mothers, getting a child ready to go out, say something like this: "Now we'll tie up this shoe; pull the laces good and tight; now we'll get the boots; let's see, the right boot for the right foot, then the left boot for the left foot; all right, coat next, arms in the sleeves, zip it up nice and tight; now the mittens, left mitten on the left hand, right mitten on the right hand; now comes the hat, on it goes, over your ears ..." This kind of talk is companionable and fun, and from it the child learns, not just words, but the kinds of phrases and sentences they fit into.

Well, I'm not so sure about this anymore. I certainly don't think this kind of talk is necessary; billions of children learn to speak who have never been spoken to in this way. And I suspect that most people who try to talk this way to children will have so much more teaching in their voices than love and pleasure that they will wind up doing more harm than good. If talk is not honest, does not have real feeling behind it—like most of the talk children hear on TV—*they will not think of it as something they can or want to do themselves,* and hence will learn little or nothing from it.

One winter morning, when we were eating breakfast, Tommy began to say "Toe! Toe! Toe!" Putting helpful expressions on our faces, we said, "Toe?" It was clear that we did not know what he meant. Again he said, "Toe! Toe! Toe!," looking furiously at us. We knew that he had been using the word to mean toe, coat, cold, and toilet. So we said, pointing at his toe, "Does your toe hurt?" Wrong. "Do you want your coat? Your blue coat?" Wrong again. "Do you want to go towet?" (family expression inherited from previous baby). Still wrong. "Are you cold?" Now we were on the right track. Asking more questions, we eventually found that someone had left an outside door open, letting in a draft, and that Tommy wanted us to close the door—which we did. This shows that a baby's speech may be more varied than it sounds. He may *know* the difference between a number of words, even if he cannot say the difference.

> This brings to mind all those questions that school people are continually asking children to be sure they know the difference between, say, P and B. If children can use these words correctly in speech, or even like Tommy understand the difference between them in the speech of others, then they know the difference even if they can't answer the questions.
>
> Such questions are another example of the dissociated teaching Professor Papert rightly complains about—facts cut off from all their natural connections with things.

When a baby shows us, by his expression, by the insistent tone of his voice, and by repeating his words over and over, that he is trying hard to tell us something, we must try just as hard to understand what he is saying. Often it will not be easy. Some people, if they don't understand the first or second time, say, "I don't know what you're saying," and give up. But we must not give up. It sometimes helps to ask the next oldest child in the family. He may be able to interpret, perhaps because he knows the smaller child better and hears him talk more, perhaps because he himself is closer to early speech and remembers what it is like. Or, if there is no other child to interpret for us, we can say to the child who is speaking, "Can you show me?" I remember seeing one mother do this with her little boy. At first he did not understand her question, and looked puzzled. She then took a step or two in one direction, pointing, and saying, "Is it in here? Is it this way?" Then she went in another direction and asked again, while the child watched, puzzled and intent. After a while he saw what her question meant, and was soon able to lead her to what he wanted to tell her about.

Once, when Tommy was very little, he came to tell me that his teddy bear was stuck between the bars of his crib. Since I couldn't understand him at first, I went through the "show-me" routine. As soon as he understood me, he led me to the scene of the tragedy. I said, "Oh, I see. Your poor teddy bear has got stuck in the crib. His head is stuck in the bars. Well, the thing for us to do is to get him unstuck and pull him out. First we have to turn him a little bit, so that his head is pointing the narrow way, and then we just slide him out." I continued to talk about the bear, and how it feels to be stuck, etc. What was the point of this talk? First, just to make some conversation, and secondly, to show Tommy our ways of saying what he was trying to say, and to assure him that we do have words for talking about such things.

I'm not at all happy about this bear episode. It's clear to me now, looking back, that even though I understood very well that Tommy could learn to speak without my teaching him, the teacher devil in me was saying, "But if you're clever, and you *are* clever, he'll learn *even more* if you do teach him." Not so. All that talk about the bear was not honest talk, but teaching talk. In fairness to myself, I must say that I didn't do much of it, perhaps because there was so much going on in the family, and so much real talk, that there wasn't much time for fake talk. But if I, or someone, had made a point of giving Tommy a dose of this kind of talk every day, we probably would have done some harm.

Bruno Bettelheim has many times pointed out that if a child's efforts to get a response from the world and the people around him fail more than a very few times, he may well decide that there is no use in trying. This throws new light on the matter of I.Q. scores. We know that so-called intelligence tests largely measure skill at understanding and using words. We also know that both high and low I.Q. scores tend to run in families. From this it is easy to infer that the kind of verbal skill measured by these tests is inherited from parents. Many educators are beginning to have second thoughts about this; but that this is still part of the folklore of our time is shown by the fact that many biologists are now talking excitedly about the possibility of treating human embryos so as to raise their I.Q. by twenty points. Clearly they still think that the I.Q. measures some inborn ability, rather than acquired skill.

It seems more likely, at least to me, that I.Q. scores tend to run high, or low, in families, because people who are skillful with words are able, most of the time, to encourage the growth of that skill in their children. Such children, when still babies, are encouraged to try to talk by hearing talk around them. When they begin real talking, they are further encouraged, because their parents (and other older people) are persistent and resourceful in trying to understand them. In a family with little verbal skill, a baby can be handicapped, not just because he hears so little talk, but also because, when he does try to talk, he is less often understood, and hence less often en-

couraged. If people do not try very hard to understand
what he says, he may come to feel that most of the time
there is not much point in saying anything.

This point about understanding seems to me even
more true now than then, even of very young babies.
The New York Times, in an article in 1981 about babies' crying, quoted Dr. Michael Lewis, professor of
pediatrics at Rutgers Medical School as saying that
even as early as the eighth week infants whose cries
are responded to are noticeably more curious, smile
more, and stay awake for longer periods. In the same
article Susan Crockenberg, associate professor of human development at the University of California at
Davis, said that the work of a number of researchers
has shown that "the more responsive a mother is to
her baby, the less it cries, the more securely attached
it gets to be and the more readily it develops trust."
Mothers who said they thought that responding to
their babies' cries would "spoil" them have been
found in later observations to have babies who cried
more.

I have long felt that the passionate anger of so
many crying two- or three-year-olds comes not so
much just from their not being able to do what they
want as from their feeling (perhaps mistaken, perhaps not) that they have not been *understood,* or
worse, that no one has even tried to understand
them, that their words have been ignored or casually
and contemptuously brushed aside. Even if in some
instances we are determined to bend a child's will to
our own, we should pay him very serious attention
when he tries to tell us what he wants. When in a
dispute with a small child, I have always found it at
least courteous and often quite helpful to keep saying, "I *hear* what you're saying, I *understand* that
you want this or that, I'm *sorry* that you feel so angry

and unhappy, but I'm not going to get you the candy bar (or do whatever it is you want me to do)."

But there is a much deeper and more important sense in which we can and often do fail to understand children. Because they are so small, clumsy, inarticulate, and foolish, and also (for those who like them) so appealing, we can easily underestimate the seriousness of many of their questions and concerns, and either laugh at them indulgently or ignore them altogether. In his recent, very short, very readable but also very profound and important book, *Philosophy and the Young Child*, Dr. Gareth Mathews, professor of philosophy at the University of Massachusetts at Amherst, makes clear from many of his conversations with young children (in many cases, his own), that many of their surprising and naive remarks and questions, which we adults are too liable to dismiss as ignorant and silly, are questions that some of the greatest philosophers in our history have been struggling with since philosophy began. Mathews also points out, kindly but convincingly, that even such close and sympathetic observers of children as Piaget and Bettelheim have consistently and gravely underestimated the intellectual capacity of children, and misunderstood or completely overlooked the philosophical implications of much of what they say.

Dr. Mathews shows us some questions that children have raised (I am sorry to have to leave out his discussions of these):

Tim (about six years), while busily engaged in licking a pot, asked, "Papa, how can we be sure that everything is not a dream?" Somewhat abashed, Tim's father said that he didn't know and asked how Tim thought that we could tell. After a few more licks of the pot, Tim answered, "Well, I don't think everything is a dream, 'cause in a dream people wouldn't go around asking if it was a dream."

Some question of fact arose between James and his father and James said, "I *know* it is!" His father replied, "But perhaps you might be wrong!" Denis (four years, seven months) then joined in, saying, "But if he knows, he can't be wrong! *Thinking*'s sometimes wrong, but *knowing*'s always right!"

Ian (six years) found to his chagrin that the three children of his parents' friends monopolized the television; they kept him from watching his favorite program. "Mother," he asked in frustration, "why is it better for three people to be selfish than for one?"

John (six years), reflecting on the fact that in addition to books, toys, and clothes he has two arms, two legs, and a head and that these are *his* toys, *his* arms, *his* head, and so on, asked, "Which part of me is really me?"

With a little reflection, we can easily see how far such questions might lead us. In the last chapter of his book Mathews describes in some detail a philosophical conversation he had with his then nine-year-old son, that went on for weeks and covered several profound and important philosophical topics, including how we know what words mean, and whether and how we could think if we didn't have any words. It is a model of how adults can and should but so rarely do talk to children, for it is above all a conversation between equals. Not that the man and the boy are or pretend to be equals in everything; both know very well that the man has much more knowledge and experience. But they are equals, first, because they work as colleagues, are equally involved in the conversation, equally eager and determined to find as much of the truth as they can. And they are equals because the man treats the boy with exactly the respect that he would want an adult colleague to treat him, takes his thoughts, confusions, and questions as seriously as he would want another adult to take his own. Again, we can only envy all children who have such adults to talk to.

When Patrick, of whom I spoke earlier, was just over two years old, he could not pronounce S, Z, SH, CH, or any other sibilant sounds. He just left them out. Words like "spoon" came out "poon." It did not take long to learn to understand him, and when we adults could not tell what he wanted to say, his three-and-a-half-year-old sister could always translate. Nobody fretted about the missing sounds. As a result, the little boy spoke confidently and freely, and before long was able to speak like everyone else. What would have happened if we had dealt with him as we deal with children in school? Instead of giving him time to correct his own speech, to grow competent and confident in making his sibilants, we would have been correcting him every time he spoke. "No, not 'poon,' 'spoon,' S-s-s-s-poon. Say it, spoon, spoon, spoon." We might have grown more impatient and angry, the child more discouraged and frightened. It would not have been long before he would have become anxious at the very thought of speaking. Perhaps he would have tried to avoid all words with sibilants in them. Perhaps he might have decided to stop talking altogether, since it always got him into so much trouble. Or he might have developed a stutter or stammer; as Wendell Johnson and other speech therapists have pointed out, this is how stutterers and stammerers are made.

Most people who write about the troubles of slum children in school claim that slum children speak badly because their parents do not correct their speech. This leads to two conclusions. The first is that any child whose speech is not continually corrected will grow up speaking like a slum child; the second is that all we need to do to cure the speech problems and defects of slum children is correct their speech often enough. Both ideas are non-sense.

Children can, do, and will learn to speak the language that most people speak around them. If a child grows up where most people do not speak what is called standard English, then we will do only harm if we try to make him think there is something wrong with his speech. It will make much more sense, as some schools are beginning to do, to teach standard English as if it were a foreign language, encouraging a child to talk and write about things that interest him, in the way that is most natural to him, all the time exposing him to as much standard English as possible.

Daniel Fader, professor of English at the University of Michigan and author of (among others) the famous and important book *Hooked on Books,* told in his later book *The Naked Children* about five black junior high school students he came to know in Washington, D.C. On the basis of school tests these children were believed by their teachers to be illiterate, wholly unable to speak standard English and barely able to speak at all. And who can blame the teachers—this was the face that these children had chosen to show to the school. What Fader found out, once the children came to know and trust him—*and we cannot learn anything important about other people until they trust us*—was that the children could read well, were very articulate, and could speak about a 95 percent standard English when they felt it was to their advantage to do so, as when they visited the University of Maryland and the children did not want to shame either Fader or themselves before their friendly college student hosts.

I spoke at a PTA meeting recently, and repeated the story of Lisa giving the name "cows" to a class of animals including cows, horses, and sheep. I explained that we did not correct her because it would be discourteous; because we were too pleased to hear her talk to be worried about "mistakes"; and because, realizing that she had done some bold and powerful thinking, we did not want to do anything to make her doubt its worth or discourage her from doing more such thinking in the future. I also emphasized that correction was in fact not needed, that the child was soon able, by herself, to get her names and classes straightened out.

A certain number of people are always upset by hearing such stories. Soon after this meeting, I got a pleasant but agitated letter from an intelligent and highly trained psychologist who had heard my talk. How, she demanded, could children possibly learn unless we corrected all their mistakes? Wasn't that our responsibility, our duty? I wrote a long reply, repeating my point and telling still more stories about children correcting their own mistakes. But she seems to be as far from understanding me as ever. It is almost as if she cannot hear what I am saying. This is natural enough. Anyone who makes it his life work to help other people may come to believe that they cannot get along without him, and may not want to hear evidence that they can, all too often, stand on their own feet. Many people seem to have built their lives around the notion that they are in some way indispensable to children, and to question this is to attack the very center of their being.

Still, even at the risk of upsetting these good people, we must question their assumption, because it is largely not true. Very recently I met Jill, the three-year-old daughter of some friends I had not seen in some time. She was entertaining me in the library, talking away and showing me this or that. At one point she said, "Do you want to see what my brother teached me?" I said, "I'd love to." She stood before me on the rug, put her head down on the floor, leaned over further and further, and finally went over in a somersault. Amazing! "Now, I'm going to do a big one," she said, and did another. While she was doing several others, I thought about how to fit into our conversation a sentence with the word "taught" in it. After a decent interval she mentioned her brother again, and I said, "Does he teach you many things?" "Oh, yes," she said. I said, "You must have been pleased when he taught you that somersault." "Yes, I was," she said. After a few more somersaults, she did something else, and said, "He taught me this, too." And our conversation went on.

Some minutes later, when her father was in the room, she showed him the somersault, and then said, "That's what Jamie teached me." I was not surprised; it takes time for children to feel confident in a new way of doing or saying something, and to this child "teached" must have seemed much more reasonable, more grammatically consistent (it is), and more likely to be right than "taught." But again, after a decent interval, I dropped another "taught" sentence into the conversation, and again, next time she had occasion to use the word, she said "taught." Nothing more was needed, or is ever needed. Children's senses are keen, they notice everything, and they want to do things like the grownups. If we speak well, and they hear us, they will soon speak as we do.

"Nothing more was needed ..." Not even that much was needed. What I did here was a mistake, not necessary, not useful, and if I had continued it for long, probably harmful. Not that much harm was done in that brief meeting; the child was too interested in me, and her somersault, to notice that I was trying to correct her speech. But if she had come to know me well, and if I had gone on with it, she certainly would have picked it up. An adult who is mainly interested in a child's somersaults and other adventures doesn't talk in quite the same tones as one who is mainly interested in finding ways to correct her speech, and children are very good at telling the difference.

As it happens, I did not see that child again for many years, so that was the end of my little experiment in speech correcting. Why, knowing already that it was a discourtesy and a mistake to correct children's speech openly and directly, did I make this experiment at all? The teacher devil in me made me do it. I just couldn't resist the sudden temptation to be so clever as to correct a word without her knowing it. Even if my experiment had worked and she had picked up my use of the word "taught," it would still have been better for her to find this out in her own time and her own way. Beyond that, if we think that every time we talk to a child we must teach her something, our talk may become calculated and fake, and may lead the child to think, like so many of today's young people, that all talk is a lie and a cheat.

I would have been less tempted to correct this child's little mistake had I not, like so many adults, been under the spell of the Bad Habit Theory of Learning. This tells us that every time a child makes a mistake, in speaking, reading, or whatever, we must instantly correct it, lest it freeze into a "bad habit," impossible to correct. The theory is simply untrue. Most of the many things children learn, and that we all learned as children—to walk, talk, read, write, etc.—they learn by trying to do them, making mistakes, *and then correcting the mistakes*. They learn by what mathematicians call "successive approximations"; that is, they do something, compare the result with the desired goal (doing it the way bigger people do it), see some of the differences (their mistakes), and try to reduce these differences (correct their mistakes). All children do this, and all are good at it; even in the homes of the busiest mistake-correctors, the children themselves correct many more mistakes than are pointed out to them.

In my closet the other day I found a yellowing sheet of notes made many years ago on the speech of Tommy at the age of four or five.

raintoats
I dot it for my birsday
toopid fool!
rash (crash) helmet
(also) shrash helmet
bring (spring)
dill (kill)
tab (stab)
betuz (because)
brack (black)
Fanta Fe (Santa Fe)
darbage (garbage)
tomin (coming)
feshin (refreshing)
tasafy (catastrophe)
organize tese tars (these cars)
flashes (glasses)
teo (mosquito)
sree (free)
Bolkswagen
fayer (sweater)
soldiers (shoulders)
fraffer (tractor)
peash (please)

As the words show, though his vowels and stresses were always correct, there was no consistent pattern in his shifts of consonants, so it was hard for people who did not know him well to understand him.

When he talked to others, some older member of the family often had to translate. But being the adored youngest of six children, he had no trouble communicating. We in the family all knew or were glad to figure out what he was trying to say, and he in turn easily understood our standard English. He did not mix up *our* consonants, even if he did his own.

In January of his fifth year, he was still talking much like those notes. When I phoned the family in March, he answered the phone, and his speech was so normal that at first I thought I was talking to his older sister. Not a trace of those consonant shifts was left. Furthermore, having heard them as "wrong" and purged them from his own speech, he became very indignant if others in the family went on using them. We had to learn to stop talking about things like "fraffers," which we did with regret, as we had come to like those words. And all of this speech correcting he did on his own; no one in the family had ever made a point of "correcting" him or trying to teach him the "right" way to talk. They wisely and rightly assumed that in time he would work this out for himself.

How was this little boy able to make such a large and rapid change in his speech? One thing is certain—no purely physical problem could have so suddenly and mysteriously cleared up. One possibility is that at first he had been too busy thinking about the ideas he wanted to get across to bother much with the actual sound of what he was saying. Then at some point, perhaps when he had become confident that he could convey his ideas, he began to listen more carefully to the actual sounds he was making, and became aware that they were often not like the sounds made by the adults. The other possibility is that, hearing his own sounds clearly enough, he had simply heard the differences between his words and other people's as differences that didn't make any difference, like someone speaking another language with a foreign accent. Suddenly, for some reason of his own, he no longer wanted to speak English with a baby foreign accent. He wanted to talk like an adult native. Having decided to, he did, in almost no time at all.

One reason we are misled about bad habits is that we use the word "habit" in two different ways: correctly, to describe things that we do without knowing it, and incorrectly, to describe things that we quite consciously make a practice of doing. The two are not at all the same. Thus when I was little I read a great deal, and seeing in books words I had not heard spoken, I had to guess what these sounded like. (Trusting myself to figure them out, I never thought of looking them up in a dictionary.) Mostly I guessed right, but not always. The word "picturesque" I pronounced "picture-skew," and "super*fluous*" became "*super*fluous." When in time I heard others say those words, I thought with mild surprise, "Oh, *that's* what they're supposed to sound like," and never mispronounced them again. Making the change was easy. I had said them wrongly not because I had a "habit" of saying them that way, but because I thought they were *supposed* to be said that way. When I learned the right way, I said them that way instead. Habit had nothing to do with it.

We tend to picture a Bad Habit as a kind of sinister creature, like a leech or a vampire bat, just waiting to fasten onto us. Smoke once, goes the warning, and you'll always smoke; read or spell a word wrongly once, and you'll do it forever. It's not true. The analogy is false, even at the purely physical level (if there is such a thing as the "purely" physical). Dr. Feldenkrais, a world-famous and very gifted physical therapist who works with people who for years have used their bodies in ways which cause them great tension and often acute pain, has found very often that when he makes them aware of what they have been doing with their muscles, and what they might do instead, they can in a very short time change the supposed habits of a lifetime. The brain, the organism, he says, is smart; it wants to do things right, and when someone "shows" it how, in a way it can understand and believe, it changes at once.

In my own work as a late-starting cellist I have in recent years made several changes in the way I hold and move the bow. In some cases I had been doing something wrong without knowing it. In other cases I had been deliberately doing something that I later came to feel was wrong, that some expert cellist had advised me to do. (Among experts there can be great differences of opinion in these matters.) In every case I was able to change with little trouble just the kind of habits that are supposed to be next to impossible to change.

The other day I made a mistake in learning the cello part of a string quartet that my friends and I were working on. I had had many lines of eighth notes, and the rhythm of them got so firmly stuck in my mind and muscles that when I came to a measure of quarter notes I saw them and played them as eighth notes. Since I then began to hear the measure that way in my mind, I went on making the same mistake. Since it always sounded the way I expected it to sound, I thought it must be right. So I worked busily away at my "bad habit." Naturally, when I played that section of the quartet with my friends, I was in trouble. At a place where we were all supposed to finish together, I kept arriving first. No matter how carefully I played, I got the same result. Could I be leaving something out? No, that wasn't it. Suddenly I saw what I had been doing wrong. I told my friends what I had been doing, laughed at myself for playing "goofissimo," and went on. Knowing what was right, I did it right. End of bad habit.

Sometimes one of us, learning our part, will play the wrong pitch, perhaps a sharp instead of a natural. Hearing the wrong note as right, we go on playing it. But when we play it with the others, it sounds wrong. For a second or two we all wonder what the trouble could be. Sometimes our coach will catch the mistake. But very often the culprit will say, "For goodness sakes, I've been playing that G natural as a G sharp." That ends the mistake. That wrong note isn't locked into our mind and muscles. Knowing it's wrong, we stop playing it.

This is not to say at all that learning never has anything to do with developing good habits, or that learning these good habits may not often take much time and effort. When we learn any complicated physical skill, music among them, we must consciously and at first awkwardly teach our nerves and muscles to do certain things, and then do them so often that in time we can do them without having to think about *how* to do them. All skilled athletes do this. Musicians play over and over again many kinds of scales, arpeggios, etc., so that when they meet them in a piece of music they can play them quickly and evenly. Jascha Heifetz, technically the greatest violinist of our time, played these simple exercises at least three hours a day, every day of his playing life. And even when we have gained those good habits, we often have to keep relearning them, putting them back into our neuromuscular systems. As Casals said one morning to a friend as he played a simple C major scale on his cello, "Every day, for fifty years, I have to *find* the E."

No, the point here is not that good habits are unimportant. They often are. The point is that if it takes a long time to develop a good habit, it will take just as long to develop a bad one. The idea that we must work hundreds of hours to make a good habit, but can make a bad one in a few seconds, is nonsense. And the point of this to us as teachers is that we don't always have to be in such a big hurry to correct children's mistakes. We can afford to give them time to notice and correct them themselves. And the more they do this, the better they will become at doing it, and the less they will need and depend on us to do it for them. The less they have to depend on us, the faster they can teach themselves.

A child who starts to talk is making a very bold leap into the world. Anyone who has learned a foreign language at home, and then used it for the first time in a foreign country, has felt for himself how bold and risky this leap is. Once, while spending a year abroad, I decided to bike from Paris to Rome. Six weeks before starting out I bought some beginning texts and began to study Italian. By the time I reached Italy I had a small vocabulary and some grammar, but I had never spoken a word of Italian to anyone. The day I crossed the border, I rode into a town called Ventimiglia. Being hungry, I decided to buy some bananas. Over and over I rehearsed how I would ask for them: *"Due kilo di banane, per favore."* It seemed easy enough. I could not see how it could be wrong. But I had a horrible feeling that if I went into a grocery store and said those words, everyone there would roar with laughter. So I grew more and more nervous the closer I came to Ventimiglia, and to the moment when I would actually have to speak. (My fears were groundless—nobody in Italy ever laughed at me, everyone was kind and helpful.) The moment arrived. There was the store. There were the bananas. No excuse to put it off any longer. I summoned up my courage, walked inside, and spoke my piece. The lady behind the counter made a gesture of acknowledgment, cut some bananas off a stalk, weighed them, and gave them to me. I paid, thanked her, and left. My Italian had worked! But this did not make me any the less nervous when the next time came to speak. It took many trials before I began to feel fairly sure that when I spoke my bad Italian to Italians I was at least getting some idea over to them.

A child learning to talk needs the kind of curious, attentive, sympathetic audience that I found in Italy. At first, he is not sure that this language business really works. Even after many years of talking, he may not feel that he can get his most important thoughts and feelings across to other people. There is no time, in all of a child's growing up, when he will not be seriously hurt if he feels that we adults are not interested in what he is trying to say. For most children, this time comes all too soon.

□ July 17, 1961

Lisa (age two and one half) is usually the first awake in the morning, after me. When she wakes, she begins to talk to herself. It is an odd mixture. Nonsense syllables, funny noises, snatches of songs, remarks about what she did yesterday and may do today all tumble out in profusion. The other day, after talking about something quite different, she paused and then said, "Going to get dressed. (pause) Dress. (pause) Shoes. (pause) Pants." Then these thoughts led to something else. She goes on talking all day. Sometimes she talks to get something she wants. Sometimes she talks to make something happen, that might uncover the meaning of what she says. Much of the time she talks just because she likes the sound of it.

She likes to talk about colors. One of her favorite words is "blue." Something about the action of lips and tongue in the "bl" pleases her, for she says it often. Whenever she says that she wants something, she usually adds, "Want a blue one, a pink one," or "I have a blue one, a pink one." She certainly does not know the names of the colors, and may not know, even in the most general sense, what a color is. What she does know about words like "blue," "yellow," "pink," and so on, is that they are adjectives. That is, they are combined with other words in a special way. Indeed, much of her talk might be called experiments with grammar, that is, exercises in putting together words in the way that people around her put them together. She makes word patterns, sentences, that sound like the sentences she hears. What do they mean? Often they may not mean anything, and are not meant to mean anything. Not long ago she said, in the middle of a conversation about something different, "I fell out of a big blue mountain into a car." My mind reeled. What was she trying to say? Then it occurred to me that perhaps she was not trying to say anything, but was making up a nice-sounding sentence, a pattern of words, using words and phrases that she knew and liked to say.

One morning at breakfast she began to say, "Pass the sugar. Pass the pepper. Pass the toast. Pass the jam." At first, we passed them along. I noticed after a while that she did not use them. Often she had no use for them; what she asked for had nothing to do with what was on her plate. She would ask for milk when she already had some, or for sugar when there was nothing to put it on. Why was she asking for these things? Clearly, because everyone else was. When you sit down at breakfast you ask people to pass things. The grownups were all doing it, so she was going to do it, too.

This may have been one reason for playing the "please pass" game, but it was not the only reason. I soon saw that, although she did not use any of the things that were passed to her, she watched very carefully each time to *see* what was passed to her. In short, she is using talk to make something happen which will, in time, help her find out what the talk means.

I don't want to make her word-experiment seem more precise than it really was. If she could have put into words her reason for looking carefully at all that was passed to her, I don't think it would have been, for example, "I'm going to ask them to pass the sugar, and I'm going to watch and see what comes up the table, and then I'll know that's what the sugar is." It was much more probably something like: "I'm going to ask them to pass things, and I'm going to watch what they do, and from that I'll probably find out something interesting, maybe what all these things are called." No doubt she had to ask for, and get, the sugar a good many times before she began, first to suspect, then to feel sure that the white sandy looking stuff in the bowl *was* what everyone called "sugar."

> I now think I was wrong about this, and that Lisa was not randomly gathering information to see what she could find out from it, but was deliberately testing her hunches about what was the pepper and the milk and the sugar.

But children are good at gathering and storing this kind of vague information—too vague to be useful to most adults—and waiting patiently until, someday, they find they know what it means. In the same way, a child hearing people say, "Shut the window," and "Shut the door," and watching to see what happens, will not say, right away, "Aha! That's the window, and that's the door." But one day he gets a hunch, and soon he knows. By such means children learn the five thousand or so words they are said to know when they first come to school.

One of the wittiest and truest remarks I have ever heard about education was made not long ago by a Catholic educator, a veteran of many years of teaching and teacher training. He was talking to a group of Catholic high school superintendents about handling your teachers, and was urging them not to be too quick to point out and correct mistakes that the teachers, given a little time, might see and correct for themselves. "A word to the wise," he said slowly, shaking an emphatic finger, "is *infuriating*." We all laughed, because he had fooled us, and because he was so right. Infuriating is just what it is. We all know the kind of person who is quick to interrupt whatever we are saying to correct some unimportant mistake. Strangling seems much too good for him. I blush to think how long it took me to break myself of just that habit.

A word to the wise, or even the unwise, is infuriating because it is insulting. When we teach without being asked, we are saying, in effect, "You're not smart enough to know that you should know this, and not smart enough to learn it." For the same reason, a question to the wise, if it is a probing question, a quiz, and not a true request for information, is often just as infuriating, because it implies, insultingly, that the person quizzed doesn't know the answer.

Many parents write us at *Growing Without Schooling* to tell about their little children getting furiously angry when their kind and loving parents, meaning only the best, try to give them help they have not asked for. In answer to one of them, I told this story:

Something happened a while ago in the office that showed me once again how strong and how fragile is little children's sense of pride and dignity, and how careful we must be not to trample on it, most of all when we mean well.

A mother came into the office with her eighteen-month-old daughter. While the mother looked over our books to see what she wanted to buy, the little one explored the office. Finally the mother had the four books she wanted, which the little girl had asked to carry. But the books were slippery, and one of them kept sliding out from between the others and falling on the ground. This began to frustrate and irritate the child. Seeing that she clearly did not *like* having the books fall on the floor, I thought I might help by putting a rubber band around them. I got one, stretched it a couple of times to show what it was, and put it around the books. She looked at it a second, saw that it was indeed holding the books together, and then burst into furious tears.

Fortunately, from many years of being with little children, I could see what was the matter. She saw me putting the rubber bands around the books as a comment on the fact that she could not hold them together. She was right, and she was offended. To her, it was as if I had said, "You're so clumsy that you'll never be able to carry those books unless I put this rubber band on." Naturally this made her ashamed and angry.

Understanding the trouble, I could easily set things right. I said, "I'm sorry, I'll take the rubber band off," and did so. Instantly she stopped crying and was as happy as she had been before. She still had to struggle with the books. But it was *her* struggle.

Most of us are tactful enough with other adults not to point out their errors, but not many of us are ready to extend this courtesy (or any other courtesy, for that matter) to children. Yet it is important that we should, because they are perceptive and sensitive, and very easily hurt, humiliated, and discouraged. For this reason I was careful, when three-year-old Jill said "teached" to me, to let some time go by before I said "taught" to her. To have said it right away would have seemed like a correction and a reproof. We should even be careful about mentioning mistakes which they have themselves corrected. They may not like to be reminded of them. Thus, while entertaining me Jill began to sing some of the chorus of "The Blue-Tail Fly." As she sang, "Jimmy crack corn, and I don't care," her (very nice) father interrupted her, to say, with pride and delight, that he had never heard her say "crack" before, that she had always said "frack." He spoke only to show his pleasure; in his shoes, I might have done the same. But the little girl, ordinarily not the least shy, became embarrassed and self-conscious, and when she started to sing the song again, could only sing "frack," and was soon eager to stop singing altogether.

I can think of a comparable experience with Tommy. Once a year, in the city where he lives, they have an annual festival, in which they burn a giant effigy of Zozobra, the King of Gloom. This great bonfire is very exciting for little people to see; for months ahead Tommy was talking about "Zorzor," and when we were going to see him. The family, when talking to each other, spoke of Zozobra, but when Tommy asked us about Zorzor, it seemed more courteous to use the same word in our reply, which we did. Suddenly, one day, not long before the festival, with no in-between experiments that we knew of, he began to say "Zozobra." A day or so later, a member of the family who had not heard him say "Zozobra" remarked that he would soon see Zorzor. Instantly Tommy said, kindly but very firmly, "It's not Zorzor, it's Zozobra."

Perhaps it is for such reasons that most children do not like to hear stories about when they were younger. Infancy is not a blessed state to them, but something to be grown out of and escaped from as quickly as possible. To them, their littleness, helplessness, and clumsiness is not cute but humiliating and they want to be reminded of it as little as possible. They don't mind, once in a while, if we don't overdo it, our telling them that they were very nice when they were little, but that is about as much about it as they want to hear. Whatever mistakes they have made, in their growing and learning, are best forgotten.

Glenda Bissex's experience with her son Paul, which she describes in *Gnys at Wrk,* suggests that this may often not be the case. He was always very interested in hearing and reading about what he did when he was younger, first exploring the world of reading and writing. The spirit behind the stories is probably what makes the difference. Children may be willing, even glad, to hear stories told about them when they were little, if the point of these stories is to show that even when they were little they were real, serious, intelligent, purposeful people, worthy of respect. But they don't want to hear stories that invite people to laugh or cry or coo over how ignorant and clumsy they once were.

I wonder whether Ruth Shinn, when she grew older, ever read her Aunt Millicent's book about her, and if so, how she felt about it. Hard to imagine that she wouldn't have liked it.

Jill's saying "teached" instead of "taught" is an example of the kind of mistakes little children often make in their talk. When we are not thinking of these mistakes as cute, we tend to think of them as ungrammatical, another example of children's unskillfulness in imitating language. The fact is, of course, that a child saying "teached" is not imitating and is not being ungrammatical. He is inventing, and in a highly grammatical way. He is not saying "teached" because he heard someone else say it; he probably never did. He is saying it because he knows—though he could not put his knowledge into words—that other verbs form their past tense by adding the suffix -ed, and he therefore supposes that the verb "teach" should behave the same way. This is in every way a reasonable assumption and a first-class piece of thinking. All the more reason why we should meet such "mistakes," not with a curt correction, but with understanding and courtesy.

When I was still teaching fifth grade, I was talking about my class to a twelve-year-old friend of mine. I happened to say that some of the children in my class had been having a conversation. At this my friend looked puzzled. She said, "You mean these kids were talking about this stuff in class?" Yes. She said, "Was this in Show and Tell?" I said, "No, we don't have Show and Tell, but there are lots of times during the day when the kids can talk to each other, if they wish it, about whatever interests them most. Don't you ever have a time in class when you can talk to other people?" She was almost too astonished to answer.

Of course I knew what she would answer even before I asked her. Bill Hull once said to me, "Who needs the most practice talking in school? Who gets the most?" Exactly. The children need it, the teacher gets it. Even in the most supposedly enlightened schools, the usual rule in almost every class is that a child talks only to the teacher, and then only when called on. In many schools children are forbidden to talk between classes or in the corridors. This leaves only lunch, when they are busy eating, and recess, when they are trying to let off a little steam built up during their long periods of enforced stillness and silence. And I have known more than a few children who have gone to schools where often they were not allowed to talk during lunch, and sometimes even during recess. After school children head for home, where their time is likely to be taken up with homework and TV, and where in any case nobody else may be very interested in talking to them. The result of this kind of education is that children of ten or even older may be no better at talking than they were at five. In fact, I have known many ten-year-olds, in a highly intellectual community, who were nowhere near as good at talking as many five-year-olds I have known.

> I still keep hearing of schools that, because it wastes time or makes the lunch room too noisy, do not allow children to talk even at lunch, and more and more even of schools that have entirely cut out recess. When, then, does the "social life" take place that schools say is so important?

This loss of skill and interest in talking affects every subject in the standard curriculum. For example, take writing. A child who does not talk will not have many things that he wants to say, and hence will not know what to write about. He will often feel that nothing he might want to say or write could possibly be of any interest to anyone else, and that if he did say or write something, others would only laugh at it. As fast as thoughts come to him, he censors them, rules them out. When he does try to express his thoughts, he finds it hard, because he has had so little practice in putting words together. Because he has never learned in practice what kinds of things make speech clear, forceful, and effective, he will have no way to judge the worth of his own writing. As they say, he will have a tin ear. The test of good writing, after all, is not whether it obeys "laws of grammar," but what it sounds like. The rules of grammar in the book will not enable him to write well. And the fact is, as a glimpse at many a learned journal will make plain, that many of our most highly educated men write extraordinarily badly.

Lack of skill in conversation is also likely to make poor readers, at least of many kinds of writing. The good reader enters into an active dialogue with the writer. He converses with him, even argues with him. The bad reader reads passively; the words do not engage his mind; he is like a bored listener at a lecture. Such a reader, studying a text, is very likely to use his mind as if it were a photographic plate, as if by staring hard enough and long enough at words on a page he could fix them in his memory. This never works. In courses like math or science, in which one must often follow instructions, turn other people's words into action, the inarticulate child often finds that he can't do it. Or he may find that he cannot separate in his mind what he understands from what he does not, or state his confusions clearly enough to enable others to help him. In short, the child in school who is not fluent with words is bound hand and foot. No doubt our schools are too symbolminded, and should give more time and scope to other forms of expression. Perhaps someday they will. Right now, it is fluency that pays. Yet, in almost all schools, hardly anything is done to help children become fluent, precise, and skillful in speech.

The so-called revolution now going on in education has so far done little to change this. In many classes doing the very latest thing in math, social studies, or whatever, the pattern of talk is what it always was. The teacher does most of the talking, and now and then asks the children questions, to make sure they have been paying attention and understand. Now and then a bold teacher will start what they call a "discussion." What happens then is usually what Bill Hull calls "answer pulling." The teacher asks a series of pointed questions, aimed at getting students to give an answer that he has decided beforehand is right. Teachers' manuals are full of this technique—"Have a discussion, in which you draw out the following points...." This kind of fake, directed conversation is worse than none at all. Small wonder that children soon get bored and disgusted with it.

Even if class discussions were open, honest, unmanipulated, and genuinely interesting to the young, and even if all children took equal part in them, they would not be enough to give most children skill in speech. There are too many children, and too little time. What is the answer? Simple enough, if we have the courage to try it. In many elementary school classes in England, children are free to work in pairs or small groups, and to talk—if they do it quietly—as they work. In classes where the children are not yet allowed to do independent work of their own choosing, there should be plenty of time set aside for children to talk to each other, about whatever interests them, without guidance or interference from the teacher. There might be times when the teacher would have to ask children to talk more quietly. But he should not control what the children talk about.

In my last fifth-grade class, I used to set aside a period every now and then as a free period. In that time the children could read, or draw, or play games (chess became very popular), or do puzzles, or, as they liked best of all, talk to each other. As time went on, I felt more and more that these periods were perhaps the most useful part of the day. Sometimes the girls' conversations would turn into whispering and giggles, or the boys' into shouting arguments. But on the whole, and more and more as the children gained experience, the conversations seemed to be serious, and very useful to all taking part in them. For one thing, at such times the distinctions between able students and less able broke down. Some of the poorest students were very interesting and well-informed talkers, and could talk and argue as equals with the most successful students in the class. To this, some teachers have said that children who were used to being tightly controlled in class would not know what to do with free time if they had it, and would abuse it. The problem is not as serious as they think, but it is real. One way to deal with it is, at first, to make free periods short, perhaps fifteen minutes or half an hour, with the restriction that talk must be quiet. There might even be some periods that could be free but silent. As the children get used to freedom and find interesting ways to use it, they can be given more of it. In such ways we can break out of the school lockstep and make the classroom a place where more and more independent study, thinking, and talking can go on.

> It can't be said too often: we get better at using words, whether hearing, speaking, reading, or writing, under one condition and only one—when we use those words to say something we want to say, to people we want to say it to, for purposes that are our own.

☐READING

When Lisa was about three and a half, she was the youngest child of a large family in which everyone loved reading and books. Books were everywhere in the house—on tables, chairs, beds, floors. Yet the family was very relaxed about reading; none of the children had been pushed into it, and nobody was trying to push Lisa. So I was taken aback when one day, out of a clear sky, she said to me, rather aggressively, "I can read!" I said, surprised, "Well, sure, I never said you couldn't." There was no point in challenging her. She knew she couldn't read; she knew I knew she couldn't. Clearly, it was very humiliating to her to know that she could not do something that everyone around her—as far as she knew, the whole world—could do. Why add to her humiliation?

Many years later a friend told me a story about his daughter, not yet a year old. She had been given a little plastic whistle, which she loved to toot. It was her favorite toy. One day one of her parents picked up the whistle, and, seeing that it had holes in it, like a recorder, began to play a little tune on it. They both amused themselves with it for a minute or two, then gave the whistle back to the baby. To their great surprise, she pushed it angrily aside. At the time her father told me the story, she had not blown it since.

The story reminds me of something that Danny once

did, when about two and a half. I had thought that he might like the Cuisenaire rods, and I was curious to see what he might do with them. So, one day when I visited his parents, I took a box of rods with me. We opened it and showed him all the little colored sticks. He was enchanted. Like glass beads to primitive people, these hundreds of pieces of brightly colored wood looked to him like the most real wealth in the world. We emptied the box out on the rug, and for a while he just sat there, picking up handfuls of the rods and letting them run through his fingers, drunk with excitement and joy, looking for all the world like a proverbial miser with his money. I know now that I should have let him go on playing with the rods in his own way, getting his own kind of pleasure out of them, taking in information about them through his eyes and his fingers, gradually exploring their possibilities. At the time, I felt I had to start him off "learning" something. So, in what I supposed was my low-pressure way, without even saying, "Watch," I took some rods from the pile and began to make a pattern of them on the floor, thinking that he would soon imitate me. Danny's father joined me, and before long we had built a simple low structure, that we thought Danny could imitate successfully. When we finished, we looked at him. He looked at us for a while, expressionless. Then, without saying a word, he came over and with one swipe of his hand knocked our little building all over the rug. Amazed, we asked, "What did you do that for?" He just looked at us. Stupidly, we persisted, and built another structure. Again, he destroyed it, looking not so much angry as determined. We tried once more; same result. Then, at last, we had the wit to see that something was happening that we did not understand, and let the little boy play with the rods in his own way.

It is certain that a child is greatly inspired and helped to learn by what are often called "competence models"— people who can do things better than he can. But we ought to remind ourselves now and then that sometimes a competence model can be altogether too competent. Child psychologists write a good deal about what they call "infant omnipotence." Their theory seems to be that infants and young children really believe they can do anything, and only gradually, as they grow up, learn how little they can do. I do not believe this is true, even of babies; I am sure it is not true even of children as young as two or three, who know all too well how little they know, or understand, or can do, and for whom this awareness is very often frightening and humiliating. This does not mean that we must try to keep our superior knowledge and competence a secret from children; it would be impossible even if it were desirable, which it isn't. But we must be aware that their ignorance and clumsiness are often painful to them, and we must be careful not to rub their noses in their own weaknesses. Parents who do everything well may not always be good examples for their children; sometimes such children feel, since they can never hope to be as good as their parents, that there is no use in even trying.

This is just as true of teachers. One of the reasons why children learn so well from children a little older than themselves may be, not just that the older child understands the language of the younger and can speak in his terms, but that he is a more helpful competence model because he is more within reach. No doubt it is exciting and inspiring for a child interested in athletics, or music, or dancing, or art, or drama, or whatever, to see, once in a while, adults who do those things superbly well. But as day-to-day examples, these experts are probably much less useful to a child than slightly older, slightly bigger children who do things slightly better than he can. I see now, as I may not have at the time, that one reason that many more children at school were interested in blowing on my bugle than on my flute may have been that, for them, I was an expert on the flute, whereas on the bugle I was a rank beginner like themselves.

But let me return to Lisa, who first taught me this, or at

least opened my eyes and my mind to it. When she was about four, I made one of my frequent visits to her family. Knowing her interest in reading, I brought with me some materials that I had been using in teaching reading at school—some charts associated with a method called Words In Color. By this time, I knew better than to try to give these materials the hard sell; children learn very early to be wary of too much adult enthusiasm. So, instead of saying, "Oh, Lisa, I've brought the most exciting things for you to look at, wait till you see them, we're going to have such fun with them . . . ," I merely left the charts in my room, where I knew she'd see them when she went in to explore. Sure enough, a few days later, she asked me, "What are those big signs in your room?" I said, "You mean those things with the colored letters all over them?" Yes. I said that they were things I had to use at school with children who were learning to read. She said, "Can I use them?" I said, "Why, sure, I suppose, if you want to." She said, "I mean, right now." So we took the charts into the living room, spread a few of them on the rug, and began to work.

Ordinarily a teacher using these charts points to certain words and asks children what they are. But I had learned by this time that even little children can get very frightened, cautious, and defensive when put into a spot where they have to give an answer which may be wrong. What I did was to give Lisa a pointer, and invite her to ask me what any word said, or, if she felt that she knew what it said, to say it herself. In other words, I was trying to put her out of danger and in control of the game. For a while, we played this way; she asked me words, I told them to her, sometimes she knew a word and would say it herself. But within a very short while, only a few minutes, she began to change the rules of the game, to play it in a different way, her way. The older children in the family had a good friend named Henry Harrison, whom Lisa knew, and she began to amuse herself by pointing to various three and four letter words on the chart and saying, "Henry Harrison!" I tried gently to steer the game back to where it had been, but no use. It was clear that she was not only tired of the game, but beginning actively to dislike it. Sure enough, in another minute or so she said she wanted to stop, we put the charts away, and for the rest of the visit she did not ask to see them again.

This was a mystery. Why, when I had been so careful not to put her on the spot, did she so quickly turn away from these materials, that she herself had demanded to use? This happened again, with some quite different materials, on a later visit. Only after some time and much thought, did I begin to suspect what the trouble had been. No matter how hard I tried to keep the game unthreatening, to avoid putting her in a spot where she might be wrong, I could not hide the fact that this was a game about which I knew everything and she nothing, and this alone was more threatening and humiliating than she was willing or able to bear.

> What I should have done is let Lisa use those charts however she wanted, give her time to fantasize and play with them (if she wanted), let her show me what use, if any, she wanted to make of them, let her ask *me* questions about them, if she wanted to do that. But even if I and she had done all those things, I doubt very much that she would have used the charts to teach herself to read, as Gattegno, their author, intended. When, a short time later, she did begin this work, what she used was real books.

It would be a great mistake to assume that this is an unusual or peculiar or unhealthy reaction. It is a very human one, as common among adults as children. Most of the time, most of us do not like at all to be confronted with someone who knows a great deal more about something than we do. Though I have recovered a lot of the child's curiosity that I lost during my schooling, I still often sense this reaction in myself. Just the other day, flying back to Boston, I sat next to two men who were having an animated conversation about advanced biology. On the one hand, I couldn't help being curious about what they were saying and the diagrams they were drawing. But even as I tried to catch some shred of meaning from all their talk, in another part of my mind I was angrily rejecting the importance of what they were talking about. I was able, for the most part, to silence my defensive thoughts, and go on listening. But the reaction was there, and strong as it is when I read, say in *Scientific American*, an article of which I can make absolutely no sense. Such reactions are natural, if nothing to be proud of. Even in the privacy of our own minds, we do not like to be made to feel ignorant and stupid. Confronted with what we do not know, we try to protect ourselves by saying that it is not worth knowing.

> I don't believe now that this was Lisa's feeling at all. Far from having decided that reading was not worth knowing, she probably wanted to learn to read very much. What she rightly resented was my taking it upon myself to teach her without being asked. When she learned to read, it was going to be by her own choosing, at her own time, and in her own way. This spirit of independence in learning is one of the most valuable assets a learner can have, and we who want to help children's learning, at home or in school, must learn to respect and encourage it.

Proud and sensitive children are particularly likely to react this way. Knowing Lisa to be such a child, I worried a little about what might happen when she got to school and had to submit to formal instruction. Would she resist it? It seemed that she well might. Fortunately she solved the problem by teaching herself to read. Nobody seems to know how she did it. In fact, this is something that, in general, we know very little about. Many thousands of children teach themselves to read, every year; we might do well to find out how many such children there are, and how they taught themselves.

At any rate, Lisa went to a kindergarten where, though the teacher did not try to teach the children to read nor spur them into reading, there were plenty of books, signs, letters, and other useful materials. Finding herself with a crowd of children no more able to read than she was, Lisa must have decided that not knowing how to read was no disgrace. Later, she must have decided that, since older people could read, they must have learned, and if they could learn, so could she. Late in November she began bringing home beginning readers and workbooks, which she worked on by herself. When I saw her again the following summer, she was reading books at about a second-grade or even an easy third-grade level.

One day she and I were sitting in the living room, both reading. From the children's section of the public library she had just taken out four books, the maximum. Picking the one that looked most interesting, she had settled herself in a big chair and had begun to work on it. I could hear her murmuring, though most of the time I could not hear what she was saying. From the tone of her voice, and her silences, I got a feeling that while there were many words in the book that she knew and could recognize at sight, there were others that she had to stop and figure out, perhaps using her rough knowledge of phonics, perhaps guessing from the context, perhaps both. Some words, she was willing to skip; she didn't feel that she had to get every one. But every now and then she would come to a word that she could neither figure out, nor guess, nor skip. On this day she found such a word. Slowly she climbed out of her chair and, holding the book, came toward me. I looked at her as she came. She had a set, stern expression on her face. Pointing to a word in her book, she asked, "What does it say?" Her look seemed to say very distinctly, "Now please don't ask me a lot of silly questions, like: 'What do you think it says?' or 'Have you tried sounding it out?' or anything like that. If I could do those things, I wouldn't be up here asking. Just tell me what the word says; that will be enough." I told her. She nodded, went back to her chair, and continued reading.

Later I asked her mother how often Lisa asked what a word was. She thought a bit, and said, "Not very often. Maybe once or twice a week, at most." Then, as an afterthought, "It's interesting, though; when she asks a word, she never forgets it." Interesting, but not surprising; the things we learn because, *for our own reasons,* we really need to know them, we don't forget. But if she only asked other people for words once, or even a few times, a week, this would only account for at most perhaps two hundred of the fifteen hundred or more words that she knew. Where had she learned the others? Clearly, she had figured them out for herself.

Another five-year-old, named Nora, taught me more about the things children do when teaching themselves to read, the problems they meet, and the ways they solve or try to solve them. I was visiting her family over a weekend. Though I had not seen Nora since she was a small baby, we were soon friends. Sometime during the day, when I seemed to have nothing to do, she came up to me with a book in her hand and asked if I would help her read it. I said I would, so we sat on the sofa and went to work. The book was *Hop on Pop,* a very good book for beginners. The pictures are interesting and funny, and the words are chosen so as to use very common sounds and words—like those in the title. Also, the book introduces new words in such a way that the child, by using the words she already knows, by looking at the pictures, and by making some intelligent guesses, can figure out almost all the words without help. So it was a useful book for a child trying to teach herself to read.

At first, it was not clear how she wanted me to help her, or what I was supposed to do. Most of the time, I just sat still and silent—a very hard thing for a teacher to do, particularly one who, like me, thinks he is good at explaining and helping. The first few pages were easy; then she began to meet more words that she did not know, and had to figure out. Only rarely, when she seemed badly stuck, did I say anything. Even then I didn't tell her the word, only suggested how she might figure it out. If she had seen it before, I told her so. If she had had words that rhymed with it, sounded like it, I told her that. If the word used entirely new sounds, so that she had to figure it out from the pictures and the general context of the story, I told her that. If she still couldn't get the word, I told her to skip it and go ahead, that perhaps next time she saw it, it would be easier to figure out. Most of the time, she went ahead, but if she asked me to tell her the word, I did.

Before long, an odd thing happened. Nora misread a word that previously she had read correctly. This happened a number of times. I found myself feeling puzzled and annoyed, as I had in my own classroom when children seemed to forget things they had supposedly learned. I thought, "Has she forgotten that word already? Or is she just being careless, not paying attention, not making an effort?" But this was not it; obviously she was reading the book as well as she could, putting all of her concentration into it. So how could she know a word on one page, and not know it on the next? It seemed almost like stupid behavior. But she was very bright, and she wasn't bluffing, or guessing, or trying to get me to do the work for her. It was a puzzle.

To understand the learning problems of another person, particularly a child, we must try to see things as if through their eyes. This is often very difficult. It is almost impossible to imagine what it would be like not to know something that, in fact, you do know. Trying to see this book through Nora's eyes, I began to realize that for someone who doesn't know how to read, and who isn't familiar with print, all words must look like funny squiggly shapes, all more or less alike. We think it should be easy for someone to remember what a word looks like from one page to the next. But we *know* the word. For a child, who has only just seen the word for the first time, it is not easy, but hard. It is hard to tell which words on a page are the same, or almost the same, and if they are different, where they are different. We readers have the expert's eye for significant detail; the child does not.

There then popped into my mind an experience I had had some years before, and had completely forgotten. While teaching the fifth grade, I ran across an ad for a British firm that makes type in many oriental languages. I asked them to send me some samples of printing in many of these languages, which they did. I thought the children would be interested in what other alphabets and writing looked like. They were not, but I was, all the more so because even then I was very much interested in the problems of a child beginning to read. One day I took a sheet of printing in some Indian language, and tried to find the words that occurred most often on the page. It was amazingly difficult. At first the page looked like nothing but a jumble of strange shapes. Even when I was concentrating on one short, common word, it took a long time before I could recognize that word at sight and pick it out of the others. Often I would go right by it without noticing it.

In the same way, it takes a child some time to get used to the shapes of letters and words, to the point where he can see at a glance that this word is like that one, and this other word almost like it, and this other word altogether different. So we must give him plenty of time and not be surprised or upset by what looks like slowness, or stupid mistakes. When a child, having looked for a long time at two words on a page, without seeing that they are the same, suddenly exclaims, "Oh, I see, they are the same!" we must not think that what he has done is trivial. We must realize that the child has made a real and important discovery.

One of the reasons why children from unlettered homes are at such a disadvantage when they start learning to read may be that they lack this familiarity with the shapes of words and letters. This may also be a reason why we should give children time to get used to, and familiar with, the look of letters and words, before beginning any kind of formal instruction. In fact, this is a very good reason, among many others, for letting the child himself decide when he wants to start to read.

Not long ago, a teacher was telling me about her work with young, disadvantaged children who could not or did not read. At one point she said, "We have plenty of books in the classroom, and they all like to use them. But they don't read them; they just turn over the pages and look at them. How can I get them interested in *reading* them?" I made a suggestion or two that seemed helpful at the time. Only later did I realize that, for children who had hardly ever seen any, this casual looking at books was a sensible and almost certainly a necessary first step to reading. Before these children could begin to think about what particular letters and groups of letters said, they had to get familiar with the look of letters in general, just as a child learning to talk must first become familiar with the sound of talk. Most children, when they start to read, have been looking at and seeing letters for a long time. This is the experience that these less fortunate children have to make up first.

There is another reason, probably more important, why a child may forget on page 6 what he seemed to know on page 5. We are so used to the feeling of knowing what we know, or think we know, that we forget what it is like to learn something new and strange. We tend to divide up the world of facts and ideas into two classes, things we know and things we don't know, and we assume that any particular fact moves instantly from "unknown" to "known." We forget how unsure we often are of things we have just learned—even things as simple as a name or a phone number. Therefore we can't understand why a child, having said correctly that the HIM on page 5 says "him," should say that the HIM on page 6 says something else.

What we must understand is that when the child figures out that the HIM on page 5 says "him," he does not *know* in the sense that we know, he is not certain, that this is so. For reasons he may not be aware of and could certainly not put into words, he has a flash of insight, a hunch, that this word says "him." He tries out his hunch, and it works. But because a hunch works this time does not mean to a child that he can rely on it next time. In fact, he may not even get the same hunch next time. Seeing HIM, he may think that it says something else. He has to get the correct hunch many times, and test it, and see it proved right, before he can feel sure of it. Each time he is right, his hunch becomes stronger and surer; but it takes a long time—longer for some children than others—before it becomes what we think of as certain knowledge.

> I am even more sure of this now than then. Children's first hunches about anything are extremely faint and tentative, the merest wisps of intuition that a certain thing may be so. Each time children test one of these faint hunches and have it confirmed by experience, the hunch becomes a bit stronger. What we might call a 5 percent hunch becomes a 10 percent, the 10 percent a 20 percent, and so, slowly, all the way to the point where they will say with conviction that they *know* that such-and-such is true— something, as I showed in *How Children Fail,* that even the "brightest" children in the "best" schools will rarely ever say.
>
> This is exactly the process I am going through in trying to learn to read music, and one of the reasons I

have been so slow to learn is that I have not been willing enough to trust my hunches, but keep saying to myself, after every note I play, "Are you sure that was right, are you sure that was right?" I am only just beginning to get over this crippling habit. And I would certainly never get over it if I had someone pouncing on me every time I made a mistake.

Teaching fifth grade many years ago, I saw this confirmed in a striking and amusing way. Trying to help some bad spellers, I had done a little work with a device called a tachistoscope, which can flash words onto a screen for very short lengths of time. I thought it might help my students look at words as a whole, and so fix their images more firmly in their minds. But tachistoscopes cost far more than the school or I could afford. So I invented a cheap one—it cost less than five cents. On a three-by-five card I printed with a black felt-tipped pen the misspelled word I wanted my student to look at. I then covered it with a blank four-by-six card, held in my hand. After telling the student to look carefully, I moved my hand very quickly, uncovering for an instant the word below. Then I asked her to spell the word aloud. The rule was that she could have as many quick glimpses as she wanted before trying to spell it. She did not have to try to spell it until she felt sure of being able to spell it right.

I was curious, first of all, to see how many glimpses they would need before feeling sure. They usually asked for several before spelling the word— even then in a faint, uncertain, questioning voice. If they missed, I would simply say "Look again" and give them another glimpse. When they spelled it correctly, I would go on to their next word. (All these words came from their own papers, the only way to work on spelling that makes any sense at all.)

Sometimes I stayed with the word even when they

spelled it correctly, as long as they didn't sound sure of it. I would begin by giving them as many glimpses as they wanted, let's say of the word "horse." Sooner or later they would say, in a quavering voice, "H—O—R—S—E?" I would say, "Look again," and give another glimpse. Again they would say, "H—O—R—S—E"—but with the voice slightly less uncertain. With every new glimpse and correct spelling the child's voice would become more certain. Eventually they would become indignant, saying each letter angrily as if *I* was the dumb student *they* were trying to teach. When they sounded really angry I would say, "Now you know it," and move on to the next word. Try as they might to short-circuit this process by faking indignation before they really felt it, they never could; it was only when they were *really* sure, only when their 5 percent hunch had turned into close to a 100 percent hunch, that they could begin to feel and sound truly angry. It was very funny to hear their voices change as their hunches became more sure; it was like seeing a pointer move slowly across a dial.

Knowing this about children's hunches makes me understand more clearly than ever why, and how, our constant checking up on children's learning so often prevents and destroys learning, and even in time most of the capacity to learn. In *How Children Fail,* I said that the anxiety children feel at constantly being tested, their fear of failure, punishment, and disgrace, severely reduces their ability both to perceive and to remember, and drives them away from the material being studied and into strategies for fooling teachers into thinking they know what they really don't know. To this I would now add perhaps even more important reasons why testing—at least, unasked for testing done by others—destroys learning.

The first reason has to do with this matter of

hunches. When we constantly ask children questions
to find out whether they know something (or prove
to ourselves that they don't), we almost always cut
short the slow process by which, testing their hunches against experience, they turn them into secure
knowledge. Asking children questions about things
they are only just beginning to learn is like sitting in
a chair which has only just been glued. The structure collapses. Under pressure, children stop trying
to confirm and strengthen their faint hunches. Instead, they just give them up. More times than I can
remember, I have heard children being tested say of
their hunches, "This must be wrong," or "I know it's
wrong." Asked probing questions, they usually say, "I
don't know." But in the privacy of their minds they
give up that newborn hunch. In its place they have
only the adult expert's answer to his own question, a
very bad substitute.

Thus there was all the difference in the world between two-year-old Lisa testing her own hunches
about the names of things on the dining room table
by asking us to pass them and then seeing what was
passed, and what might have happened if we had little quizzes at every meal—"What's this, Lisa? And
what's this?"

Rachael Solem, one of our readers (and volunteer
helpers), wrote us at *Growing Without Schooling*
about her four-year-old daughter's response to questions:

Occasionally when I'm reading her a story I will
ask her a question about it, to test her comprehension. She will invariably say, "I don't know." But
she can re-tell that story, with many details and insights, to her younger brother. She also feels she
has the right to ask me silly questions about things
we are doing—how many apples, what is the num-

ber on that bus—just as I ask her. And because I answer, it becomes a game of talking about things rather than just little quizzes from me. I used to ask questions about the numbers or letters on buses, etc. to test her eyesight in an underhanded way. Then she began to describe to me things she was seeing, and I realized her eyes are far keener than mine. For example, though having no particular interest in cars (none she's shown us, anyhow), she told me that the difference between a car we were seeing and a car belonging to one of our friends was that the tail light curved around the side on one and not the other. Sure enough, same model car, but two different years—and the curve of the lights is barely discernible.

In their new and useful book, *On Learning to Read,* Dr. Bruno Bettelheim and Karen Zelan tell about two children who were so deeply shamed and insulted by the stupid material they were required to read aloud and the equally stupid questions they were continually asked that they could not and would not respond to them at all.

Fourth and fifth graders who had left the beginners' books behind described their resentments to us quite clearly. One rather quiet boy, who preferred to read or work by himself and rarely participated in class, spoke up all on his own and with deep feeling. He had felt so ashamed to say the things written in primers that he could not bring himself to do it. And although he now liked reading a lot, he said he still had a hard time reading aloud.

Dumb questions not only insult and anger children but often confuse them enough to destroy some of what they have already learned. They may in fact know the answer to these questions. But they then think, "That answer couldn't be right, it couldn't be that easy, or they wouldn't have asked me the question in the first place." So they don't say the correct answer they really know. What's worse, they often give it up in their mind. Instead, they may grab desperately for some other answer, or say nothing at all.

So, much of the time all we get from our endless checking up and testing are children who will not give even the correct answers they know because they don't feel sure enough of them; or children who, even though sure of their answers, remain silent or give wrong answers instead because they are so offended by the questions, or because they fear a trap has been set for them. And on the basis of these wrong answers and nonanswers, we adults keep on making wrong and harmful judgments about what children know and what and how they need to be taught. Because of these wrong judgments we label many, perhaps millions, of these children as having some kind of supposedly incurable "learning disability."

The worst damage we do with all this testing is to the children's own confidence and self-esteem, their belief that others trust them to learn and that they can therefore trust themselves. For every unasked for test is above all else a statement of no confidence in the learner. That I check up at all on what you have learned proves that I fear you have not really learned it. For young children, these repeated votes of no confidence can be devastating.

Once I was invited to an all-day conference and dinner of a state association on "learning disabilities." At dinner I sat next to the wife of the president of the association. Early in the meal she said to me, "Our children will always be failures, but at least they'll know it's not their own fault." Later she described the way in which her own son, then about five years old, learned officially for the first time that he was a failure. His parents, worried and ashamed that he seemed to be learning more slowly than other children, took him to some kind of center for an extensive series of psychological tests. Finally, his mother told me, he was given a puzzle-type test to put together. Even at the three-year-old level, he couldn't do the test, just looked at it, said, "I can't do it! I can't do it!" and burst into tears. I said how sorry I was. But after a moment's reflection, I suddenly had a terrible hunch. I said, "That puzzle that he couldn't do—did it have written on it what age level it was for?" Not seeing the point of my question, she said, "Of course." Just to be certain, I asked again, "It was written right on the puzzle, 'three years old,' or something like that, where anyone could see it?" She said yes. Appalled, I sat silent; this was not the time or place to argue about it, even if there was anything to be said.

But later I have thought often of that scene in the psychologist's office as the child must have experienced it. It is a scene out of nightmare. For many months, perhaps years, he has sensed that his parents were worried about him, even ashamed of him. Finally, in an atmosphere heavy with tension and dread, he is taken to a strange place, where strange people peer at him, ask him peculiar questions, and tell him to do peculiar things. Clearly all these people think there is something wrong with him as well. Finally they tell him to put together a puzzle on which is plainly written that it is intended for three-year-olds. One way or another, the boy figures this out, and realizes that all these adults, his parents included, don't think he is even smart enough to do what any three-year-old can do. Faced with this overwhelming vote of no confidence, he breaks down. Why should he not? If none of these people have any confidence in him, how could he have any in himself? And it may well have been clear to him, as his mother's remarks later made it clear to me, that his parents were in some way *relieved* that he failed; they could tell themselves (and everyone else) it wasn't their fault.

By such means these adults destroyed most of the confidence and intelligence of that child. Perhaps by now he really *is* "learning disabled." But they and their incessant anxious testing surely did a lot to disable him.

As I pointed out in *How Children Fail,* the children who always forget things in school may not forget so much because their memories are bad as because they never dare trust their memories. Even when they are right, they still *feel* wrong. They are never willing enough to bet on their hunch that something is so, to turn it into a conviction that it really is so. Working with bad spellers, for example, I have often found that their first hunch about how to spell a word is often correct. But they don't trust that hunch. They think, "It must be wrong," and try to find some other spelling of the word, which leads them to write something that *is* wrong, and thus undermines their confidence still further.

Therefore, when Nora made mistakes in reading I resisted the temptation to correct them, or even point them out. It would probably have made her nervous and timid, afraid to try out her hunches, concerned instead to figure out ways to get the answer out of me. Nobody, not even adults, likes to be corrected. We do not have the self-confidence of Sam Johnson, who, asked once by a lady how he happened to misspell a word in something he wrote, answered, "Sheer ignorance, Madam." Few adults, and fewer children, can take correction in such a spirit; for most of us, it is a heavy and painful blow at our precarious self-esteem.

But I soon found, to my great surprise, that there was a far more important reason for not pointing out Nora's mistakes. Left alone, not hurried, not pressured, not made anxious, she was able to find and correct most of them herself. It was most interesting to note how she did this. When she made a mistake, she rarely noticed it, at first. But as she read on, I could feel growing in her an uneasy sense that something had gone wrong, that something she had said didn't make sense, didn't fit with other things she was saying. Let us say that on one page she read HIM incorrectly—perhaps as "Tom." At first, she might be satisfied with this. But then, on the next page, she would find something that was inconsistent with that first reading. She might find HIM, where it couldn't mean "Tom." Or she might find TOM, and read it correctly. Or she might find some other words with the *i* or the *o* sound. At any rate, she would begin to be aware that something on that earlier page had not been quite right. At first she tried to ignore this feeling. She didn't want to go back; she wanted to go ahead and finish the book. But this awareness of something not quite right would not let her alone. It nagged her, like a stone in a shoe. Finally, after fidgeting and squirming, she would turn the page back in an irritated way and try to find what she had done wrong. Most of the time, she was able to find her mistake and to correct it.

This happened often. Not every time; some mistakes she never became aware of, perhaps because there was nothing in the text immediately following to make her aware of them, perhaps because she was so interested in going ahead that she couldn't be bothered. But most of her mistakes she caught. Like many or most young children, she had a strong desire to see things fit together, make sense, come out right. And not just that: she had the ability, when things didn't fit, to find out where they had gone wrong and to put them right.

   Wanting to be helpful, and to save them (and their pupils) trouble, I have said this to a great many teachers. For a while I was astonished at how angry it made many of them to hear this. I see now that it threatened their need to feel that children cannot learn without them.

   It's important to note that Nora, in noticing and correcting her mistakes, was much helped by the fact that she was reading a real story which she already knew and liked. In *On Learning to Read* Bettelheim and Zelan show very clearly that in reading. as in everything else, children seek out *meaning*, which is to say, whatever helps them make the most sense of the world they live in. If, as is more and more true of school reading books, there is no meaning in the text, just a few easy words repeated in almost nonsensical ways over and over again, or if, as is also too often true, whatever meaning there is in the text seems uninteresting, unreal, and false, children will either refuse to read the text at all or, by changing words in it, will "correct" it to make it more interesting and true. The trouble is that teachers too often respond to these "corrections," these word substitutions, as if they were nothing but careless and stupid mistakes. In our efforts to make reading easier for children by giving them ever easier books to read, we have only succeeded in making it more and more dull and false, and therefore harder. We can hardly ever hurt children by putting too much information within their reach. As long as we don't try to force them to learn it all, they will use what they need and set the rest aside for later. But we can very easily bore and confuse them by giving them too little information.

What we must remember about this ability of children to become aware of mistakes, to find and correct them, is that it takes time to work, and that under pressure and anxiety it does not work at all. But at school we almost never give it the time. When a child at school makes a mistake, say, in reading aloud in a reading group, he gets an instant signal from the environment. Perhaps some of the other children in the group, or class, will giggle, or cover their mouths with their hand, or make a face, or wave their hand in the air—anything to show the teacher that they know more than the unfortunate reader. Perhaps the teacher herself will correct the mistake, or will say, "Are you sure?" or will ask another student, "What do you think?" Perhaps, if the teacher is sympathetic and kindly, as many are, she will only smile a sweet, sad smile—which from the point of view of the child is one of the severest punishments the school has to offer, since it shows him that he has hurt and disappointed the person on whose support and approval he has been trained to depend. At any rate, something will happen to tell the child, not only that he goofed, but that everyone around him knows he goofed. Like almost anyone in this situation, he will feel great shame and embarrassment, enough to paralyze his thinking. Even if he is confident enough to keep some presence of mind in the face of this public failure, he will not be given time to seek out, find, and correct his mistake. For teachers not only like right answers, they like them right away. If a child can't correct his mistake immediately, someone else will correct it for him.

The result of this is a great loss. The more a child uses his sense of consistency, of things fitting together and making sense, to find and correct his own mistakes, the more he will feel that his way of using his mind works, and the better he will get at it. He will feel more and more that he *can* figure out for himself, at least much of the time, which answers make sense and which do not. But if, as usually happens, we point out all his mistakes as soon as he makes them, and even worse, correct them for him, his self-checking and self-correcting skill will not develop, but will die out. He will cease to feel that he has it, or ever had it, or ever could have it. He will become like the fifth-graders I knew—many of them "successful" students—who used to bring me papers and say, "Is it right?" and when I said, "What do you think?" look at me as if I were crazy. What did *they* think? What did what *they* thought have to do with what was right? Right was what the teacher said was right, whatever that was. More recently I have heard much older students, also able and successful, say very much the same thing. *They* could not make any judgments about their own work; it was up to the teachers to decide.

> One of the most important things teachers can do for any learner is to make the learner less and less dependent on them. We need to give students ways to find out for themselves whether what they have done is correct and makes sense. In arithmetic there are many ways to do this, some of which we have suggested in *Growing Without Schooling*.

Many children learn to read like Scout Finch, heroine of Harper Lee's *To Kill a Mockingbird*. She learned by sitting in her father's lap while he read to her aloud, following with her eyes the words as he read them. After a while she found she knew a lot of them, and from what she knew had enough information or intuition about phonics so that she could start figuring out words for herself. A friend told me just the other day that his younger brother, when about four, had done just this. As he grew more skillful in figuring out what word his father or mother would read next, he began to see if he could say it under his breath, before they got to it. One day his father paused in his reading and heard the little boy reading away softly to himself, before he realized that he was being noticed.

One father I know used to read to his daughter, when she was about three, out of an illustrated Mother Goose.

By the time she was four she knew the book so well that, as soon as he turned to a page, she could recite, almost word for word, all the verses there. This must have been a great help to her when she began, as she soon did, to teach herself to read. From this book she could draw on a fund of words that she could already recognize. From these words, in turn, she could begin to get an understanding of phonics—relationships between written letters and spoken sounds—that would help her figure out other words.

It will probably help many children get started in reading if their parents read aloud to them. However, this isn't some kind of magic pill, and if the reading isn't fun for both parent and child, it will do more harm than good. Tommy, at least when I last saw him, had never shown much interest in being read to. Once, on one of our shopping expeditions downtown, I bought him a book, which I let him pick out himself in the bookstore. This was very exciting for him. As soon as we got home, he asked me to read the book to him. He would not let me stop until I had read it all, and through the whole reading he sat quietly and absorbed—unusual for him. But he never asked me to read it again, and showed no particular interest when I suggested it. At that particular time in his life, other things interested him more.

Even children who like being read aloud to, like Danny, don't like it when the parents don't like it. One evening, just before his bedtime, he asked his mother to read to him. She took a picture book from a nearby pile, and began, with a sigh—she was tired. The book was not particularly interesting, and she had read it many times before. She did her best to make it sound interesting, but children are quick to sense our feelings, and Danny soon began to squirm and fidget. Because the reading was no fun for her, it was no fun for him. Soon he said he didn't want to hear any more.

There's nothing wrong with telling a child, if we don't

like a book or get tired of reading it, that we don't want to read it. He will enjoy our reading more if we read something that we like, as well as he. As a matter of fact, since we will probably be asked to read aloud any book that we get for a child, we would do well to make sure that we like most of these before we get them

> I mean, like them enough so that we will be glad to read them not once or twice but many times.

There's no reason to feel, either, that we must always read aloud to little children from "easy" books that they can "understand." If we are reading something we like, with great expression and pleasure, a child may well like it, at least for a while, even if he doesn't understand all of it. After all, children like hearing adults talk, even though they can't understand much or most of it. Why not reading as well? Once, when teaching first-graders, I decided to try reading aloud to them something more difficult than the very simple stories they were used to. My choice was *The Odyssey for Boys and Girls,* by A. J. Church—a book I loved when small, but which many teachers would feel was much too advanced or difficult for first-graders. This class, however, liked it very much, and on subsequent days asked me to read more of it.

> By now we have had hundreds of letters to *Growing Without Schooling,* many of which we have printed, about children learning to read by being read aloud to. But if parents read aloud to children only *so that* children will learn to read, the whole thing will be spoiled. The only good reason for reading aloud is the joy of sharing with children a story you love. Any who don't feel that way about reading aloud ought not to do it. The children will find other ways to learn to read. I taught myself to read *before* other people began to read aloud to me.

Not long ago, the mother of a seven-year-old child who was not yet reading told me that he had asked her, "Why should I learn to read? I can tell what all my books are about just by looking at the pictures." Books for little children, beginning readers, have so few words and so many pictures that many children may not be sure where the story is coming from. They may think that it is in the picture, and that in reading we are just telling a story about the picture. When I was little, children's books contained mostly words and very few pictures. We knew that if we wanted to find out the story, we had to learn to read the words.

> Bettelheim and Zelan make this point very strongly in *On Learning to Read.* As the publishers of our school basal readers have over the years consistently used fewer and simpler words, they have at the same time used more and more pictures.

Remembering this, I one day took into a classroom of three-year-olds a book with no pictures in it at all, sat down in a corner, and in a quiet voice began to read it aloud. After a while, some of the children began to notice, and listen. One by one, they came over to see what I was reading. When they looked in the book, and saw no pictures, they were at first surprised. Then, after more watching and listening, quite a number of them would point to a word on the page and ask, "What does that say?" I would tell them. None of them stayed for long—it wasn't a very interesting book. But they all grasped the vital idea, new to many of them, that in some way those black marks on the page *said* something.

I have recently heard from his mother that Tommy, who a year ago was very little interested in books, reading, or written words, is now very much interested in what those words say. He continually asks her what is written on cans, bottles, cereal boxes. He likes big words even more than little ones, and he finds it mysterious and exciting that the label that said FRUIT COCKTAIL yesterday still says it today—*always* says it. And indeed it is mysterious and exciting that, in writing, we should be able to freeze and preserve for as long as we want such perishable goods as thought and speech.

I remember the first time I discovered that a written word *said* something. The word was LAUNDRY. I was about four, perhaps a bit younger. Young enough so that nobody had yet started to teach me that words said things. We lived in New York City. In our walks through the streets, to the park or elsewhere, we passed many stores, with their signs. Most of these signs said nothing that would help a child know what they were saying; that is, the grocery signs were Gristede's, First National, A & P, the drugstore signs were Rexall's, Liggett's, and so on. But wherever there was a laundry, the sign over it said LAUNDRY. Ten, twenty, a hundred times, I must have seen that sign, and under it, in the window, the shirts and other clean clothing that told me that this was a place where things were washed. Then, one day, I realized that there was a connection between those letters over the store, and the shirts in the window, and what I knew the store was doing; that those letters over the store told me, and were there to tell me, that this place was a laundry, that they *said* "laundry."

That is all I can remember about teaching myself to read.

Jean was a very bright, alert, and articulate child, but she did not learn to read in the first grade. Her parents, and we at the school, thought this was odd, because she was so bright. She didn't seem afraid of reading; she hadn't tried to learn and failed; she just hadn't tried. Her parents, being unusually sensible, didn't fuss or worry, and they persuaded the school not to fuss and worry either, but to let Jean stay with her class. At the end of her third-grade year, though as lively, articulate, and curious as ever, she still was not reading. The school and her parents talked it over, and decided to offer her a choice. They pointed out to her that the fourth grade did a great deal of reading, that almost all their learning came from books, and almost all their talking was about books. It would be very hard, and dull, and confusing for her if she did not read. Did she want to go ahead with her class anyway, or would she rather take another year in the third grade, to catch up? Jean thought about this a while, then said that she would like to stay with her class. By the following winter she was reading as well as any of her very bright and able classmates.

> I later knew a boy, taught at home by his parents (both of whom worked during the day), who did not begin to read until after he was eight. When he was eleven he moved to a new town and wanted to go to school so that he could meet some other children, and also find out something about what school was like. The school gave him the usual reading tests, on which he scored at the twelfth-grade level. But of course he didn't have to spend hours a day being taught reading skills and being tested to be sure he had learned them. He could use that time *to read.*

Here is a copy of a letter, written by the mother of a boy who is at one of the schools in which children are not required to attend classes but learn when, and what they like, with whatever help from the older people around them they may choose to ask for. The boy, who had been having great difficulty in his conventional school and had not learned to read, went to this school when he was seven. Two years later his mother wrote:

[He] has not, until the last month or so, attended a single class ... yet in taking the Standard Achievement and I.Q. tests we find he is reading into the tenth grade, doing math into the ninth grade, working with electronics and in several other areas that are not offered in public schools, even to the high school student.

The electronics suggests how this seeming miracle was accomplished. There are no electronics manuals, texts, and instruction books written for young children. To use them, you must be able to read words like "resistor," "capacitor," "potentiometer," and the like. No doubt this boy had to have help at first; but in learning to read the basic terms of electronics he undoubtedly got enough information about letters and sounds to enable him to read any words he met. To work in electronics you must also know arithmetic, up through the decimals, so he had to learn that, too, along with a good deal about electricity and electric circuits.

Timetables! We act as if children were railroad trains running on a schedule. The railroad man figures that if his train is going to get to Chicago at a certain time, then it must arrive on time at every stop along the route. If it is ten minutes late getting into a station, he begins to worry. In the same way, we say that if children are going to know so much when they go to college, then they have to know this at the end of this grade, and that at the end of that grade. If a child doesn't arrive at one of these intermediate stations when we think he should, we instantly assume that he is going to be late at the finish. But children are not railroad trains. They don't learn at an even rate. They learn in spurts, and the more interested they are in what they are learning, the faster these spurts are likely to be.

> Not only that, but they often don't learn in what seems to us a logical sequence, by which we mean easy things first, hard things later. Being always seekers of meaning, children may *first* go to the hard things, which have more meaning—are (in Papert's

word) less dissociated from the world—and later from these hard things learn the "easy" ones. Thus children who read well certainly know a lot of "phonics," but they have probably learned at least as much phonics from words as they have learned words from phonics. No one taught me that the letters PH say the sound "fff." I figured it out, probably from hard words like "photograph" and "telephone."

I think of an "utterly hopeless" student I once knew, now grown up and a skillful and successful commercial photographer, who when she first took up serious photography at about age fourteen learned in a few months, because she needed it, all the arithmetic she had never been able to learn in ten years of school. Such stories are by no means rare.

It may be true enough that in learning purely physical skills, such as sports, gymnastics, ballet, or playing musical instruments—though not even these are "purely" physical, nothing is—we generally have to learn easy movements before we learn hard ones. That is how the body works. But it is not how the mind works. What makes things easy or hard for our minds has very little to do with how little or how much information they may contain, and everything to do with how interesting they are and, to say it once again, *how much sense they make,* how connected they seem to reality.

This is not to say that all children, left to learn on their own, would find something that interested them as much as electronics interested the boy I just spoke of. It is to say that when they learn in their own way and for their own reasons, children learn so much more rapidly and effectively than we could possibly teach them, that we *can afford* to throw away our curricula and our timetables, and set them free, at least most of the time, to learn on their own.

I would now say "all of the time." Children do not
need to be made to learn, told what to learn, or
shown how. If we give them access to enough of the
world, including our own lives and work in that
world, they will see clearly enough what things are
truly important to us and to others, and they will
make for themselves a better path into that world
than we could make for them.

Nowhere is our obsession with timetables more needless and foolish than in reading. We make much too
much of the difficulties of learning to read. Teachers
may say, "But reading must be difficult, or so many children wouldn't have trouble with it." I say that it is *because* we assume that it is so difficult that so many
children have trouble with it. Our anxieties, our fears,
and the ridiculous things we do to "simplify" what is simple enough already, *cause* most of the trouble.

How great, in fact, is the task of learning to read? What
information, what relationships must be learned, in order
to do it? What we have to learn are the various ways in
which the letters of written English can represent the
sounds of spoken English. How many such sounds are
there? About 45. How many letters, and combinations of
letters, are needed to make these sounds? About 380.
Granted, it would be nice if for each sound there were one
and only one letter, as in Italian. But 380 letters and letter-
groups is nothing to get into a panic over. How many
words does the average child know when he comes to first
grade? Five *thousand* or more. And a great many of these
words have many more than one definition, as a quick
look at the dictionary will show, so that the child knows
many more than five thousand word meanings. And this
is not all. He knows a great many of the enormous number of English idioms that cause such trouble to foreign-
ers. Moreover, he knows most of the grammar of the
language as well. Though he may not know their names,
there are hardly any of the constructions of English that

he cannot understand, or use in his own speech. And this is just as true of children in countries whose grammar is much more complicated than English, full of case endings, verb endings, genders, agreement, and all kinds of things we don't have to bother with. All over the world, children acquire this extraordinary amount of information, most of it by the time they are six, and most of it, as I have described, by themselves, without anything that we could call formal instruction. Compared with this task, the task of learning to read even English is very, very small. To be sure, it can't be done overnight; but it certainly doesn't deserve all the worry and agony that we put into it. All we accomplish, by our worrying, simplifying, and teaching, is to make reading a hundred times harder for children than it need be.

> Since then the teaching of reading has become much more "scientific," fragmented (five hundred skills!), and dissociated from both the reality and the pleasures of real books, real newspapers and magazines, real letters from real people. And our reading problems have grown much worse.

When I went to Europe, and began relearning my long-forgotten school French, and learning Italian from scratch, I was much helped by signs. In those days, at least, most European stores, like our laundries, had a sign over them telling what kind of store they were. This made it easy to learn these words by myself. Also helpful were signs like Entrance, Exit, Men, Women, Telephone, No Parking, Emergency Use Only, Bus Stop, Gas, Restaurant, and so on. It occurred to me later that it might help children build up a mental reserve of known words if there were many such signs around them in the home. I thought of making, on three-by-five cards, such signs as Door, Window, Kitchen Sink, Chair, Table, Stairs, Light Switch, and putting them in the right places. I suggested this to a friend who had some small children. She laughed and said, "The older one would just tear them all off, and the younger one would eat them." This set me back a bit. But later, when Lisa was four, and again when she was five, I made a number of these signs, and put them around the house. At first she seemed not particularly interested in them, though she did look at them, and perhaps learned something from them. When she was a bit older, she became quite interested, and wanted to make some herself.

When Tommy was four I decided to make some for him. By this time I had decided that it would in the long run be more useful to him if I wrote more than one word on each sign, thus: This Is A Lamp, Clothes Closet, This Is The Washing Machine. Though it might be harder at first to figure out or remember what each word said, it would give him more data, from which he could figure out such words as "This," "A," and so on. He was very enthusiastic about it, watched me make the cards, followed me around when I put them up, and asked me about them. Following the lead of Sylvia Ashton-Warner, I said that I would make a sign that said anything he wanted it to say. He showed himself very much like the older children—about nine or ten is the great age for this—who cover the doors of their rooms with notices warning people to stay out, on penalty of the most horrible punishments, up to and including death. We had put up in the yard a tent for him to play in, and he immediately asked for a sign saying "Do Not Go In This Tent." I made it for him, and he put it on.

Then *he* wanted to make signs. I said, "Fine!" and gave him some cards and a felt-tipped pen. In the back of my mind was a hope that he would start trying to copy some of the words I had written, or would at least use some of the letters I had written. But he didn't see the task that way. As he saw it, you thought of something you wanted to say, and then you made some marks on a card, and then that was what the card said. What marks you used were not important. Most of his were rough O's and U's. He plunged himself into the task, and soon had his signs all over the place, usually next to one of mine.

Here I made a mistake, showing how addicted I can still be to narrow and supposedly efficient ways of learning. I began to feel that Tommy was so interested in making his signs that he was not interested in looking at or copying my "real" signs. And indeed he wasn't; the task, as he saw it, was to get cards stuck up everywhere with marks on them. So I decided that this activity probably wasn't very useful, that he was too young for it, wasn't learning anything from it. I stopped making any new signs, and put away the cards and felt-tipped pen. After a while, perhaps most foolish of all, I began to take some of his signs down, leaving my own up. I thought, why confuse him, why not just leave up the ones with real letters on them? Only later did it occur to me that it would have been very useful for him to discover, by himself, that my signs were different from his. This might have led him to see—not study, just see—some of the ways in which they were different.

Only later yet did it occur to me that what he had discovered in making his signs was the most important thing he could have discovered—that writing is a way of expressing one's thoughts, a kind of magic, silent speech. What difference did it make that I could not tell from his marks what he was trying to say? What counted was that he really felt he was saying something. It is this feeling about writing that so many children never get in school, and that makes all their work with both writing and reading seem so dead, artificial, and impersonal. If from the start they could think of writing as a way of saying something, and reading as a way of knowing what others are saying, they would write and read with much more interest and excitement.

I see now that Tommy's first sign making has the same relationship to writing English as an infant's first babbling has to speaking English. I should have encouraged him to go on babbling in writing. After a while, almost certainly, he would have begun to think about ways to make his writing like other writing. It would also have been easy to show him, tactfully, that many people could read conventional writing, whereas only he could read his own. In time he would have begun to be interested in making a writing that other people could read.

I regret this mistake more every time I think of it. Did I offend or discourage Tommy when I took down his signs? He never complained to me about it, and he was not a boy to keep quiet if he thought he had been wrongly treated. But I often wonder whether to some extent it is because of this that he has never been much interested in writing, of any kind. He likes to talk, but not write. For that matter, he has never cared much about reading.

It may be that no matter what I had done or not done, his main path into the world would always have been the path of tools and machines, making, fixing, and building things, rather than the path of written words. But we can explore the world along many paths, the more the better, and it troubles me a little to think now and then that I may have blocked this particular path. Children trying out new things are like plants putting out little green shoots. We must be careful not to cut them off.

At any rate, it's a mistake I would never make again. Many parents have written to *Growing Without Schooling* about their small children's "writing." One family I met later sent a card their youngest child had written to me, covered with many lines of wavy marks—a child's Rosetta stone. I wrote back thanking the child for the nice letter. Soon, like Julia in the "Fantasy" chapter, below, she will write letters that we all can read. Many other children learn to read by writing first, and if the mechanics of writing were easier (one reason I like typewriters), perhaps many more would. These writing children begin with a very personal but logical kind of phonic spelling. Then, just as when younger they gradually adjusted their speech to match the speech they heard around them, so as they learn to read and see more written words they gradually make their writing more like the writing around them.

A wonderful example of this, the best study of a particular child's growth and learning over a number of years that I have ever seen, is Glenda Bissex's book, *Gnys at Wrk,* which I have already discussed in the chapter "Learning About Children." Her son Paul essentially taught himself how to write, and also to read, though the writing came first, in time and in importance. Like the children just mentioned, he began with scribble-writing. One of his first efforts was a sign, intended to say to his mother, "Welcome Home." His first readable message was an indignant note to her: while busy reading, she had not noticed that he was trying to ask her something. After a while he went away, soon to return with a piece of paper on which he had printed in large letters, RUDF. She wisely read the message correctly— "Are you deaf?"—and gave him the attention he sought. Her quick response must have been one of the reasons why he went on writing messages.

Years ago a friend of mine, the English teacher (and writer of books about English) James Moffett, wisely said, "You can't write writing," meaning, you have to write *about something.* As Mrs. Bissex, herself a teacher of English, makes clear in vivid example after example, Paul did not "learn to write," learn what schools would call the skills of writing, so that *later on* he could use them to write something. From the beginning he wrote because he had something he wanted to say, often to himself, sometimes to others. About his first writings, she says:

> Paul himself described what he was doing as "writing" rather than "spelling." ... Had his main interest been in spelling *words*, he would have written word lists; what he wrote, however, were *messages*. He cared about what he wrote, not just about how he wrote it.

Even in the first six months of his writing, these messages took very different forms, including (she gives examples of all of these) signs, lists, informative notes, letters, labels and captions for objects or drawings, a story, a greeting card, a board game, directions, statements, a newspaper, and a book. In the following years he continued with these forms, adding to them Valentines, shopping lists, instructions, "report cards" for the family dog and three cats, a cookbook, four more newspapers (with funnies, news, weather, and advertising), licenses and ID cards for his toy animals, schedules for himself, rules for using his electric train, business letters (sending away for things), quizzes (to self), and a diary. Clearly, his writing was strongly connected in many ways to the world around him.

The only time he ever wrote lists was when, once in a while, he would challenge himself by trying to spell some hard words. Mrs. Bissex makes this very good point about children and challenges:

> A challenge is something that will stretch your powers, with the likelihood of confirming them; you want to take on a challenge because you have confidence enough that you can succeed. A threat is a task that seems beyond your powers to accomplish or cope with. *In setting his own tasks* Paul

was able to keep them at the challenge level. He was not content to repeat his accomplishments but spontaneously moved on to harder tasks. . . . He set up a progression of increasingly difficult tasks for himself as many other children spontaneously do. How much might self-set challenges occur in school learning if time and space were allowed for them to happen and be observed?

As Alison Stallibrass so clearly shows in her book *The Self-Respecting Child,* and Millicent Shinn in *The Biography of a Baby,* all children do this as they grow up—until they get to school. What all too often happens there is that they learn to see school challenges as threats, which they usually are, not just because you have a good chance of failing to accomplish them, but because if you do fail you are almost certain to be criticized, shamed, or even punished. They become so used to dodging and escaping these daily threats that they fall more and more out of the habit of challenging themselves, even outside of school. Their school-learned fears infect the whole of their life. The world, which had once seemed at least neutral if not actually friendly and tempting, begins to look more and more like an unpredictable and dangerous enemy.

In this, as in so many other things, we do things backwards. We think in terms of getting a skill first, and then finding useful and interesting things to do with it. The sensible way, the best way, is to start with something worth doing, and then, moved by a strong desire to do it, get whatever skills are needed. If we begin by helping children feel that writing and reading are ways of talking to and reaching other people, we will not have to bribe and bully them into acquiring the skills; they will want them for what they do with them.

I know of a number of schools—there may be many more that I don't know of—in which there is nothing whatever of what we think of as formal instruction in reading, yet in which children learn to read just as well as in conventional schools. Classes are large, forty children per teacher. Nor are the children special; they are of average I.Q., and often come from homes in which little reading is done. How do they learn? Why do they learn? What happens?

In most of these schools incoming five-year-olds, who do not read, are put in classes with six- and seven-year-olds, who do. This takes care of most of what we call the problem of motivation. Little children want to be able to do what bigger children can do and do. There are many different kinds of materials in the classrooms that children can read, or use to discover how to read. There are books, pictures with self-explaining captions, pictures drawn by children and described by them, stories written and illustrated by children, groups of rhyming words, and the like. In short, a wealth of materials, evidence, which the children can take in and from which they can make discoveries. Also, there are many people from whom they can get advice and help, when and if they want it.

> The schools referred to here were mostly British "infant schools" (for children of five through seven), about which I wrote in *How Children Fail*. During the sixties and early seventies many of these schools—enthusiasts said as many as one-third, skeptics said more like 10 percent—were trying to run schools on the principle that children learn best and remember most when they have not just the freedom to move about and talk in the classroom, but beyond that, a great deal of choice in what they learn and when and how they learn it. There was much talk in those days about the "revolution" in primary school education in Great Britain. It seemed for a

while a kind of wave of the future. But even when it was at its peak, I began to fear it might not last long. In an introduction to the book *Open Education in the Informal Classroom*, edited by Charles Rathbone (New York: Citation Press, 1971), I wrote:

What is the future, what are the prospects of the revolution in British primary education? The contributors to this book do not discuss this directly, but from their tone one gets the feeling that the revolution is established, secure, and bound to grow. I am not so sure, for a number of reasons.

In their chapters Charles Rathbone and Roland Barth state very clearly and fully the assumptions on which open education are based. It would be natural and tempting to assume that ... many or most of the parents of primary school children in Leicestershire and in other counties having open schools more or less understand what these assumptions are and accept them. I think this is very far from the truth. Primary schools in England have been able to make changes on a wide scale largely for two reasons. In the first place, there is a tradition that schools and teachers know best, that what they do is none of the parents' business, and that parents should not stick their noses in school affairs.... Secondly, and much more important, the parents of almost all these children do not expect in the slightest that their children will later go on to a university but rather that they will leave school at fifteen or sixteen and take their places somewhere in the working or lower middle class.... In short, most British parents have not seen or felt their society as being very upwardly mobile, or felt it their chief duty in life to shove their children up the socio-economic ladder, or seen school and success in school as a way to do this.

Though I do not know, I suspect this attitude is changing, and as it changes, as adults tend more and more to see school as a place where children start a race that will go on all the rest of their lives, the primary school revolution may be deeply threatened. Indeed it is already threatened by members of a self-styled elite who want to keep Britain a rigid and hierarchical society. These enemies of open education see much more clearly than most of its supporters the long-run political and social consequences of this kind of schooling. My teacher friends in new British primary schools do not think that the ground they have gained can be lost. I hope they are right, but I fear they may be overconfident. . . .

The contributors to this book have themselves done almost all their work in open education with young children. . . . In my visits to Leicestershire and in many discussions there with primary school teachers and heads (principals), I have never heard of any movement to carry into secondary education the kinds of reforms they have carried out in their own schools, or indeed any thinking or discussion about what reformed secondary education might be like. . . .

This seems to me a mistake and a quite serious one. . . . The best [of the British infant schools] *are* wonderful places, no doubt about it. But they are, with very few exceptions, cut off from the world and from the problems and crises of our societies and times. They avoid the question of how a young person may best grow up in these times and deal with these problems, even the problems of their next and very different school. . . . The British primary schools act, on the whole, as if the outside world was not there or was there only as a kind of Given that nothing much could be done about. . . . They seem to say, in effect, "Within these walls you can be the director of your life, free, responsible, making choices and acting on them. After you leave here, that is all over, and you will have to live like other people, doing what you are told, taking what comes to you." Thus these schools are less a part of the whole of a child's life than an interlude away from it—a breathing spell, or as another British open educator (Lyward) once put it, a "respite." ...

I only wonder whether an educational revolution as profound as open education can survive in the long run unless it is or becomes a part of a wider and deeper notion or vision of life and social change. Without some such connection, some such vision, I fear that it may either lose its vitality and capacity for growth or that it may be isolated and destroyed by those who see more clearly to what social and political consequences it might someday lead.

It was not long before my fears began to prove well founded. The people who dislike and distrust both children and human liberty, and there are many of these in Great Britain as everywhere, began to attack the open infant schools. A so-called study was written, published, and widely publicized in Great Britain and here, supposedly showing that children educated in open schools learned less than children educated traditionally. Though it may have been honest in intent, the study was a model of bad and worthless educational research. In the first place, it drew its findings largely from a county that had done no outstanding work in open education, and studiously avoided the many cities and counties where the best work had been and was being done. It drew the line between open and traditional schools solely on the basis of what the schools called themselves, and thus completely missed the vital difference, immediately obvious to me when I visited schools in Leicestershire, between schools that really believed in the principles of open education and practiced them with imagination and enthusiasm, and those which neither understood nor believed in those principles and only practiced them, grudgingly and skeptically, because that was what someone over them seemed to want.

Even among the best schools in Leicestershire, an outstanding county in open education, I saw several of these pseudo-open schools. They were clearly not working. Children know all too well when people respect and trust them and when they don't, and schools which pretended to be open when they were at heart traditional, that is, based on a distrust of children and their desire and ability to learn, were in many ways worse, more anxious, more full of contradictory, "double-bind" messages, than traditional schools that never pretended to be anything else.

Beyond that, this study judged children's learning solely on the basis of standardized test scores. Naturally, the traditionally schooled children, who were in all probability coached for these tests as many open-school children were not, would be likely to do somewhat better, though this difference was in fact very slight. But as I pointed out in *How Children Fail,* these test scores are frauds. Even in highly selective private schools, most of the fifth-graders I taught did not know more than a small part of the mathematics that their test scores supposedly showed they knew, and regardless of their reading scores, only a handful really liked to read or would read unless made to. The authors of the British study made no effort to find out how much of the "learning" in their traditional schools was genuine and lasting; indeed, it probably never occurred to them that it might be otherwise. Nor did this study make any effort to find out how much children in open schools might have learned that was not tested on the tests, and since much of their learning was precisely of this kind, the test scores grossly misrepresented what the open schools had accomplished. With all this, the difference in test scores between the traditional and open schools was so slight—a matter of a few months—as to prove nothing. Even if we set aside all I have said about the shallowness and impermanence of school rote learning, there is no reason to believe that the tests are accurate to within a matter of months.

But people will seize any excuse for believing whatever they want to believe. As the British author Leila Berg has shown in her many books, children are no more generally liked in Great Britain than here. For the same reasons as most Americans, reasons I have described in *Instead of Education* and *Teach Your Own,* many or most people in England strongly disliked the idea of little children actually enjoying school. Whatever humane changes had been made in infant schools, changes that, as I said before, were rarely extended into the junior schools and not at all into the secondary schools, were slowly or not so slowly undermined and done away with. When the then Labour Party prime minister James Callaghan said in a major public speech on education that what Britain needed was "round pegs for round holes," it was clear that this educational revolution had come to an end, and for just the same reasons that had put an end to all earlier revolutions of the same kind. Needless to say, what children were or might be learning was not one of those reasons.

In a number of these classrooms the teachers were making imaginative use of tape recorders. I have described earlier how helpful it is for many children to hear a story read aloud, while they follow the words with their eyes. Teachers with forty students cannot do this reading themselves. What they had done was dictate onto a tape a number of the books that were in the class. Often I saw three, four, sometimes even six children sitting around a table, listening over headphones to a story being read aloud, while they read or followed the same story in a book in front of them. There is much here that we can borrow, and perhaps add to and improve.

In many elementary school classrooms children dictate stories, directly or through a tape recorder, to their teacher, who writes out the stories and returns them to their authors. For many children, these stories are much more exciting to read than some old book. By such means many children who had not been at all interested in learning to read have become interested. In some inner city schools, the children, bored with the commercially available readers, which have nothing to do with life as they know it, are writing their own readers.

Until recently we have been somewhat limited in what we could do with tape recorders by the fact that the machines were too difficult for children to operate and too easy for them to damage. Those whirling wheels! All that lovely tape, just aching to be spilled out on the floor! It was more than most teachers dared risk. But now, with the development of cassette-type recorders, we have machines that are so simple to operate that children could easily be taught both to record and play back on them without supervision. This would make it possible for a teacher, perhaps with the help of some children, to record a tape library to go with many of the books in their book library, so that at any time a child who wanted to hear a book read aloud, and read it at the same time, could easily do so. Or, if there were children of different ages in a class, the older ones could often write out stories that the younger ones had dictated.

It was not long before educational publishers in the United States did in fact begin to publish such cassettes, and I saw quite a few of them in schools I visited. But the ones I listened to (full of hope) were disappointing—too elaborate and expensive, with not very good stories, and these usually read in the dreadful, false, condescending, cutesy-wootsy voices that educators tend to use with young children. Even so, some children may have gained something from them. But what I had hoped to see didn't happen, that children using these cassettes could hear stories they liked and chose for themselves, or even had dictated themselves, and beyond that, that these stories could be read in a natural voice by people they knew, perhaps teachers, perhaps parents, perhaps even their friends or themselves. None of this need be difficult or expensive to do. Good cassette recorders and tapes are cheap, durable, and easy for even young children to use, and there are now a number of companies that will copy cassettes very cheaply, so that teachers (or parents or librarians or whoever) could easily make as many copies as they needed of whatever stories proved most popular.

For the time being, as far as I know, not much of this is being done in schools. But it could very easily be done by other people—librarians, or best of all, people teaching their own children at home.

□SPORTS

☐ June 6, 1965

We took Tommy to the pool today—our first trip this year. Right away, he had an accident that would have discouraged most infants his age. He was standing on the first and second of the steps leading down into the shallow end of the pool. This was as far as he wanted to go; he had refused my invitation for a "ride" in the water. Instead, he walked about on the steps, looking at the water, and feeling it with his hands. Suddenly, as he walked around, he stepped off the edge and dropped in over his head. His older sister, watching close by, had him out in a second, coughing and spluttering, but not visibly frightened. After a short time out of the water, to rest and get his breath and courage back, he was in again. Now he asked for the ride he had refused earlier, I took him in my arms and walked about in the water, which came up to his waist and chest. He clung to me tightly, holding on, as babies do, with arms and legs. Once in a while I would duck down in the water far enough so that it came up to his shoulders, but as he did not seem to like it, I did not do it often. At no time did he relax his tight grip of arms and legs, and after a short time he wanted to go back to the steps. This was all he wanted to do today.

☐ June 9, 1965

Today Tommy was much more eager to get into the water and to take his first ride. He clung to me less tightly, and did not mind it, even enjoyed it, when the water came up to his shoulders. After we had done this a while, I thought I might be able to get him to let me hold him without his holding me. I began by gently loosening the grip of his legs. He did not resist, and seemed pleased to have them free in the water as we walked around. Then, holding his body very firmly in my hands, I was gradually able to get him to loosen his arms around my neck, and to hold on to my arms instead. Thus I could tow him around in something like a true swimming position. After a bit of this I urged him to kick his feet, and moved his legs to show him what I meant. He liked this and began to kick—as he does everything else—vigorously. Now and then, for a short time, I could get him to let go of my arms and have his hands free in the water. Once or twice I was even able to get him to paddle.

His progress in exploring this new element of water was not steady and uninterrupted. The courage of little children (and not them alone) rises and falls, like the tide—only the cycles are in minutes, or even seconds. We can see this vividly when we watch infants of two or so, walking with their mothers, or playing in a playground or park.

Not long ago I saw this scene in the Public Garden in Boston. The mothers were chatting on a bench while the children roamed around. For a while they would explore boldly and freely, ignoring their mothers. Then, after a while, they would use up their store of courage and confidence, and run back to their mothers' sides, and cling there for a while, as if to recharge their batteries. After a moment or two of this they were ready for more exploring, and so they went out, then came back, and then ventured out again.

In just this way, this baby in the pool has his times of exploration, and his times of retreat and retrenchment. At times he let me tow him around freely, kicking his feet and paddling his hands. At other times he gripped my arms fiercely, pulled himself toward me, and by his gestures and expression showed me that he wanted to be held in the same tight and enveloping grip with which we had begun. Or he might even ask to go back to the steps, or to be lifted out of the pool altogether. Then, a few minutes later, he would be back in the water and ready for more adventure.

At one time or another I have watched a number of parents trying to teach their very little children to swim. On the whole, they don't get very far, because they are so insensitive to this rise and fall of courage in the child. Is it because they don't notice? Or because they don't care? Perhaps they feel that the child's feelings are unimportant, to be easily overridden by exhortation and encouragement, or even anger and threats. More probably, people who don't care much how a child feels will not notice much how he feels. In any case, such would-be teachers, even when they are not wholly unsuccessful, lose a great deal, since a child who is allowed to return to babyhood for a while when he feels the need of it, to fill up his tank of courage when he feels it run dry, will move ahead into the unknown far faster than we adults could push him.

Of course, Tommy has always been an exceptionally bold and adventurous baby. Very few children, however carefully and respectfully treated, progress as fast as he does. But the principle is always true. If we continually try to force a child to do what he is afraid to do, he will become more timid, and will use his brains and energy, not to explore the unknown, but to find ways to avoid the pressures we put on him. If, however, we are careful not to push a child beyond the limits of his courage, he is almost sure to get braver.

Tommy's sister Lisa, for example, was much more tim-id than he is. When she first went to a pool, she would not do anything more than sit on the top step and splash her feet, and her expression and manner showed that she thought that even this was a risky business. It was weeks before she was willing to get as much as waist deep, or to allow any of us to give her a ride. It was not until the following summer that she would let us tow her around without her holding on tightly with her arms. But we respected her natural timidity and caution. The result was that she wanted, and learned, to combat her fears and overcome them. Now, at the age of six, she is a fearless skiier, going down difficult trails with children twice her age. In the summer she works hard at learning to swim, which she does as well as most of her friends.

☐ June 10, 1965

Today there was a rope stretched across the shallow end of the pool, to make an enclosed space for the little children. Tommy was very interested in this rope, and particularly in the two blue-and-white plastic floats that helped hold it up. He seemed not at all interested in going on from where we had left off the day before, in learning to kick and paddle. Instead, he wanted to investigate the rope and the floats. At first, like any adult, I thought this would divert him from learning to swim. But I was wrong, for he soon discovered that with the rope he could support himself in the water without any help, and used the rope to explore further into this new element. When he first grabbed the rope and tested its strength and reliability, I gradually relaxed my grip and gave him less and less support, until, at least as it seemed to him, the rope was doing all the work. Of course, he was largely supported by the buoyancy of his own body and by the small plastic float he was wearing.

At first I stayed very close to him when he was holding the rope. Then, very gradually, as he got used to the idea of my not holding him, I moved farther and farther away, to give him more sense of independence. The feeling of not being held was very exciting to him. It clearly made big demands on his courage, for after holding the rope alone a short while, he would say, "Hold me." Then, after a moment of being held, he would say, "Don't hold me," and I would let him go again. As time went on he wanted to be held less and less, and even told me, now and then, to go away. At about this time he discovered that the plastic floats on the rope could be slid along it. This became a very exciting game, and for most of the rest of our time in the water he busied himself with pushing the floats from one end of the rope to the other. He also discovered that while holding on to the rope he could let his feet swing underneath it, so that he was in effect floating on his back. He liked this, though getting right side up again was something of a struggle.

There were many other children in the pool, swimming, splashing, leaping about, and jumping in and out. This made another problem for Tommy. Water was being continually sprayed in his face, and now and then a wave would come up over his mouth, and even his nose. I did not fully realize, until I watched him, that one of the most important and subtle skills that a swimmer must develop is a reflex that automatically blocks his mouth and nose whenever the water rises over them. The expert swimmer does this without thinking, and indeed often learns to breathe through the upper part of his mouth even when the lower part is under water. This baby, naturally, had no such skill. He didn't know how to keep water out of his mouth and nose. He did not even understand that this had to be done. Quite the reverse, in fact; when a wave rose up over his face it so startled him that he was very likely to gasp in surprise, and thus take water down all pipes. Then followed much choking, coughing, spluttering, and often a loud burp. Fortunately it was about as easy for him to get the water out as to take it in. He didn't like it when this happened, and almost always needed to be held for a moment afterward, but he never cried or asked to leave the pool. Now and then he would say indignantly, "Too much peoples!" To which I could only agree.

I have since read that in their first year of life babies have this nose-blocking reflex, and that they swim very easily and naturally, like fish. But apparently children who can and love to swim at one year, unless they keep on swimming regularly, will lose this reflex and this skill by the time they are three or four and will have to learn all over again.

A child finds it easier to learn to be aware of when his nose or mouth is under water, and to act accordingly, in a pool that is not too rough. But this pool was small and crowded, and being in dry country, had no overflow gutters to keep the waves down. We had to find ways to deal with the situation. One helpful game turned up quite by accident. I was holding him close when he got a small surprise mouthful of water, which he instantly and instinctively blew out in my face. I made a great event of this—grimaced, coughed, choked, spluttered. He thought this was terribly funny, and quickly did it again, putting his face in the water to get new mouthfuls to spray at me. This game had several uses. He could see that a grownup could choke, gasp, and cough, and that he was not the only one to whom such things could happen. Also, he could see that getting a mouthful of water need not be an accident or a calamity. Finally, he could feel that *he* was deciding and controlling whether water was going into his mouth, or out. When he had done this a while I thought I could get him to blow bubbles in the water, and did it for him. He showed no interest in imitating me, so I dropped it.

□ June 12, 1965

Today was the most adventurous day of all. As soon as we got into the water he asked me to take him for a ride. So I towed him for a while around the shallow end. He did not hold on to me, but kicked and paddled vigorously. I was able to hold him very lightly, and after a while, gave him no support whatever. I said to him, "You're swimming, you're swimming!" and from his excited expression it was clear that he knew this was so. Finally I took my hands away from him altogether, and held them out of the water, to show him and his mother that he was truly on his own. A few seconds of this at a time was as much adventure as he could stand, so I was careful to give him a little contact and support before he could be worried by not having it.

Later, while he was resting and warming up in the sun, I did some swimming of my own. As I came to the deep end, there he was with his mother, who told me he wanted to jump off the diving board and have me catch him. I said, "Are you kidding? You're sure he wants to do that?" He insisted, climbed up on the board, walked out to the end, and without a second's hesitation jumped off. I caught him and towed him over to the ladder at the side of the pool. Back he came for a second try, and a third, and he would have gone on if there had not been a crowd of bigger children waiting for a turn on the board. But this adventure brought on a crisis. Having jumped off the board, he felt that the whole pool was rightfully his. Next time we began to swim, he asked me to give him a ride on the deep side of the rope. As soon as he got over the rope he headed straight for the deep end and began swimming with all his might. I followed along, and when we got to where I could just stand, I turned him back toward the shallow end. He said he wanted to go all the way to the deep end, and turned right around again. I turned him back. He protested, and turned again. Soon his mother, and then the life guard, joined me in telling him that he had to stay at the shallow end, that he wasn't big enough or a good enough swimmer to swim at the deep end. For a while he argued, as best he could, but when he realized that we were really not going to let him swim in the whole pool, he began to cry, or rather, to roar, with disappointment, humiliation, and rage. We could not appease him. It must have seemed to him that he had proved himself, had earned the right to use the whole pool, and that in keeping him in the shallow end we were just discriminating against him.

> It seems to me now that we were very foolish and mistaken in what we did. Why did we feel we had to make such an issue out of this? If I had it to do again, I would say, "Okay, swim to the deep end if you want, and I'll just swim along with you." What harm could it have done? He could not sink—he had his floater on—and if he had run out of energy or nerve, or taken in a big mouthful of water, I could easily have towed him to the side of the pool. He had indeed earned his chance to swim to the deep end, and I don't blame him in the least for being indignant that we denied it to him and, after all his good work, gave him this ringing vote of No Confidence.

☐ June 16, 1965

Bad weather has kept us from the pool for a few days. Today the sun brought us back again. As we drove down in the car, Tommy said to me several times, "Don't hold me, John. I do it by myself." He was clearly rehearsing in his mind what he would do when he got to the pool. It seemed to me that this was the kind of mental operation that many experts say children of this age, and indeed considerably older children, cannot do. When we arrived, and had put his plastic bubble on, Tommy went right into the water and without any help or support from me began to swim. The bubble, riding up between his shoulders, kept him in a fairly vertical position, so that he had to work very hard to make forward progress. Only when another child, playing, or jumping into the pool, gave him a surprise faceful of water, did he stop swimming, and look around for help and support. As soon as he had coughed and spluttered out all the water, he was off again. In this way he made three or four trips across the entire shallow end. This used up most of his store of energy and confidence for the day. Most of the rest of the time, he was content to have me tow him around, or to hang on and play with the rope.

☐ June 18, 1965

Today he learned for the first time how to deal with water coming up over his face. He began the day's exploration, as he had done several times before, by jumping off the steps into my hands. However, he must have been feeling a bit more timid than usual, for he asked me to hold him, not just in my hands but in my arms. We had not done this for some time. In this way I would take him back to the steps, from which he would jump off into my hands again. After doing this a few times, he felt bolder, and was willing to swim back to the steps, I giving him only token support. This soon became no support at all; as soon as he reached me he would turn around and swim to the steps or the edge of the pool. After some experiments he found that he could turn himself around in the water, and go in whatever direction he wanted. This was also very exciting. Several times he turned himself in a complete circle, just to show he could do it, and for the fun of doing it.

During one of our breaks I watched a man trying to

teach his three small children to swim. He was a perfect example of the kind of parent I have described, who thinks that by superior will and brute force he can make his children learn whatever he wants to teach them. As we arrived at the pool he had his little daughter, about four years old, in his arms, and was moving her about in the water. She did not resist, but she was stiffly motionless, and looked uneasy. After not much more than two or three minutes of this, the father, a young ex-athlete run to fat, decided that she was ready for serious instruction. His plan was to hold her in the water in a swimming position, that is, face down, or belly down, while she paddled and kicked. In its proper time, not a bad idea, but this was not the time, or anywhere near it. The little girl suddenly found herself snatched loose of her grip on her father, and suspended helpless over this new, and still strange and frightening element. She went rigid in his hands, arched her back, as if to lift herself out of the water, and struggled to get loose. No use. Her father held her tightly, and said, in a louder and louder voice, "Kick your feet! Move your hands!" The little girl began to scream, partly in terror and anger, partly in the hope that if she made enough noise her father would have to stop. For a while he countered with threatening shouts of his own: "Rink! Rink! You stop it! Do you hear! There's nothing to be afraid of! Be quiet!" But she held the stronger hand. The pool was surrounded by people, and as her screams got louder and louder, more and more disapproving eyes were turned on him, until he gave up, and furiously lifted her out of the pool. Not long after this he repeated the process with a little boy. Before our short stay at the pool was over, he had reduced all three of his children to tears and terror.

The pool was very crowded that day, kids were jumping in and out, and the seas were running unusually high. For the first time Tommy began to be able to deal with the problem of water in his face. Now and then he would breathe or swallow some down, and have to be held until he got rid of it. But more and more, he was able to keep his mouth closed, or if water did get in, to spit it right out again. He was no longer much troubled by spray flying in his face. He accepted this as part of being in the water. In this, as in other ways, he showed that he was beginning to feel that the water was his element, and that he was at home in it.

Here my visit came to an end, and with it my reports on Tommy's progress. The Styrofoam plastic bubble he wears is buoyant enough to support him with very little effort on his part. It seemed to me that the next step was to free him of his dependence on this bubble, so that he could support himself entirely by his own buoyancy and effort. One way to do this might be to carve little hunks off the bubble so that it would gradually give less and less support. Another way might be to take him in now and then without the bubble, holding him up with hands, or by a belt around his waist, and gradually reduce this support. Perhaps in a year or two he will himself decide that the bubble is babyish, and that he no longer wants or needs it. Whatever method is used, our experience so far makes it clear that when we use a child's natural desire to explore the new and unknown, and to gain some control over it, without trying to force him faster or further than he feels ready to go, both pupil and teacher have the most fun and make the most progress.

Tommy did learn to swim a year or two later. But as he grew older and began going to school, he became very interested in competitive sports, and in his New Mexico home swimming was not a big competitive sport or indeed something that very many people did. None of the boys who became his best friends cared much about swimming, and many of them may not even have known how. So, though in

the sports he loved—soccer, basketball, skiing, running—he became an outstanding athlete, he never
became more than a competent swimmer. No matter; he knows he can do it if he wants to, and if he
ever finds himself living near the ocean, he will
probably draw on his skiing experience to become a
good surfer.

Recently, Manfred Smith from Maryland wrote us
at *Growing Without Schooling* about his three-year-
old daughter learning to swim:

Last year, we decided that Jamie ought to have
swimming lessons. At first, it seemed like a good
idea. By the second lesson, it was becoming obvious that Jamie hated it. We dropped out after the
fourth. Yes, we were quitters. For the rest of the
summer, Jamie was constantly worried that she
had to have lessons and did not like to go into the
big pool. This year, Jamie never entered the big
pool but instead spent lots of time "swimming" in
the baby pool. The baby pool we have here is nice
in that it gets deeper at one end. Jamie would
spend hours with her head under the water, swimming sideways, backward, etc.

About three weeks ago, she walked up to me and
informed me that she was ready to go into the big
pool by herself now. She then proceeded to walk toward the pool. Had I not gotten up, I have no doubt
that she would have jumped into the pool. Well, we
walked on over to the big pool, I picked her up and
lowered her into four feet of water—and she
SWAM. We spent over an hour in the pool that day.
She would jump head first into the pool and swim
toward me. All in all, she could swim at least fifteen feet. Now we spend lots of time in the big
pool.

We just returned from the beach where Jamie

had great fun with the ocean. She not only would swim in the ocean, she bodysurfed waves! Jamie is three years old. When kids are ready, they will do what they want to do.

A mother wrote to *Growing Without Schooling* about a similar experience:

> Z took swimming lessons at age four and again at five, for a couple of weeks each time. He was just on the verge of *really* swimming when he decided he didn't want any lessons—and hasn't had any for about a year and a half. But we've been going swimming weekly. Last week, he took off on his back. When he realized he had gone all the way across the pool he just kept swimming laps until he had done seven! This week he went across on his front (using his own style, of course) and, combining it with swimming on his back, did twelve laps!! Then, just to let us know he is not ready for complete independence, he wanted to jump in and be pushed back to the side just like our one-year-old.

A very common pattern in children's learning. First, a great bold leap forward into exciting new territory. Then, for a short while, a retreat back into what is comfortable, familiar, and secure. But we can't predict, much less control, these rhythms of advance and retreat, exploration and consolidation, and this is one of the main reasons why the learning of children can't, or at least shouldn't, be scheduled.

In the field of sports we see clearly how much children can learn without anyone teaching them anything. At one elementary school where I taught, we had a rather poor athletic program, mostly due to lack of space, partly to lack of time. The fourth, fifth, and sixth grades had a half-hour recess period in the morning, and an hour sports period in the afternoon. Only in the afternoon could we play softball, and then we had to play in a paved yard that was big enough to hold an infield, but not much more. After two years that yard was lost to softball; part of it was fenced in for smaller kids to play in, and much of the rest was turned into a parking lot. Also, the afternoon sports period was cut down to a half hour, and we were moved into another yard a good deal smaller than a tennis court. In most of such practice as we had, I, or David Hardy, the sixth-grade teacher, would rap out balls for infield practice, or occasionally pitch for batting practice. Fourth-, fifth-, and sixth-graders would do the fielding; third-graders, sometimes even second-graders, would run the bases.

With such limited time and space for practice, we did not expect to get much of a softball team, all the more so as the boys in the school were not outstandingly athletic to begin with. Yet, year after year, we were able to field a competent softball team that could hold its own against other boys of the same age. How did these kids manage to learn this very complicated game? David and I certainly didn't teach them. There was no time, or room, for anything that could be called instruction. No, they learned by watching each other, and imitating. Year after year we would see the same thing happen. Here would be a boy in the third or fourth grade who seemed so hopelessly clumsy, unathletic, and ignorant of all the rules and skills of baseball that it looked as if he could never learn to play. Two years later that same boy would be a competent and often an expert player—and many of them did almost all of their playing at school. They learned, as I say, by watching the older boys who did it best, and trying to do what they did.

As a matter of fact, they learned, on the whole, much better than the boys at another school, at which I taught, where there was far more play space, more time given to sports, and where teachers tried to teach softball. The boys in this school spent a good deal of their sports time standing around watching while someone "explained" something to them. I was then still under the spell of the idea that if you are determined enough you can teach anybody anything. I remember a couple of boys that I was trying to teach to bat and throw. I can still see their sullen but resigned faces, feel their limp, uncooperating muscles, practically hear their thoughts. Here was school brought right out into the playyard, where they were supposed to be having fun, or at least a moment's respite from school. Small wonder we did not get far. If, instead, they had had a chance to play with, and see, and imitate bigger boys, how much better things might have gone.

☐ART, MATH, & OTHER THINGS

One morning, in the first-grade classroom, two little girls, very close friends, got big pieces of paper, and pencils, sat down at a table, and got ready to draw. After some thought, one began to draw a very large tree. She started at the bottom of the page and drew two lines, which came together for a while and then went parallel up the page, almost to the very top before they began to spread out again. Then she made a fork in this trunk, near the top. From the two main branches so obtained she drew several smaller branches, which she began to cover with leaves. All the while, the other little girl watched, and did nothing. After a while I said to her, "What are you going to draw?" I was not insistent, only curious. She said, "I don't know what to draw." I said, "Why not draw another tree?" She said, without any hesitation or shame, "I don't know how."

It was a surprise and revelation to me. Though I like to look at much drawing and painting, I know very little about it. There was almost no art in my own schooling. I can only remember one art class, and one picture that I tried to paint—an owl sitting on a limb of a dead tree, with a full moon behind it; for me, a rather ambitious work. I never finished it. As a result of my inexperience, I had the naive idea that artists just look at what is in front of them and copy it, getting better at this as they go along. Only recently have I learned that life does not copy itself on paper, and that to make, with lines and colors, an image that looks like something real, takes technique. There is a trick, or many tricks, that have to be learned, practiced, and perfected.

Still, it hadn't occurred to me to think of this in children's terms, as children would see it. I thought that at their more primitive level, art was just a kind of copying. So when this child told me that she did not know how to draw a tree, I was startled. It was on the tip of my tongue to say, "Well, just look at one." But I thought again. I remembered reading once that many primitive people cannot recognize either drawings or photographs of even the most familiar objects and surroundings. We say, we believe, that a picture looks like life, but it really doesn't. Pictures are flat; life has depth. The business of turning real objects into flat pictures is a convention, like language, and like language, it must be learned.

A picture of a tree, I realized, has somewhat the same relation to a real tree that a map of a town has to the town. The map is like the town, in many ways; but in making a map we put some things in and leave others out. The same with a picture. This little girl, looking at the complicated piece of reality we call tree, with all its colors, shapes, textures, masses, light and shade, did not know which of these qualities to represent with a pencil, nor how to do it.

Two or three days later, I saw the same girls, sitting at a table again with big pieces of paper before them. But this time there was the familiar tree on both pieces of paper, the roots coming in to make the trunk, the trunk going almost to the top of the page, the two forked branches, the smaller branches sticking out any way, the green leaves. I said, "Ah, I see you're drawing a tree." She gave me a pleased smile, and then, nodding toward her friend, said, "She showed me how." And then went on with her work.

The children, of course, were not drawing a tree but what they had learned to recognize as a symbol of a tree, almost like a large hieroglyph. The lines they put on the paper did not look to them like a tree; they *meant* tree. And as far as their ever being able to draw a real likeness of a tree, or anything else, that was exactly the trouble.

Though I have long amused myself by making doodles and designs, I have never been good at drawing or thought that I could be. Being able to draw real likenesses of things or people seemed, as being able to play musical instruments once had seemed, a mysterious and almost magical talent. It was only this past year, when I read for the first time Betty Edwards's book *Drawing with the Right Side of the Brain,* that I understood why I and most people draw so badly, and what people do who draw well. In the past I had looked at a number of books about how to draw, but none had made the mystery less mysterious, or changed in the slightest my feeling that I could probably never master it. But this book makes me feel that if I wanted to spend time on it, and not so much time at that, I could learn to draw well. I doubt that I will do it—music pulls me much more strongly—but I am sure the possibility is there.

What the book makes clear to me is that the reason so many of us cannot draw well is that, like the two little girls, we have filled our minds so full of visual symbols for things that for the time being we are unable to see their true shapes. Thus we have in our minds a collection of symbols about human faces: eyes look like this, noses like this, mouths like this. When we try to draw a real face we put these symbols on paper, eyes on top, nose in the middle, mouth below. But we are troubled because the shape doesn't look like anyone. What we have to learn to do is to forget or put aside our symbol of what all noses look like, and instead really see the shape of the one particular nose in front of us. This takes a little knowledge, a few useful tricks, and some thought and practice. But it is not a life work, or even a work of years; drawings done by some of Betty Edwards's pupils and published in her book show that people apparently without talent can learn it in a few months.

In the same class was another girl who loved to draw as much as any child of that age I have ever known. She worked hard and quickly, and turned out picture after picture. The walls of the room were covered with them. All of them were interesting, both to me and the other children. She always drew more or less the same thing—a house, with people in and around it. But she varied the drawings in many ways, in the shape of the house, in the kind of garden and trees that grew around it, in the people and the things they were doing.

These pictures were large and full of life and activity. What was most remarkable about them was the extraordinary amount of detail she put into them. When she put grass around a house, she didn't just make some slashes of green crayon; she drew blades of grass, and colored them. When she drew flowers, she put on leaves and petals. Her people always had five fingers on each hand, and in the right proportions; and on each finger she put a correctly shaped fingernail. Afer a while she began to put curtains inside the windows of her houses, carefully pulled aside, like the curtains in a real house.

Some of the people who have made a fad or cult of psychoanalyzing children's art might at this point make learned noises about this child's obsession with detail, compulsive character, etc. There might be a tiny fragment of truth in this, but no more than that. This was a very gay and energetic little girl, one of the leaders in her class. She drew as she did because she liked to look at things and draw them the way she saw them. Art was her way of expressing much of what she was learning about life. It sharpened her eye as well, and gave her an idea of what next to look for. And not only her eye, but the eyes of many of her classmates. A number of them, without thinking of it this way, made themselves into a kind of school under her leadership, like the schools of the old Italian masters. They drew pictures like hers, or used her ideas and developed them in their own ways. The kind of carefully and surely observed detail that she put in her pictures began to appear in others' work as well. Children would go up—I used to hear them—and look at one of her drawings, and notice that the people had fingernails. "Look!" they would say. "They even have fingernails." It seemed a wonderful achievement. Then they would think of putting some fingernails on the people in their own pictures, and they would look with a new eye at their own fingernails, to see what they really looked like, how they were shaped, how big they were. Or they would begin to try to find some details that this little girl, their leader, had not yet thought to put in.

I wish I could report that this tremendously productive and self-renewing process continued and grew throughout the year. It didn't. This was not because of the teacher, who was a very understanding and gentle woman, and gave these children much more time for art than would most first-grade teachers. But she was under the pressure of the curriculum, the academic lockstep, and both she and the children were under the pressure of the nervous parents, worried about their children's "progress"—that is, whether the Ivy League express was running on schedule. The children began to feel, after a while, that there was no time for art, that it was not serious—and six-year-olds in school are very serious. They are also very sensitive to what adults value. They show a parent or teacher a picture, and the adult says, in a perfunctory voice, "How nice, dear." Then they take home some idiot workbook, whose blanks they have dutifully filled in, and their parents show real joy and excitement. Soon the pictures get shoved aside by the workbooks, even though there is more real learning in a good picture than in twenty workbooks.

When, in later years, the children do draw pictures, they are very likely to draw them more as an escape from real life, like the war scenes of third-grade boys, or the horses that ten-year-old girls interminably draw, than as a way of getting in touch with real life. Not that art as a way of expressing fantasy, fears, and hopeless wishes hasn't value. But this kind of drawing is liable to be furtive and trivial, done on the edges of notebooks and homework papers. It is no longer bold and serious.

I certainly don't agree anymore that third-grade boys drawing pictures of war are trying to escape from reality, and I can't think how I could have been dumb enough to think that in the first place. In our world any boy of eight knows very well that wars exist, and that in them grown men kill each other with bombs, rockets, bullets, etc. Moreover, he knows that when he grows up he may be expected to try to kill other people who will in turn be trying to kill him. For brutally mistreated children, this may seem a perfectly natural extension of the world they already live in. For most eight-year-olds, coming from the shelter of the family, living in a world in which they are still fairly well treated, and hearing adults talk all the time about not hitting or hurting other people or destroying property, this must be a very strange, difficult, and frightening piece of reality to have to come to grips with. Aside from that, of course, death itself is a very powerful and mysterious subject for children, boys or girls.

When I was very young, hardly more than six, if that, my father brought to our apartment one day a friend who was an artist. After a while he took out a big drawing pad and a soft pencil and began to draw. Before my fascinated and unbelieving eyes, there began to appear on the paper—a knight! In full armor! It was a miracle. One minute, blank paper; then, a line here, a line there, the hand working smoothly and surely; and there he was, almost as real as life. I would not have been much surprised if he had stepped right off the page. Certainly there was nothing that I wanted, then and for some time, as much as to have been able to do what that man did—put life on a page with a pencil. It seemed a superhuman skill; I couldn't imagine being able to, but I would have given anything to have been able to do it myself.

It is hard to imagine a child in school today having such an experience. It is good that they are allowed and encouraged to paint big, sloppy, colorful pictures with poster paint, without anyone leaning over their shoulder telling them to do it this way or that way, or that what they have done is wrong. But there are possibilities in art that they can hardly have dreamed of, as I would never have dreamed of anyone being able to make that knight. They ought to be able to see more of those possibilities. They should at least be exposed to the idea that art can be, not just a diversion, but a very powerful way of getting in touch with and expressing reality. In short, they should meet some people who can make real things appear on paper. No doubt many children would not choose to explore reality in that particular way; they would rather do their exploring through books, or construction, or machines, or experiments in any one of a number of sciences. But some children would choose the way of art, like the girl in the first-grade class, and their serious work would be a great benefit to themselves and many children around them.

There are far greater possibilities in children's art than I dreamed of then (or most people dream of now), and much more to say about it than there is room to say here. What most opened my mind on this subject was a letter that a parent, Tom Wesley, sent us a few years ago, and which we printed in *Growing*

Without Schooling (issue #9) and later in my book *Teach Your Own.* He said in part:

Mariko [his daughter] began to draw when she was six months old. Everything she did was treated as important art. By the time she was one year old she could draw better than anyone around her. Knowing that she could do something better than anyone, even better than the ever-competent giants around her, emboldened her strokes. . . . At one year of age she was given an easel and some tempera paints. On her second birthday she got non-toxic acrylics, the medium she has preferred since.

[In] the children's art scene in San Francisco we made the surprising discovery that Mariko is a child artist who does not paint children's art . . . especially so since she began using acrylics, because it is always assumed that children's art should be done with water colors. For obvious reasons acrylics are easier to use than poster paints or tempera but they cost more. I know people who make five or six times my subsistence wage who tell me they can't afford acrylics for their children. What this really means is that they think children can't do anything worth that much.

With the letter he sent some colored photographs of five paintings his daughter had made with acrylic paints between the ages of twenty-six and thirty-eight months. The paintings are stunning. Three of them would stop you dead in your tracks if you saw them in an exhibition of adult art. The colors, the shapes, the drawing, the design, the underlying idea of the paintings, are extraordinary. Most adults, even those who respect children, would find it hard to believe that these paintings were done by a young child, and indeed, almost every "expert" in children's art to whom Mr. Wesley showed these paintings flatly refused to believe it.

Later Mr. Wesley wrote us another letter, full of practical suggestions about art materials and techniques, and saying in part:

I'm a real crank about worthless children's art supplies, the way children's art is exhibited, and all the other adult assumptions and myths about children's art.... We have always bought the best art supplies for Mariko despite my subsistence income. The results into her ninth year have constantly amazed us. Her use of materials went approximately from crayons and felt pens at six months to easel and tempera at one year, to acrylics at two. Acrylics have since been her favorite medium.... I quote her on why she prefers them: "They go on better and when you put them on thick they're shiny. Tempera paintings get dull and powdery. They won't last. There are lots more nice acrylic colors." But in all the books on children's art I have read in Japan and the U.S., and in all the shows of children's art in Tokyo and the Bay Area, I have never seen an acrylic painting by a child.

My reward for buying her an expensive camel-hair brush is to see the sensual pleasure she gets from the delicate feel of a new brush and to see the interesting way a new brush influences her painting. For some time she has been painting on masonite boards or other hardboard. I buy big sheets at a builder's supply, cut them into 2' × 4' or other sizes, lightly sand them, and prime them with good latex paint.

Speculations about the interplay of light, the reflection and absorption of colors are endless....

Since before she was one year old, Mariko has been getting excited about colors and their relationship.

I agree strongly with Mr. Wesley that even very young children should be given or have access to art materials of high quality, and shown how to use them carefully and well, just as we would show them how to use any other quality tools. Freed of the limitations of bad tools, they can then begin to explore, express, and enlarge their own artistic powers. We should not assume that they will be too clumsy, impatient, and uncaring to use these tools properly. As by now many letters to *Growing Without Schooling* have made plain, even very young children want to do things well, or at least as well as they see us do them. They are perfectly able to learn how to use many kinds of tools, including sharp woodworking tools, cooking tools, musical instruments, and cameras, that most people would insist they could not use.

A musical friend of mine, who just for the fun of it has taught himself (in middle age) to speak and write fluently in Chinese, showed me not long ago a calendar of children's paintings from mainland China.* Like Mariko's paintings, it makes nonsense of our conventional ideas about what child painters can and can't do. On each page is a beautiful reproduction of a painting done by a Chinese child, with a charming photo and brief biography of the child. Granted, these children (age four through twelve) were the winners of a big competition, and so are perhaps not typical of most Chinese children. Still, the paintings, done with brushes and what looks like

---

*1982 *Children's Art Calendar*, Guoji Shudian (China Publications Centre, P.O. Box 399, Beijing, People's Republic of China)

some kind of water-based but very vivid paint, are astonishingly beautiful in both design and color. I hope it may prove to be easy for us to get these calendars in the United States; they will certainly be an inspiration to many children and adult friends of children.

It is ironical that China, a country vastly poorer than we are, should attach so much importance to children's art and devote so much energy and resources to it at the very same time that all over our country we are taking art—admittedly most of it not very good—out of our schools.

At any rate, I will insist once again, and more strongly than before, that art is a very powerful and essential way for many children both to explore the world around (and inside) them and to express much of what they have learned and felt about it. It is not a "frill" but a central human activity and need, one we neglect at our peril.

Art can exercise the brain, as well as the eye and hand. I said in *How Children Fail* that the test of intelligence was not how much we know how to do, but how we behave when we don't know what to do. Similarly, any situation, any activity, that puts before us real problems that we have to solve for ourselves, problems for which there are no answers in any book, sharpens our intelligence. The arts, like the crafts and the skilled trades, are full of such problems, which is why our skilled artists, artisans, and craftsmen are very likely to be sharp-witted people. Their minds are active and inventive; they have to be.

An example of this came up not long ago. A friend of mine, when a grown man, started to paint. When he had been at it a year or two, I asked how it was going. He said fine, but there was one problem he couldn't seem to lick— he couldn't get water to lie down. Seeing my blank face, he explained. He liked to paint landscapes, and was getting fairly good at them; but every time he tried to paint a lake or pond, his water didn't look like water at all; it looked like a sheet of blue or green or gray glass sticking straight up out of the ground. He showed me a couple of pictures, and it was so. We parted, but I couldn't get his problem out of my mind. I kept asking myself, what is it that, seen by the eye, tells our brain that what is in front of us is a horizon surface of water and not a vertical sheet of glass? What are the cues and clues?

One day, walking down by the Charles River, I began to look carefully, to see if I could find an answer to the question. Of course, there are many. If there are waves, they seem bigger close up; at a distance they lose their individual identity and fade into a rough texture. If there are things along the bank, they get smaller as the bank gets farther away; in other words, perspective tells us that the edges of the body of water are not all the same distance from us. If the water is calm, things are reflected in it. Even where perspective gives us no sure sign that some parts of the body of water are farther from us than others, color change would do it—things farther away are fuzzier, more blue and gray. For some reason, finding the answer to this question gave me great satisfaction. I had solved a mystery, and saw, and thought, a little more clearly than before.

Because I am ignorant and unskilled in drawing and painting, I could not give many ideas or much inspiration to the children I worked with. But I was able to do a couple of small things that aroused their curiosity and interest, and these possibilities for learning and growth stretched out into the future. After teaching fifth grade for four years, I spent a year as a kind of roaming teacher, developing ideas and materials, most but not all connected with teaching math. Most of the materials I wanted to use I had to make myself. Usually my raw material was the cardboard that laundries put in shirts. It was cheap and easy to work with. Some of the time, I worked in my own office-classroom, but as time went on I did a good deal of my manufacturing in other classrooms, the teachers permitting, where children could see what I was doing, and if so inclined, wonder about it, and perhaps imitate it.

One day I was in a first-grade classroom and, for the first time in that room, began to make some small, open-topped cardboard boxes, of just such dimensions that various sizes of Cuisenaire rods would fit neatly into them. I had a drawing board, a T-square and triangles, a ruler, and a sharp knife to cut the cardboard. All this material was interesting to the children. Every now and then, in the midst of their normal class business, they would come over to the corner where I was working and watch me for a second or two before leaving. Sometimes they would ask what I was doing, to which I would reply, "Oh, just making something."

By the time I had finished a few boxes they could see what my work was all about. They wanted to make some of their own. So, when there was time in their schedule, the teacher gave them pieces of a heavy paper known as oak tag, and some scissors, and told them to go ahead. Off they went. By watching me, or each other, or by thinking, or by trial and error, they all figured out that to make a rectangular box with an open top you had to cut out a piece in the shape of a heavy cross. At first these shapes were very crude, the sides not carefully measured, if at all, and the corners not square. But children have a great deal of what might be called a sense of workmanship. When they are not bribed or bullied, they want to do whatever they are doing better than they did it before. So they began to make their boxes more carefully, trying to figure out how to cut them so that the sides would join evenly along the edges, and so that the top of the box would be smooth. Nobody asked me for advice. Now and then someone would watch me doing it for a while, and that was all. Then they went back to work.

I watched their work for a bit—not as long as I would have liked. I had other classes to work with, and some special classes to teach, and a number of kids to "tutor," which meant cramming them in the hopes they could pass some kind of test. So I didn't have as much time as I would have liked for leisurely exploration, or to pursue a promising lead. And the first-grade teacher, naturally, felt she had to get through her curriculum, and get those children ready for second grade. So they were not able to spend enough time making boxes to explore and develop some of the mathematical possibilities that lie in such work—making boxes of exact dimensions, making boxes to hold certain quantities of wooden cubes, making boxes of shapes other than rectangular, and so on.

However, in the short time that they were working on them, one little boy did a remarkable piece of work which in time might have led him and the class in directions I had never even thought of. Incidentally, he had been one of the more troublesome members of quite a troublesome class. After making a few boxes with open tops, he began to think about the problem of making a box with a closed top. He soon figured out what shape piece he had to cut out in order to do this. Then, looking at his closed box, he began to think of it as a house, and drew a door and some windows on it. But this wasn't a very interesting or house-like looking house. He began to think how he might make a house that really looked like a house, with a peaked roof. I didn't see him work on the problem, and don't know by what steps he managed it, but within a few days his teacher showed me a cardboard house, with peaked roof, that he had cut out in one piece. It was well made, too; the sides and the roof fit together quite well. And he had cut out, not drawn, the doors and windows, before folding the house together. A most extraordinary piece of work.

In such work are many possibilities for further exploration and learning. This particular child, and class, had no time to explore them. But in a different kind of class and school, they might have gone on to do quite a number of things. We can imagine them making models of many differently shaped objects; or making models of one object, but in various sizes, the shape remaining the same but the scale changing. Children are very interested, indeed fascinated, by the idea of scale. That things can be made the same shape, that is, to look the same, but some of them bigger than others, is a great mystery and wonder to them. One teacher I knew made, for demonstration purposes, a giant set of Cuisenaire rods, which her children loved to look at and work with. With this somewhat in mind, I made, of cardboard, a miniature set of Cuisenaire rods, to about two-fifths the scale of the real ones. A number of first-grade children were much taken with them. They were amazed and delighted to see that relations that held true for the real rods also held true for these miniature ones.

There are also great possibilities in scale drawings. I remember when I was little seeing somebody make a big copy of a small picture by putting the small picture on a grid—squared or graph paper—and then transferring it to a bigger grid. I think I even did it once or twice myself, and was always amazed to see that it worked. But this was not part of our regular schoolwork; if we did such things, we had to do them at home, or if we did them in school, we had to be careful that nobody saw us. I can easily imagine, however, that a class of young children, starting with a small line drawing, could be fascinated with the idea of making that drawing bigger and bigger, until they had a copy big enough to cover a large part of a wall or a chalkboard. This, in turn, could easily lead into the idea of coordinate points, graphs, and analytic geometry, representing pictures by things that were not pictures, but functions. Or, in another direction, it could lead to the idea of making accurate drawings, to various scales, of real objects, and from there to measurement, not only of lengths but of angles, and to mapmaking.

It is easy to see how much arithmetic there would be in

this. One of the fundamental ideas behind most of what we do in school is that children should and must spend many years memorizing a lot of dull facts before they can begin to do interesting things with them. This is a foolish way to go about things, and it doesn't work. Most children get so fed up with learning the dull facts that they quit before they get enough of them to do, or even to want to do, anything interesting with them. And even of the children who do learn all the facts, most have their wits so dulled in the process that they can't think of anything interesting to do with them, but just go on accumulating more and more—which accounts for too much of the activity in our graduate schools and universities. But if we get the horse in front of the cart where it belongs, if we get children to do things that require them to find and make use of otherwise dull and useless facts, they learn these facts very rapidly—like the boy I described who, as a result of working on electronics, gained nine years of skill in reading and math in two years, and without ever going to a formal class.

Another time, I introduced the first grade to the idea of isometric drawings. It is easier to show what they are than to say. Suppose I have a cube in front of me. An isometric drawing of that cube would show three faces of that cube, the top and two sides, and would be so drawn that all the edges were the same length. The vertical edges of the cube would be shown by vertical lines on the paper; the horizontal edges, by lines going to right and left at sixty degrees to the vertical.

Isometric drawings are used by draftsmen to give three-dimensional views of objects. There is a kind of paper called isometric paper, on which are ruled vertical lines, and lines going up to the right and left at sixty degrees to the vertical. With a ditto machine I made some of this paper, and took it down to the first grades. At first I used it to make colored patterns, using pastel crayons or colored magic marker. Some interesting shapes and patterns came out, and it wasn't long before the children were asking me if they could have a piece of paper so that they could do some of this themselves. Which they did.

I have since learned that there is a similar kind of projection called axonometric, which I think children (or adults) might find easier to draw and more interesting to look at. It is like isometric (vertical lines in space are vertical on the paper), but all horizontal surfaces appear in their true shape. Thus, the top of a cube drawn in axonometric would be a square (see sketch).

In some of the Michelin Green Tour Guides, of New York, for example you can find axonometric drawings of some of the major buildings. And a German company, Bollmann-Bildkarten-Verlag KG, Braunschweig, West Germany, publishes a whole set of maps of different cities, most of them in Germany but also including New York, in which all the buildings are drawn in this way. The map of New York is astonishingly intricate and beautiful. Looking at it is almost like flying over the city in an airplane. It is hard to believe that Mr. Bollmann himself drew all those hundreds of intricately detailed buildings. Young children would probably not make much of it, but many older children, especially those who knew New York, might find it fascinating, and a few would surely be tempted by the problem or task of making an axonometric drawing of a building that they knew, or even, perhaps, of some structure they had made of Lego or other blocks.

One day, while I was in a first-grade class, half visiting and watching, and half working on my own work, the idea came of making an isometric drawing of a house with pitched roof and dormer windows. This raises some interesting problems, as anyone will find out who tries it. The main part of the house was easy to draw, as were the doors and windows, and the roof was quite easy. But when I began to try to figure out how to make the dormer windows fit into the roof, things became more difficult. Here again, as I puzzled and worked on this, children began to drift over now and then for a few seconds, to see what I was doing. After a while some of them wanted to try to make some isometric drawings. First they drew simple boxes; then they began to draw flat-roofed houses, with doors and windows. Sometimes, drawing their windows, they would forget that a line that in life was horizontal had to go up at sixty degrees to the vertical in the drawing; but when they had made this mistake, they would almost always notice, after a while, that it looked funny and wrong, or someone would point it out to them. Then they would come over to take another look at mine, to see how I dealt with the problem. Some of them even began to grapple with the problems of drawing a pitched roof—which for a first-grader is hard. Again, we had little time to pursue this activity, but it was clear that the children were very interested in it, and might have learned a lot from it. Like the work we did with boxes, it stretches out in several directions. We can imagine children making isometric drawings, to various scales, of a number of real objects; or exploring the relations between conventional scale drawings, which show front view (or elevation), side view, and top view; or going from one kind of drawing to the other. And still more interesting problems and possibilities would arise if we introduced the idea of perspective. Little children, like primitive painters, do not get much depth into their drawings, because, like the little girl with the tree, they don't know how, and have never even considered the problem. Suppose they were challenged with this? We could hardly expect little children to discover the idea of perspective for themselves, though here as in other places they might surprise us; but they could certainly see for themselves the need for it, and would be delighted to see that there was a way of drawing railroad tracks that looked the way railroad tracks really do look.

I said earlier that art, in this very strict sense of representing the appearance of things on paper, exercises the mind as well as the eye. Once I asked my fifth-grade class to draw me a picture of a bicycle. Instantly thumbs went down on the panic button. What kind of bicycle? The kind you ride, the kind that you see out in the school yard, a regular two-wheeled bicycle. Boy's or girl's? I don't care. So they began to draw. There was no question here of prior skill; only one or two of the children in the class really liked to draw for pleasure—this after years of school "art," in schools that believed, or said they believed, that art was important. And even they didn't like to draw bicycles. After some time, except for one or two deliberate failers who refused even to try, the children gave me their pictures. They were extraordinarily revealing. The kids in the class who were intelligent, whose minds were still active, who were still interested in how things were instead of right answers and staying out of trouble, drew bicycles that looked more or less like bicycles. They may have been wrong in detail, here and there, but their bicycles made some sense. Clearly, they had thought, as they drew, about how a bicycle is made and works. They had all drawn some kind of frame; the wheels were attached to the frame; there was some way of making the wheels go round. But the other children, the defeated, drew the most extraordinary collection of shapes. They had very little connection with a real bike, or for that matter, with each other. I could usually make out what were supposed to be wheels, but they were rarely connected to anything else at all. Two or three vague parts of a bicycle floating in the air is what most of them looked like. So I took a number of these children outside, with pads and pencils, and set them down in front of a bicycle, and asked them to try again. The results were hardly any better. With the bike right before them, they could not see how it was put together, or if they could, could not hold that knowledge in mind long enough to transfer it to paper. It seemed as if their schooling had been for so long so far removed from reality that they were no longer able to see reality, to grasp it, to come to grips with it.

If children could do more of the kind of work I have described and suggested, they would get, not just knowledge, but skill. This is important to a child. To be able to do something well, to get visible results, gives him a sense of his own being and worth which he can never get from regular schoolwork, from teacher-pleasing, no matter how good he is at it. There is too little opportunity for this in school. In my own high-priced and high-powered education, there was virtually none; until I was about thirty, the only things I ever *made* were some model airplanes, and those out of school, and only when I was nine and ten. This was, and is, a mistake. Maria Montessori showed, among other things, that children could make, and like to make, movements that are careful and precise, as well as movements that are exuberant. Some of the time, at least, children like to be careful, when it is the work or the situation, and not some grownup, that demands it. We should give them many more opportunities and ways to use and develop skill and precision.

An afterthought. I hope no one will mistake me as saying that we should scrap our present curriculum, then make a new curriculum out of what I have been talking about, and put it in place of the old one. I am only suggesting some of the things that children might like to see done in school, and might like to do themselves, were they free to choose. But they must be free to choose whether to explore the world in this way, or any one of a number of other ways. If we merely substitute *Isometric Drawing I* or *Model Building I* for *Arithmetic I,* with the same old business of assignments, homework, drill, and tests, we will have gained little, and probably nothing.

During the year that I was doing the work just described I took over one of the first-grade classes for a week while the teacher was out. It had been her custom each morning to put some arithmetic problems on the board for the children to see when they came in—problems which they could do while waiting for the organized day to begin. These were usually problems in addition. There were rarely more than two numbers to add, and the sum was rarely over 10, never over 20, because the children had not learned—i.e., been told—how to do such problems.

One day there was a happy accident. I had forgotten to put the problems up. Two or three children came in early, saw no problems, worried for a while, and then asked if they could put some problems up. (All little children, and some maybe not so little, like to write on the blackboard.) I told them, sure, go ahead. They began by writing some of the kind of problems that had been up there. But after a while they grew bolder, and began to write problems like $70 + 20 = ?$ Quite often they would get into an argument among themselves as to what was the right answer. They were never willing to leave a problem unless they felt they knew how to do it. Usually they would manage, within a short while, to come to an agreement, and usually the answer they agreed on was correct. It is hard to get honest agreement on any answer that is not correct. Only rarely did they appeal to me, and then only when they got into an argument in which a number of them were all sure they were right. After a while they began adding things like 200 + 400, or even 230 + 500, or 340 + 420. Step by step, making their problems more complicated all the time, the children—not all of them, but a good many— worked out for themselves most of the rules for doing addition. In a week—working only a few minutes a day— they covered material that the school was prepared to spend years teaching them.

At the end of the week, just as they were beginning to get going, I had to leave, and so wasn't able to give their work the kind of nudge that might have led them to consider the problems of carrying, or of subtraction. But I saw enough to make me feel that if arithmetic were treated as in fact what it is—a territory to be explored, not a list of facts to be learned—children, at least many children, would move into it faster than we would have dreamed possible.

Thus, in the prospectus of the Green Valley School (Orange City, Florida) George von Hilsheimer, who founded this and other schools and institutions based on human freedom, writes:

> Students who begin at this school have no fear of math. We have had the pleasure of seeing five-year-olds doing math for their bedtime "story" and complete the Workbooks for Kindergarten, First, Second and Third Grades *in four nights.* We cannot offer the hope of this progress to summer students, nor to regular students entering after the first grade.

One day, this same year, I found myself thinking of the boy in fifth grade who had told me that between 100 and 200 there were 164 whole numbers. I had felt. intuitively, that children felt that numbers grew more dense, so to speak, as they grew bigger; in short, that there were more whole numbers between 900 and 1,000 than between 100 and 200. Even if they had some common sense about small numbers, this began to leave them when the numbers got big enough—as may well be true of all of us—and their heads began to swim, and their guesses grew wilder and wilder.

I thought first- and second-graders might be interested to see how numbers grow, and also to get a concrete idea about the size of certain numbers. One day I bought one of the rolls of paper that go into an adding machine, brought it into the first-grade classroom, and without a word to anyone, began to measure off dots on the roll, two inches apart. When I had a number of these I began to label them—1, 2, 3, 4, 5—a number over each dot. Before long, as always happened, someone came over to look. They asked what I was doing. I told them to watch. They watched for a while, then went away; others took their place. Now and then a child would say, "What's that for?" It seemed to me that the question meant, "Are we going to have to do something about this?" and I usually didn't answer. If a child asked point blank whether he was going to have to make one, I said, "Goodness, no!" As this went on, the numbers grew. The word got around as I neared 100, and children came around to watch me write it. It was like the magic moment when a whole lot of 9's on the car's odometer (the thing that tells you how many miles you have gone) turn into O's.

Eventually someone said, "Where did you get the paper?" I named the store. "How much did it cost?" Twenty-five cents. "Can I have one?" I said, "Sure, if you'll pay for it." I thought this would be the end of it. Not at all; next day a couple of the children showed up with a quarter for their own rolls. I brought them, and they went to work. Before long there were more than a dozen first- and second-graders working on their own number rolls. Some of them just wrote out the numbers, not spacing them carefully; others copied me in making the numbers a uniform distance apart. The numbers grew and grew. Many children continued up into the hundreds. I kept working on my roll—eventually I had to splice a new roll to the old—until it reached 1,500 or so. But two boys, both interested in numbers and competitive to boot, took their rolls home to work on, and before long had passed me, getting close to 2,000.

People may say, did say, in fact, "What good is all this? What are the children learning?" Meaning, of course, what questions can they answer, what tests can they pass, as a result of what they were doing? I am not sure what the children learned. Different ones probably learned different things. I suspect they learned something about the rate at which numbers grow, and about the meaning, in concrete terms, of some of the numbers they had been working with in arithmetic. One day, when my tape had become fairly long, up to about five hundred or so, we unrolled it to its full length. We had to go around the room and then out in the hall to get to the end. Children walked curiously and eagerly up and down the length of the tape, saying, "Here's 200," "Here's 400," and things like that.

I had many plans for continuing this the following year, but the money that was supporting this work—a few thousand dollars a year—ran out, and I had to stop. Not without a certain bitterness, when I thought of the kind of money that was being spent in education, and the things for which much of it was being spent. It seemed that number rolls could be used in a great many ways, leading into multiplication, factors, large numbers, proportion, scale, measurement, mapmaking—who knows what?

But the matter of freedom, to choose how to do this, or to choose not to do it, is all important. Long before the "New Math" had ever been heard of, before the great boom in curriculum reform was under way, Bill Hull was trying to get his fifth-grade classes to do some real, original, problem-directed thinking. One piece of equipment he used was a balance beam, a piece of wood balanced at its midpoint, with places along the arms to put weights. The children were supposed to figure out the principle of the beam, so that, whatever weight we put on one side, they could balance it with weights on the other. In *How Children Fail* I described some of the work that very bright fifth-graders did with this beam. One girl, that I can remember, seemed to know how to do at least the simple balancing problems—two weights on one side balancing one on the other. Hardly anyone else in the class could consistently work out even simple problems; most of them never got beyond the guessing stage. And this in spite of the fact that we—or so we thought—had done everything possible to set up a situation that would make discovery more easy. We worked with the children in small groups; we gave each child an easy problem; we encouraged the other children in the group to say whether they thought this solution to the problem was correct, and if not, why not. We thought we had set up in our class a laboratory in miniature, and that the children would accordingly act like scientists. But we hadn't, and they didn't, for just this reason, that it was our problem they were working on, not theirs.

Two years later, when I was teaching my own fifth grade, I borrowed some extra balance beams from Bill, to see whether my students could make anything of them. I put these beams, and some weights to hang on them, on a table at one end of my classroom. Then I had a piece of undeserved good luck. Before I had a chance to do any talking or explaining or instructing about these beams, some children came in early one morning and saw them. "What's that stuff?" they said. I said, "Oh, some junk I got from Bill Hull." They said, "What's it for?" I said, "Nothing special; mess around with it if you want to." Three or four of them went down to the end table and began to fool around. As other children arrived they went down to watch. By half an hour later, almost all the kids who had been working with the beams knew how to work them—including some who were not good students. I gave one of them one of the problems that had in earlier years given very able students so much trouble. She solved it easily and showed that she knew what she was doing. I said, "You have any trouble figuring that out?" She said, "Oh no, it was cinchy."

Not long after, Bill Hull and some other friends of mine were developing a very ingenious and powerful set of mathematical and logical materials (now produced by the McGraw-Hill Book Company in New York City) called Attribute Blocks or A-blocks. These are a set of wooden blocks, of various colors, sizes, and shapes, with which children can play a wide variety of classifying games, and with which they do a great many things that experts on such matters have said they would be unable to do.

They developed these materials by having small groups of young children, mostly five-year-olds, come into their office-lab-classroom and work with them, that is, play various games, do puzzles, solve problems. (Some of the games now incorporated into the unit were invented by the children.) They found a very interesting thing about the way children reacted to these materials. If, when a child came in for the first time, they tried to get him "to work" right away, to play some of their games and solve some of their puzzles, they got nowhere. The child would try to do what he was asked to do, but without joy or insight. But if at first they let the child alone for a while, let him play with the materials in his own way, they got very different results. At first, the children would work the pieces of wood into a fantasy. Some pieces would be mommies and daddies, some children; or they would be houses and cars; or big animals and little animals. Then the children would make various kinds of patterns, buildings, and constructions out of the pieces of wood. When, through such play and fantasy, the children had taken these materials into their minds, mentally swallowed and digested them, so to speak, they were then ready and willing to play very complicated games, that in the more organized and businesslike situation had left other children completely baffled. This proved to be so consistently true that the experimenters made it a rule always to let children have a period of completely free play with the materials, before asking them to do directed work with them.

David Hawkins, professor of philosophy at the University of Colorado and formerly director of the Elementary Science Study, has written perceptively and eloquently on this question, in an article called "Messing About in Science," which appeared in the February 1965 issue of *Science and Children*, and also in the June 1966 quarterly report of Educational Services, Inc. He says in part:

[In science teaching, and other aspects of elementary education] there is a time, much greater in amount than commonly allowed, which should be devoted to free and unguided exploratory work (call it play if you wish; I call it work). Children are given materials and equipment—*things*—and are allowed to construct, test, probe, and experiment without superimposed questions or instruction. I call this phase "Messing About." ... In some jargon, this kind of situation is called "unstructured," which is misleading; some doubters call it chaotic, which it need never be. "Unstructured" is misleading because there is always a kind of structure to *what* is presented in a class....

Let me cite an example from my own recent experiences. Simple frames, each designed to support two or three weights on strings, were handed out one morning in a fifth-grade class. There was one such frame for each pair of children. In two earlier trial classes, we had introduced the same equipment with a much more "structured" beginning, demonstrating the striking phenomenon of coupled pendulums and raising questions about it before the laboratory work was allowed to begin. If there was guidance this time, however, it came only from the apparatus—a pendulum is to swing!

In the front hall of the Urban School, an evening summer school in Boston where I teach English, we have one of these pendulum frames. Some students (high school age), as they come in, fool around with the pendulums. Others do not. One boy came in the other night, looked suspiciously at the pendulum for a while, and then said, "What's it supposed to be doing?" Children who have spent much time in school no longer surprise me with such questions. I said, "It's not *supposed* to be doing anything. Shall we tell it to do something?" He didn't get the point of the joke, or even know that I was joking. Nor did he even so much as touch the pendulum. It was dangerous. If he didn't know what it was "supposed" to do, he wasn't going to try to make it do anything; it might do the wrong thing, and someone might think it was his fault. It was a small but striking example of the feeling described in *How Children Fail,* on the part of many children, that nature and the universe are not only inconsistent and unpredictable but even unfriendly and treacherous.

I started messing with the pendulums myself. I knew, not as a rule I had memorized, but as part of my mental model of how the world works, that short pendulums swing back and forth more rapidly than long ones. I had forgotten the exact relationship between length and rate of swing. My faint hunch was that if one pendulum was half as long as the other, it would make two swings for the other's one. I tried this out, found I was wrong, adjusted the short pendulum until it was making two swings for one of the other, and estimated by eye that its string was one quarter as long. From this I re-created the rule. As I was busy with this little project, one of the other teachers, a very lively and intelligent woman, began to watch me. After hardly more than a few seconds she began to say,

with some real anxiety in her voice, "What rule is it supposed to be following? What's the rule that applies to
what it's doing?" I laughed and said, "Why don't you just
watch it for a while, and see what you see?" But she could
not, or would not, play this childlike game. After some
more rather nervous talk about the rule, and how she
never had been able to remember those rules, and never
had been any good at science—all good standard defensive strategies—she went off about her business.

To return to Professor Hawkins:

In starting this way I, for one, naively assumed that a
couple of hours of "Messing About" would suffice. After
two hours, instead, we allowed two more and, in the
end, a stretch of several weeks. In all this time there
was little or no evidence of boredom or confusion. Most
of the questions we might have planned for came up
unscheduled.

Why did we permit this length of time? First, because
in our previous classes we had noticed that things went
well when we veered toward "Messing About" and not
as well when we held too tight a rein on what we wanted the children to do. It was clear that these children
had had insufficient acquaintance with the sheer phenomenon of pendulum motion and needed to build an
appreciative background, against which a more analytical sort of knowledge could take form and make sense.

In other words, to use my own way of putting this, until
their mental models of the world had enough pendulums
in them so that talk about pendulums would mean something to them. This applies just as strongly to reading, or
numbers, or arithmetic, or history, or geography, or language, as it does to science. Children need what we rarely
give them in school—time for "Messing About" with
reading—before they start trying to learn to read, to make
the connections between letters and sounds. They need

time to build up in their minds, without hurry, without pressure, a sense of what words look like, before they start trying to memorize particular words. In the same way, they need time for "Messing About" with numbers and numerals, before they start—if they ever should start—trying to memorize addition facts and multiplication tables. They need to know how big 76 is, or 134, or 35,000, or a million. They need to see, again without hurry or pressure, how numbers change and grow and relate to each other. They need to build up a mental model of the territory before they start trying to talk about it. We teachers like to think that we can transplant our own mental models into the minds of children by means of explanations. It can't be done.

Professor Hawkins continues:

Second, we allowed things to develop this way because we decided we were getting a new kind of feedback from the children and were eager to see where and by what paths their interests would evolve and carry them. We were rewarded with a higher level of involvement and a much greater diversity of experiments. Our role was only to move from spot to spot, being helpful but never consciously prompting or directing. In spite of— because of!—this lack of direction, these fifth-graders became very familiar with pendulums. They varied the conditions of motion in many ways.... There were many sorts of discoveries made, but we let them slip by without much adult resonance, beyond our spontaneous and manifest enjoyment of the phenomena. So discoveries were made, noted, lost, and made again. I think this is why the slightly pontifical phrase "discovery method" bothers me. When learning is at the most fundamental level, as it is here, with all the abstractions of Newtonian mechanics just around the corner, don't rush! When the mind is evolving the abstractions which will lead to physical comprehension, all of us must cross the line between ignorance and insight many times before we truly understand.

This is exactly the process I am trying to describe in the chapter on reading, where I tell about the five-year-old teaching herself to read. "When the mind is evolving the abstractions. . . ." In practice, this means that you get a faint hunch, lose it, get it again, test it, lose it again, get it again—and all this many times over. You think that a word says such and such; it seems to work; you meet the word again, and try a new hunch; it doesn't work, causes an inconsistency; you correct the mistake, and go on. After many times, you know the word. You have not memorized it, you know it. It is part of your model of the way things are; you could no more "forget" it than you could forget that if you drop your shoe, it will fall to the floor, not rise to the ceiling.

One other point. Professor Hawkins rightly says, "All of us must cross the line between ignorance and insight many times before we truly understand." Not only must we cross that line many times, but, in the words of the old spiritual, nobody else can cross it for us, we must cross it by ourselves. Being shoved or dragged across does no good.

Professor Hawkins again:

This (Messing About) phase is important, above all, because it carries over into school that which is the source of most of what children have already learned, the roots of their moral, intellectual, and esthetic development. If education were defined, for the moment, to include everything that children have learned since birth, everything that has come to them from living in the natural and the human world, then by any sensible measure what has come before age five or six would outweigh all the rest. When we narrow the scope of education to what goes on in schools, we throw out the method of that early and spectacular progress at our peril.... To continue the cultivation of earlier ways of learning, therefore; to find *in school* the good beginnings, the liberating involvements that will make the kindergarten seem a garden to the child and not a dry and frightening desert, this is a need that requires much emphasis on the style of work I have called "Messing About." Nor does the garden in this sense end with a child's first school year, or his tenth, as though one could then put away childish things. As time goes on, through a good mixture of this with other phases of work, "Messing About" evolves with the child and thus changes its quality. It becomes a way of working that is no longer childish, though it remains always childlike, the kind of self-disciplined probing and exploring that is the essence of creativity....

If you once let children evolve their own learning along paths of their choosing, you then must see it through and *maintain* the individuality of their work. You cannot begin that way and then say, in effect, "That was only a teaser," thus using your adult authority to devalue what the children themselves, in the meantime, have found most valuable. So if "Messing About" is to be followed by, or evolve into, a stage where work is more externally guided and disciplined, there must be at hand what I call "Multiply Programmed" material; material that contains written and pictorial guidance of some sort for the student, but which is designed for the greatest possible variety of topics, ordering of topics, etc., so that for almost any given way into a subject that a child may evolve on his own, there is material available which he will recognize as helping him farther along that very way. Heroic teachers have sometimes done this on their own, but it is obviously one of the places where designers of curriculum materials can be of enormous help, designing those materials with a rich variety of choices for teacher and child, and freeing the teacher from the role of "leader-drag-ger" along a single preconceived path, giving the teach-er encouragement and real logistical help in diversifying the activities of a group.

We must recognize that there are some teachers who like being "leader-draggers." They like to feel that they are at every moment in control, not only of the child's body, but also of his mind. They like to feel themselves the source and the sole source of all knowledge, wisdom, and learning in the classroom. Some such teachers are moved by a love of power, of which the classroom gives them plenty; others, by a deep and sometimes desperate need to feel useful, necessary, and even indispensable to their students. Both kinds are strongly threatened by any suggestion that children can and should learn on their own. Many other teachers would like to give their stu-dents more independence and self-direction but are held back by a fear of the standardized tests by which their pu-pils, and they themselves, will be judged. In any school whose main business is preparing children to get high scores on achievement tests, Regents exams, Merit Schol-arship exams, college boards, and the like, we are not likely to see much open-ended, independent student work. It must be said in fairness, too, that so far not many of the curriculum reformers and educational revolution-aries have shown much interest in it either. They tend to be so sure that the path they have marked out for their students is the best of all possible paths that their main concern is how to lead or drag them down it as fast as pos-sible.

Professor Hawkins again:

There is a common opinion floating about, that a rich diversity of classroom work is possible only when a teacher has small classes. "Maybe *you* can do that, but you ought to try it in my class of 43!" I want to be the last person to belittle the importance of small classes. But in this particular case, the statement ought to be made that in a large class one cannot afford *not* to diversify children's work—or rather *not* to allow children to diversify, as they inevitably will, if given the chance. So-called "ability grouping" is a popular answer today, but it is no answer at all to the real questions of motivation. Groups which are lumped as equivalent with respect to the usual measures are just as diverse in their tastes and spontaneous interests as unstratified groups.... When children have no autonomy in learning everyone is likely to be bored.

The question of small classes is one I hear every time I speak. My answer is that in a small class you may be able to maintain at least the illusion that you have complete control, and that everyone is doing the same thing at the same time; in a large class it becomes impossible. Given fairly docile children, in classes of about twenty, a teacher has a chance of being a reasonably effective policeman. In a class of forty, it can't be done. There are too many to watch. The large classes which exist in many of our schools, and which are, if anything, going to get bigger rather than smaller, require that we find ways to break the academic lockstep, and get our students learning on their own. This is above all essential in our cities, where many children, unlike children in the suburbs, cannot and will not submit to being bored all day long. Many people talk as if our problem was to make city schools as good as the ones in the suburbs. This is not the problem at all. We have been able to afford boredom and miseducation in the suburbs because the children have been willing to put up with it—though we may not be able to afford it there much longer. We can't afford it in the city, because the children won't put up with it, and we have no way to make them. Nothing less than real education will solve the problems of our city schools—and real

education means the kind of learning Professor Hawkins
is talking about.

Some social studies teachers asked me once, at a meeting, how students might explore and learn independently
in their field. For part of an answer, I told a few stories.
The first is about a seven-year-old boy. One day he saw,
and read, I think in the *National Geographic,* an article
about underwater swimming. Like most kids he was very
interested in the scuba equipment, and even more in the
varied and colorful fish the divers were seeing and catching—in the whole idea of an underwater world with a life
of its own. Excited, he talked to his mother about the article. Soon after, she found him another article about
divers. This time, however, they were not diving for fish,
but for treasure—vases, bowls, implements, and weapons—lying deep in the hold of a ship that three thousand
years before had sunk in the Mediterranean. Everything
about this story fascinated the boy, above all the idea that
these strange and beautiful objects had been lying there,
unknown, forgotten, for so long. He became interested in
the pre-Homeric civilizations of Crete and Mycenae that
had made these treasures. Helpful adults found him some
books about them, which he read. In them mention was
made of Homer and the Trojan War, so he read some
abridged versions of the *Iliad* and the *Odyssey.* Somewhere in his reading about Troy he read about the seven
cities of Troy, and about Schliemann, the archaeologist
who dug them up. He was fascinated with the idea that a
city might simply disappear under the ground, and another city be built right on top of it, and so seven times
over; he was equally fascinated with the idea of patiently
bringing those buried cities into the light again. This
made him want to find out as much as he could about archaeology. When I last heard of him, he was reading everything on that subject that he could get his hands on.

The next stories are about a one-room country school
taught by Julia Weber (now Gordon). She wrote about her

work in a book called *My Country School Diary*, now out
of print, though its publisher, Harper & Row, may bring it
out in paperback.

> For a while the book did come back into print, in a
> Delta edition for which I wrote an introduction. At
> the moment it is out of print again. I hope someday it
> will come back a third time. It is a very important
> book about teaching and what it means to be a teach-
> er, and the best argument I have ever seen against
> the too often heard complaint that the schools can't
> do this or that because they have no money.

The children in the school were in grades 1–8. Much of
the time, of necessity, they worked independently. At other times they discussed things, as a class. In these discussions many questions were raised, and it was Miss
Weber's custom to write down many of the unanswered
questions on large sheets of paper and post them on the
wall, where the children could see them and be reminded
of them. The students did not have to find answers to
these questions; they were not curriculum, or homework.
But they were free to pursue any that particularly interested them. Some questions were never answered. Others
caught the curiosity of the class, and led them on some
wide-ranging explorations.

One such question came up early one spring, when the
children were getting ready to put away their winter
clothes. The clothes had to be cleaned before they were
put away, and someone asked why they couldn't be
washed. Many of them knew that it was because the wool
would shrink. But why did wool shrink, and what happened when it shrank? Nobody knew. Perhaps they could
find out if they looked at wool through a microscope. Un-
fortunately, they didn't have a microscope, and couldn't
possibly afford to buy one. All right, they would borrow
one. They wrote a letter—I believe it was to the state uni-

versity—asking if they could borrow a microscope, and explaining what they wanted to use it for. Incidentally, the children always wrote such letters, and they were writing them all the time, since their tiny school had to borrow most of the books and equipment they needed.

Here, it seems to me, is the answer to the current super-stition, made fashionable by Dr. Conant and others, that we have to have giant school-factories because we can't get good education in a school unless it has all the latest equipment. In making our schools ever larger we have lost much more of value than we have gained, and what little we have gained by having all this expensive materi-al in each school we might well have accomplished in other ways. There could have been, as in some parts of the country there still are, central libraries from which books or equipment could be borrowed, or mobile librar-ies and laboratories that visit schools in turn. Someday, if we get over our notion that bigness in education means efficiency and quality, we may revive some of those ideas.

At any rate, the microscope eventually arrived—the children had had many other things to work on while they were waiting for it. There was much excitement while they carefully unpacked it, and read the instruc-tions for using it, and learned to use it. Soon they were ready to examine some wool fibers before and after wash-ing. They discovered that the fibers of wool have joints, rather like a telescope, and that for some reason these slide in together when the wool is washed. Then, having looked at wool, they decided to look at a number of other fabrics under the microscope—linen, cotton, rayon. They noticed the different appearances of the fibers them-selves—and noticed also that the appearance of the cloth depended on the way it was woven. This in turn got them interested in weaving, and after some discussion they de-cided they wanted to weave some cloth of their own, us-ing the simplest kind of tools. More letters were written, and after a while they had all they needed to spin and weave cloth, beginning with raw wool. They decided on wool because it was the easiest to work, using simple tools. They got raw wool from a neighbor who owned sheep; then they washed it, carded it, spun it, and wove it. Someone in the class thought it would be interesting to find out how much work it would take to make the cloth. They decided to keep records of time spent on the project, and so developed or discovered the idea of the man-hour as a unit of work—a very important concept in economics.

When they had finished weaving their small square of cloth, their records showed that seventy-two man-hours had been spent. Seventy-two hours for this tiny square of cloth! How long would it take to make a whole suit? This brought in a good deal of arithmetic, plus the problem of calculating the area of an odd-shaped object. When they found out how long it would take, at their rate, to make a suit, they began to wonder how people like the early colonists ever managed to find time to make their own clothes. They also began to see how great and real was the need for specializing labor, and laborsaving devices.

The cloth project led the children in a number of different directions. For one thing, they wanted to dye the cloth, so they had to find out about natural dyes, how they were made and used. Since most of these came from plants, this led into botany. They made some dyes, and tested them. They also got interested in other kinds of wool fabric. Their piece of homespun did not look much like the wool garments they were used to seeing and wearing. What caused the difference? How many different kinds of wool were there? The children took to asking everyone they saw wearing wool what kind of wool they were wearing. They found out that there were many kinds of wool. Someone began to note, on a map, the kinds of animals that gave wool, and the parts of the world they lived in. This led them to wonder, and to discuss, why some kinds of wool cost more than others. After talking and reading about it, they decided that it had to do with the animal, how hard he was to raise and keep, how much wool he gave, and also with the difficulty of making the wool into cloth, how far it had to be shipped, and so on. More genuine economics, and some geography on the side.

At the same time they became interested in the difference between woolens and worsteds (which I don't know), and the weaving process and industry. They could see how better machines would reduce the price of cloth. Who invented the first machines? To get answers to such questions they had to order books from the county library. Dr. Gordon told me that in a year the class of thirty-five children borrowed seven hundred books. They found that many of the early machines were invented in England. Why there? Partly because there was already a certain amount of division of labor, so that they were in effect ready for the factory mode of organization. What were factories like? They visited a textile mill in New Jersey, read about the early factories and the conditions of labor, talked about the effect of machines on employment, examined the effect of machines on a nearby township, considered labor unions and labor legislation. And so on.

Now, not all the children did all of these things. On the other hand, these were not the only things that the children did. While they were exploring these questions, they were exploring many others as well. And while it was true that only a few of the children might do the actual research on the invention of the first weaving machines, they would always report to the entire class what they had found out, so that almost all the discoveries made were shared by all the children.

Here is another of their projects. The older children used to put out a small school newspaper, which appeared every few weeks. One day a student said, "If it takes us so long to put out this little paper, how come people are able to put out a great, fat newspaper every day?"

The question was interesting to the class, as it has always been to me. They decided to look into the matter. After some letters, they were able to visit a large newspaper plant. They were so interested in the typesetting and printing processes that they began to investigate the whole history of type, printing, and bookmaking. This made some of them curious about the history of writing and writing materials in general. They began to study the earliest alphabets, and such writing materials as papyrus, parchment, and so on. Before long they decided to make—write, type, and bind—a book of their own, about the complete history of writing, printing, and bookmaking. It was a big job; they had not quite finished by the end of the school year, and a number of them came to school for a week or more after school ended, so that they could finish. Dr. Gordon showed me their book. It was a wonderful piece of work: well organized, clearly written, elegantly illustrated and typed, and strongly bound—a real book. In making it, they had gone from today's daily paper all the way back to the beginnings of history.

These stories show us a number of things about the ways in which children learn. They see the world as a whole, mysterious perhaps, but a whole none the less. They do not divide it up into airtight little categories, as we adults tend to do. It is natural for them to jump from one thing to another, and to make the kinds of connections that are rarely made in formal classes and textbooks. They make their own paths into the unknown, paths that we would never think of making for them. Thus, for example, if we decided that it was important for children to know about the Trojan War, or archaeology, would we start by talking to them about scuba divers? Certainly not. Even if we did, there are many children for whom this would not be a good beginning, or a beginning at all. Finally, when they are following their own noses, learning what they are curious about, children go faster, cover more territory than we would ever think of trying to mark out for them, or make them cover.

People have often said to me, nervously or angrily, that if we let children learn what they want to know they will become narrow specialists, nutty experts in baseball batting averages and such trivia. Not so. Many adults do this; the universities are full of people who have shut themselves up in little fortresses of artificially restricted private learning. But healthy children, still curious and unafraid, do not learn this way. Their learning does not box them in; it leads them out into life in many directions. Each new thing they learn makes them aware of other new things to be learned. Their curiosity grows by what it feeds on. Our task is to keep it well supplied with food.

Keeping their curiosity "well supplied with food" *doesn't* mean feeding them, or telling them what they have to feed themselves. It means putting within their reach the widest possible variety and quantity of good food—like taking them to a supermarket with no junk food in it (if we can imagine such a thing).

□FANTASY

A six-year-old friend came into our office the other day with her brother and mother. While her mother talked to me and her brother looked over the books on our shelves, the girl made a beeline for the electric office typewriter she had been using the day before. I gave her some paper and soon she was "typing," seeing how fast she could make the machine go, probably enjoying some fantasy of competence and power—her mother is a good typist, and she has often heard her at work. For a while, as we talked, her mother and I could hear this busy clatter of keys. Then it began to slow down, and soon became very deliberate, a letter or two, a silence, then another letter or two. I said to her mother, "Now she's started to look at what she's doing, writing something real."

After a few minutes the child came into our office and said briskly to us, "At first I was only doing nonsense, then I got tired of nonsense." With that she gravely handed us some "forms." At the top of mine she had typed her name, her own zip code, and her telephone number. Further down the page, each one on its own line, were typed the words "naem," "adress," "zip," and "number." After each word she had made a long underline (she had figured out herself how to do this) on which I was to fill in the needed information.

As I began to do this, I asked whether under "number" she wanted my Social Security number. No, what she wanted was my phone number. When our forms were filled out, she went back to make some more, each a little more official-looking, and asking for a little more information than the one before. On the final few she drew a rectangle colored in with green crayon. Her mother explained to me that these represented bank checks.

About these checks, her mother later wrote us at *Growing Without Schooling:*

> Our checks fascinate Vita. I always give her our old checks to play store with and she often keeps a stack of them on her little desk (made from a wooden box) in the living room. Three or four times now she's asked me to explain how checks work—how they represent money. And she wants to know where our money is, and if the bank gives us the *same* money we put in, and so on. She likes to watch me attempt to balance the checkbook. But mostly she likes the physical sensation of holding a bundle of checks in her hands. It is a very grown-up feeling.

In this chapter I will say something very simple, that may not often have been said before. *Children use fantasy not to get out of, but to get into, the real world.*

There has been much talk in child psychology about "infant omnipotence," as if children's fantasies were a way of escaping from the real world into a world in which they could do anything. But children, at least before they meet the ready-made fantasies of TV, don't want to be omnipotent. They just want not to be impotent. They want to be able to do what the bigger people around them do—read, write, go places, use tools and machines. Above all, they want, like the big people, to control their immediate physical lives, to stand, sit, walk, eat, and sleep where and when they want.

Children, at least at first, do not dream of going faster than a speeding bullet or leaping tall buildings with a single bound. Those fantasies are made up by adults. It takes years for children to grow used to these and to build them into their own fantasy lives. Children may imagine large and powerful creatures chasing *them*. But they rarely have fantasies in which they can make everyone else do what they want, or own or blow up the world.

Of course, children these days are very early hooked by the mass media. We are seeing something new in human history, a generation or two of children who have most of their daydreams made for them. To watch children whose fantasies were truly their own, we would have to catch them very young. But even as recently as the late forties and early fifties, when I first began to pay attention to children, the "pretend" games they played with each other were more likely to be games like house, in which someone would be the mommy and someone the daddy and someone the baby, or maybe school or doctor. They didn't run around pretending to be Superman. Such fantasies must be learned from the adults who invent and sell them.

When my sister and I were about five and six, we used to visit our grandmother in Maine in the summer. There were no children our age anywhere near us, and by modern standards, not much to do. So we spent many happy hours in various kinds of fantasy play. One of our favorite games was Train. Going to Maine was a great adventure, because it meant sleeping on the train, very exciting. When I had the upper berth, it was even a little scary, as I used to fear that the upper berth might snap shut on me, like a giant clam. Later, when I understood a little more about how things worked, I would inspect the berth very carefully to make sure there were bars or locks to prevent it from closing. But even with that fear, the trip was wonderfully exciting, eating dinner in a dining car, watching the sleeping car being made up for the night, climbing in through the heavy green curtains, peeking out the window at the countryside at night. (Overnight trips on trains are still one of my favorite things to do.)

So when we were at Granny's house nothing was more natural than that we should relive the adventure of getting there. Outside the house Granny had a number of those folding canvas armchairs known as director's chairs. Jane and I would tip the chairs forward so that they were resting on their arms, with their backs in the air. We'd tip them over in pairs, legs facing away from each other, the tops of the backs of the chairs touching each other. Then we'd drape some of Granny's old towels over the backs and sides of the chairs. The little space thus enclosed became for us the lower berth on a train. We'd crawl into those spaces (one lower berth for each) and spend hours there. Talking about what? I wish I could remember. But we played this game day after day. We didn't pretend to be the conductor or engineer. We just pretended to be ourselves, riding on the train.

A few years later our fantasies had been taken over, partly by radio serials, which our parents knew about, and partly by a form of crime literature called dime novels, which they did not. We bought and read these dime novels in secret, and hid them carefully. When we ate breakfast with our five-year-old sister (but not parents), Jane and I often pretended to be taking part in various fantasy adventures. Sometimes these would revolve around some episode in the radio serial "Buck Rogers," which we could listen to if our father took the late train home from work. But often our morning adventures had to do with our favorite dime novel, *The Spider.* The Spider was the alias and alter ego of a rich young man named Richard Wentworth, a kind of knight-errant against gangs of organized criminals, a different one each month, and each one armed with some kind of fantastic superweapon; a poison gas that killed at a touch, an explosive (made from eels!) that would destroy an entire city, a plague that could infect millions, and so on.

Even then, at ten, I indentified myself more with the author of *The Spider* than with the hero. Part of my fantasy life was trying to think up mass-destroying weapons that the author had not thought of. I even imagined writing a story about it and later seeing the magazine with the name of my story and a cover illustration of my superweapon in action. The only one of these I can remember was a weapon—I had just read about liquid air, which fascinates most kids when they first hear of it—that would freeze everything it touched. A year or two later I had begun to read a monthly magazine called *The American Boy* and used to daydream about writing stories for it. I even began a couple, thought out the plots, even typed out ten or more single-spaced pages. That was as far as I could get, because I knew absolutely nothing about what I was writing about—when I picked a topic, it wasn't because I knew anything about it but only because no story about that topic had yet appeared in the magazine.

Later, as an adult, I thought very little about children's fantasies, or use of fantasy, until the early sixties, when I was beginning to observe and write

down the things that went into the original version
of this book. I was then much less interested in children's fantasies than in how they thought about the
world and tried to solve problems in it. But one day,
three or four years after we had taught fifth grade
together, Bill Hull told me something that made me
begin to consider fantasy in a new way. He and two
friends and colleagues were studying children's re-
sponses to a new set of materials that Bill had de-
vised to introduce them to different ways of
classifying things and even to the beginnings of symbolic logic. Bill had used these materials successfully with children of eight or ten, and now wanted to
find out how five-year-olds would react to them and
use them. But when he and his colleagues gave these
materials to some five-year-olds and asked them to
do some simple things with them, the children could
do nothing. No amount of explaining made any difference. They were completely blocked. Then the
adults tried a new tack. They gave the materials to
another group of young children, but before saying
anything about them or asking the children to do
anything with them, just let the children play with
them however they wanted, calling them people or
animals or houses or whatever, until they seemed a
bit bored with this and ready to do something more
interesting. Then, when they gave these children the
same tasks, they did them with no trouble at all. But
the free play had to come first. Before the children
could think of these things as the mathematical abstractions they were to the adults, *they had to make
them real,* a part of their own living world. This is
what their fantasy did, and what it was for.

I thought about this episode often during the next
few years, in which I also began to understand better
the uses and importance of fantasy in my own life.
During those years I was invited to speak at a Mon-

tessori convention, and to prepare myself I read some books about Montessori theory and practice. From them I learned that Maria Montessori and her followers did not approve of children's fantasizing. They felt that children should be exploring the "real world," and that their fantasies were nothing but an escape from this. Of course, some Montessori people disagreed with this. But even now many or most traditional Montessori schools probably discourage children's fantasizing.

Thus, two of the particular kinds of materials used in Montessori schools everywhere are called the Pink Tower and the Brown Stair. The Pink Tower is a set of wooden cubes ranging in size from about an inch on a side to about four inches on a side. The children are supposed to make these cubes into a tower, the largest cube on the bottom, then the next largest, and so on up to the smallest cube on top. The idea is that by doing this they will gain a clearer notion of relative size, of "bigger than" and "smaller than," of order. The Brown Stair is a set of brown wooden rods, all of them about an inch square in cross-section, but of different lengths. Here again the children are supposed to make these into a stair, the largest rod on the bottom, going a step at a time to the smallest one on top. From this the children are supposed to be learning something about the idea of length.

Children seem willing to spend quite a bit of time building this Tower and Stair, and no doubt learn something useful from it. But what the traditional Montessori schools are very firm about is that children cannot use these materials to do *anything else,* can't make them into trains or houses or people or whatever. If they do, the teacher is supposed to come up and say, "That's not how we use the Tower, or Stair," and show them what they are supposed to do.

If they persist in playing fantasy games with the materials, the teacher is supposed to say to them, "You're not ready to use these yet." In practice, this seems to work—soon all the children learn to use the materials the "right" way. They also learn that their fantasies are not legitimate and must be kept secret.

To whatever extent the Montessori schools may still think and act this way, I think they are much mistaken. For the fact is that in trying to make these pieces of wood into trains or trucks or mommies and daddys, the children are by no means trying to escape reality. On the contrary, they are trying to put as much reality as they can *into those blocks*. It is the adults who are trying to take all the reality out of the blocks except the abstract notions of "size" or "length." It is the adults who are in fact saying that nothing is important about these blocks except what can be measured—for that is what the children are supposed to do with them, measure them against each other. Let me be clear about this; it is the fantasizing children who want to add reality to these blocks, and the adults who want to take it away.

In any case, as Bill Hull's experience made clear, even from the point of view of teaching size and length, the traditional Montessorians are mistaken. Whatever it is they want children to learn from these blocks, the children would learn *faster* if they were allowed to play freely with them.

In Australia in the summer of 1981 a friend gave me a copy of a report by Caroline White, "An Investigation of Beginning Writing," done for the publication *Occasional Papers* of the Centre for Language, Reading, and Communication Studies of the Adelaide College of the Arts and Education. It is a fascinating and delightful report and shows another kind of fantasy at work. Over a twelve-week period Caroline White studied the writings of a group of eight five-year-olds. She describes the beginning of the project:

Early in August 1980 (the children having been in school since June), I asked class members to write down a list of their favorite foods. Many grunts, groans, and scribbles, and wrinkled-up faces later, I collected the lists and selected eight pieces of work. I chose six children whose work most closely approximated correct spelling and two children who very confidently supplied me with masses of scribbled symbols. These two girls "wrote" to their classmates regularly and seemed to get much pleasure from their scribbles.

I then talked to these eight children, explaining that I had to do an assignment for College and I needed them to help me. The children agreed to "write" to help me. Some children were reluctant because they felt that they did not know how to write; the task was too difficult. These were the children I considered had managed the first task quite well. *My "letter writers" saw no threat and talked the others into helping me!* [emphasis added]

Caroline White reports that just before the September holidays Julia (one of the "letter" writers) wrote her first "Rumplestiltskin" story, which she reproduces in the report. It is a mass of letters, or letterlike shapes, arranged more or less roughly in lines on the page, but not in words, that is, groups of letters. These lines of scribbles mean nothing to us. But they meant a great deal to Julia; she meant to say something, and thought she was saying something, as she wrote them. Ms. White reports that she borrowed the "story" and then lost it over the holidays.

Julia was very upset about this; she said it wasn't "finished." She continued to write like this, though in time more of her symbols were actual letter shapes, and she grouped them more and more in wordlike bunches. But she always *meant* something when she wrote them and always expected Ms. White to know what she had "said."

Children like Julia could write prolifically at the responsibility-free scribble stage. But the next step proved to be a traumatic one for some of the writers, as they realized that their readers could not in fact read their scribbles. Five weeks after I had begun the study I realized that Julia would be likely to experience this trauma soon. I wanted to alert Julia's mother. On the morning I had planned to talk to her, she came in with the news, "Julia won't write to Grandma anymore because Grandma can't read it!"

That's so sad! During the rest of this short study, Julia refused to do any more "real" writing, that is, writing which she meant to say something. What she did was to make lines of random letters copied from books. She knew the letters were correct, but she knew they didn't say anything. Poor Julia!

Earlier in this book I describe some three-year-olds using my electric portable typewriter at a school. In a memo written soon after I had begun this work I wrote:

The children do not, for the most part, seem to make any connection between the keys they hit and the marks they make on the paper. In fact, they don't seem to be very interested in the marks on the paper. They know that marks are there, but don't seem to care what they look like.

A number of children have to some degree or other grasped the idea that the typewriter is a device for saying things. But it does not occur to them to ask me to show them how to say what they want to say. Quite often, as they bang keys in any old order, they will announce that they are saying this or that. In a low-key way, I try to pronounce what they have written, and tell them that that is what they have said, but they just think I am being silly. For them, the typewriter works by will power. To want to have said something is to have said it.

One little boy has learned that when I write his name the first key I hit is J. The other day, when another little boy was typing, the first one said, pointing to the J, "That's my letter, don't hit that letter." Another child was banging out a whole string of letters at top speed when all at once he said, "Oops! I made a mistake."

These children were not trying to learn to type. They were not *trying* to do anything. Their reality-fantasy was that they were *doing* just what big folks do—using the typewriter, by hitting the keys very fast, to say something. As far as it was in their power to do what the grownups do, they would do that. In time they would get "tired of nonsense," and begin to think about how to do or write something more real. Their fantasy having pulled them a little way into reality, the reality of adults typing on typewriters, they would now want to learn how to do it even more like the adults, that is, so that other people really could read the results. What a happy day it must have been for Julia when she finally wrote a letter that her grandma really could read.

In their efforts to organize and understand the world around them, children use fantasy and play in at least two ways. First, they use it to test reality, to do what adults do with mathematical models and computers, i.e., ask the question "What would happen if . . .?" Children's models of reality are of course very crude; they have little experience. But in their fantasy play and games they stick as close as they can to reality rules as they understand them. When young children are playing with trucks in a sand pile, pretending to build a road or a dam or whatever, they set themselves real problems, about how to get this load from here to there, and solve them as legitimately as they can. That is, if they meet an obstacle as they roll their trucks this way and that over the sand, they don't jump or fly over it but try to find a way to drive around it, as any real truck would. They are not pretending to be a superman who can lift up trucks. They are only pretending to be real truck drivers driving real trucks. In short, as in all their games, they are trying to enlarge the boundaries of their own experience.

Here, from the first part of the chapter "The Doll Game," in Nancy Wallace's as yet unpublished book about home schooling, is her description of a part of one day's worth of a game which her children Ishmael (ten) and Vita (six) play day after day.

Margery, the Victorian doll mother, is in the garden harvesting potatoes. Gently, with care not to intrude, Ishmael helps. The potatoes are blue and green marbles which they pile into little china pots. At the edge of the garden, feeding on pink paper flowers, are the barn yard animals—a red plastic sheep, a glass pig, and a white metal horse. The animals are no more than half an inch high, whereas Margery must be a towering six inches. Nobody minds this incongruity. The rest of the members of the Victorian doll family are idling their time away in the second story of their block house, which is in the middle of the rug on the bedroom floor. Thomas, the father, is staring at the grandfather clock, Auntie-Governess is standing over a wounded toy soldier who is lying in a bed of paper towels, and the Victorian children are sitting at a table covered with a flowery table cloth made by Vita.

Across the blue-velvet-ribbon river, things are more lively. Vita is helping her family of wooden Fisher-Price "Little People" to have a picnic. They are outside their modest block house standing around a table, complete with a red checkered table cloth, and they are drinking from a little green bottle of champagne and a slightly larger mug of frothy beer. For food they have a large bowl of roast beef.

Suddenly, all eyes turn on the mother. "Look, I've had a baby!" Vita helps her exclaim. Sure enough, lying on the floor right next to Mother is a tiny plastic baby. Vita helps everyone crowd around in admiration and then she takes the father away to find a cradle and a bottle for the baby. When it is comfortably settled, the Little People continue with their picnic.

"Br-r-r," says one of the picknickers. As if brought back to reality, Vita calls across the river and through the wooden evergreen forest to Ishmael, "What season are they having?" "Fall," he answers. "Fall?" she complains. "But we haven't even had winter yet and I thought fall came after winter. And anyway, if Margery is digging potatoes, it must be summer, because Nancy harvested our potatoes in the summer." Patiently, Ishmael explains, all the while working with Margery in the potato patch, "No, Vita, fall comes between summer and winter—you know, it's when the leaves turn color and we have frosts. I know Nancy harvested the potatoes in the summer, but that was because we had an early frost. Sometimes there are frosts around here in the summertime. Most people, though, harvest their gardens in the fall and that's why they have Jack O' Lanterns at Halloween and big dinners at Thanksgiving. After that comes Christmas, but then there's lots of snow and it's winter." "Oh," says Vita thoughtfully as she feeds the baby and helps Mother put a rug over it to keep off the chill. "Well, let's have Halloween then." . . .

Back at the potato patch, Ishmael helps Margery load the last of the potatoes into pots and put them into the stone house next to the Noah's Ark barn. "Well," he says to Vita doubtfully, "I guess if they only eat a potato a day they'll get through the winter." "Hey, I know, Ishmael," says Vita. "If you trade us some wool from your sheep we'll give you our pig, since we already have all the roast beef we can eat." "Well, OK. But is your pig dead or alive?" "He's dead. We'll smoke the meat and it'll last for a couple of months anyway, and come spring, the glass pig will have piglets again and we won't have to worry about meat."

And the game goes on. When we think about it a bit, what these children (and many others like them) do in their play is remarkable. They are at one and the same time writing a play and directing and producing it. This would be hard enough for many of us adults to do, even working all by ourselves, but these two children are working as partners. Whatever one of them introduces into the play, the other one must deal with. And like any serious writer of plays or novels, they have to play fair. They can set the stage as they choose, and there start whatever events they want. But once they have set the event in motion, they have to let it take its natural course. As Nancy Wallace points out later in the chapter, every part of this doll game comes from real life. The children who played it lived in the country, grew much of their own food and cut their own firewood, and had to think about having enough for the winter; they knew people who raised, butchered, and smoked meat; they had friends who were having babies; and so on.

Children also try to use fantasy to make sense out of reality, make a mental model of reality that works. Because they have so little experience, this is hard to do. They are like someone trying to put together a jigsaw puzzle with only 10 percent of the pieces—they have to invent imaginary pieces to fill in all the gaps. We adults don't like to do this. If we can't be sure we have all or nearly all the pieces, then we won't work on the puzzle. But little children can't wait till they have all the pieces, that is, all the information and experience they need to make a coherent and sensible model of reality. They have to make some kind of sense of it *right now*. Their fantasy grows out of reality, connects to reality, reaches out to further reality. Six-year-old Vita explores the mysterious adult world of money through her mother's canceled checks, or through the "forms" she types up on our office typewriter. Others reach out in other ways.

Janet Sarkett wrote to *Growing Without Schooling* from Arizona about her four-and-a-half-year-old son learning to read:

Lately, he's taken to drawing elaborate and detailed pictures of his favorite subjects such as rescue helicopters, deep sea divers, hydrofoils, pirates, and police. After a drawing is completed, I ask him to tell me about it. He replies with a good one sentence description, e.g., "Pirate Sam had a sword"; "Four divers on a submarine"; "This hydrofoil is one hundred feet long." I write this on his picture (with permission) or on a separate sentence strip. He chooses whichever color of felt marker he wishes. We read the sentence together a few times. ... Next step is to write the individual words on 3 × 5 cards, using a felt pen which corresponds to the color of the picture. I mix up the cards, he matches them to the appropriate word on the sentence strip or picture. He duplicates the sentence, using the cards, thinking of them as cars of a train. The period is always the caboose and the capital letter the engine. ...

For this little boy to call the first letter of a sentence "the engine" and the period "the caboose" is to fill his word learning with reality, to hook it up more strongly and unforgettably with what he already knows and cares about, *to take possession of it.* As Seymour Papert says in *Mindstorms,* anything is easy to learn if we can assimilate it to our collection of models. This is what children do, and are good at doing—connecting new experiences and ideas to the ones they already have. Fantasy is often their way of doing it. And it is something that, no matter how clever we may be, we cannot do for them. We cannot predict, or plan, or control their fantasies, or bend them to our uses. All we can do is put on their mental dinner plate, as on their real dinner plate, the kinds of food we know they like to eat.

Carol Kent wrote us from Texas about her son's love affair with trains:

For his second Christmas we got him a little wind-up train that ran on a small circular track.

Robert was delighted! The following Christmas we rode to Florida and back on the train, and took along a tiny plastic train with ten cars which he played with during the ride. In the spring of his third year we bought him a wind-up train.... It had a circular track, and a black steam engine with shiny silver driving rods, a coal car, hopper car, and a bright red caboose. Robert loved that train, and although he soon dismantled it, he learned to assemble the track himself, and for many months he could be seen stretched out on the floor, gazing fixedly beyond the stark hulks of his torn-down train cars set up on the track, into the train realm of his imagination....

On the 4th of July, 1979, in the Museum of History and Technology we came upon the train exhibit, featuring among other things a great steam engine flanked by signal lights. Every ten minutes or so the sound effects of a steam locomotive would fill the room and the signals would begin flashing and ringing, as if the locomotive was pulling in, then out of the station. Robert was ready to stay there all day, and we did stay for several repetitions. He had a railroad hat, which he happened to have worn that day, and from then on he wore it whenever we left home. We learned of a genuine steam excursion from Alexandria to Charlottesville later in the month, and signed up for the trip.

The trip really sold Robert on trains. Every week we *had* to check out one of the four or five train books at the library. Robert became "Robert the Railroadman," and his hat and bandanna were necessary apparel. He rode his tricycle—his "Steamer"—almost constantly, making locomotive sounds with such earnestness and ferocity that pedestrians frequently observed him with pained looks. Then Robert discovered train songs on some of his records. He would sit huddled next to the record player with his hat on and his poor old black steam engine clutched tightly, playing the songs over and over. When I found a recording of steam train sounds shortly before Halloween, it was an instant success.

I figured we would get Robert a new wind-up train for his fourth birthday, and was dismayed to discover that the genre had completely dried up. There were no wind-up trains for sale. The hobby store sold model trains, but the cheapest good one cost seventy-five dollars. Of course Robert's eyes were lit with trains when we left, and he made the situation quite clear to me: he needed one of those. I explained to him, "Robert, those trains are very expensive and are made for older children. You take your trains apart, but those trains cannot be taken apart. They must be handled very carefully. You must grow up some more before you get one of those." He touched my hand and looked at me very seriously. "Mama, I already grew up!" he said.

For Christmas Robert received from his grandparents a brand new railroad hat, two bandanas, a steam train photograph, and a great big railroadman's flashlight. He sat right down with his new hat and flashlight to listen to train records. Next day we received a generous Christmas check from his other grandmother. We voted unanimously to put it toward the train. With the check and his savings, Robert had the money to get his choice. At a big hobby shop downtown he found and bought a steam engine, a diesel engine, a hopper car, a flat car, a red caboose, and a cattle car complete with eight tiny cows, a stock loading platform, and a livestock truck.

[After setting up the train and showing Robert how to run it] we have brought George Zaffo's BIG BOOK OF REAL TRAINS home from the library many times, and happened to have it on hand over the Christmas holidays. It features double-page illustrations of all the train cars, with a short paragraph describing each. I came into the schoolroom one day as Robert was telling Susie his "train story." He gave me the book and asked me to help. He wanted me to prompt him if he forgot the text. First he placed the little steam locomotive and tender on the track. Then he began, "The engine comes out of the roundhouse. It is cleaned and oiled. The tender behind the engine carries coal and water. The locomotive is ready for a trip." After finishing the locomotive page, he carefully coupled the hopper car to the tender and recited, "A steel hopper car carries coal and gravel...." He said the entire text for each of the cars on his train, with only a couple of corrections. A few days later we made a Tinkertoy lantern, and Robert learned to do all the lantern signals given in the book. He hung all his train pictures on the walls beside the train table. Sometimes at night he likes to come into the schoolroom in the dark and watch the train by the light of his flashlight.

The above was written on Robert the Railroadman's fourth birthday. He is now almost six, and I'll have to find out where his love for trains has taken him. Meanwhile it is touching and exciting to read about it. We are fed by our fantasies as much as by our food. They open the world to us. Robert's engines pull him into reality just as much as they pull his freight cars down the track—or as my fantasies pull me along. Before I can begin the huge labor of writing a book I have to imagine the book, finished—and not just finished, but published, successful. Until the book has become real in my mind, I can't make any headway writing it.

In *Mindstorms,* Seymour Papert, professor of

mathematics and of education at M.I.T., tells about one of his most important pathways into the world:

Before I was two years old I had developed an intense involvement with automobiles. The names of car parts made up a very substantial portion of my vocabulary. I was particularly proud of knowing about the parts of the transmission system; the gearbox, and most especially the differential. It was, of course, many years later before I understood how gears work, but once I did, playing with gears became a favorite pastime. I loved rotating circular objects against one another in gearlike motions, and naturally, my first Erector set project was a crude gear system.

I became adept at turning wheels in my head and at making chains of cause and effect: "This one turns this way so that one turns that way so . . ." I found particular pleasure in such systems as the differential gear, which does not follow a simple linear chain of causality since the motion in the transmission shaft can be distributed in many different ways to the two wheels, depending on the resistance they encounter. I remember quite vividly my excitement in discovering that a system could be lawful and completely comprehensible without being rigidly deterministic.

I believe that working with differentials did more for my mathematical development than anything I was taught in elementary school. Gears, serving as models, carried many otherwise abstract ideas into my head. I clearly remember two examples from school math. I saw multiplication tables as gears, and my first brush with equations in two variables (e.g., $3x + 4y = 10$) immediately evoked the differential. By the time I had made a mental gear model of the relation between x and y, figuring out how many teeth each gear needed, the equation had become a comfortable friend. . . .

One day I was surprised to discover that some adults—even *most* adults—did not understand or even care much about the magic of the gears. I no longer think much about gears, but I have never turned away from the questions that started with that discovery: How could what was so simple for me be incomprehensible to other people? . . . Slowly I began to formulate what I still consider the fundamental fact about learning: Anything is easy if you can assimilate it to your collection of models. . . .

I find myself frequently reminded of several aspects of my encounter with the differential gear. First, I remember that no one told me to learn about differential gears. Second, I remember that there was *feeling, love* in my relationship with gears. Third, I remember that my first encounter with them was in my second year. If any "scientific" educational psychologist had tried to "measure" the effects of the encounter, he would probably have failed. . . .

A modern-day Montessori might propose, if convinced by my story, to create a gear set for children. Thus every child might have the experience I had. But to hope for this would be to miss the essence of the story: *I fell in love with the gears.*

It is mostly through our fantasies that we get our first collections of models. The first step is almost certain to be at the level of dream, romance, love. Automobiles were a source of mystery and delight for the two-year-old Seymour before he had any idea what was in them. The first gears he ever saw must have seemed beautiful, wondrous objects before he began to figure out how they worked and how they might be used. I have said that four-year-old Robert the Railroadman was pulled into the world by his trains. But we could as well say that Robert's trains, real, model, and imagined, pulled more and more of the world into him. The two processes are, after all, the same; as we move farther and farther into the world, we take more and more of it into ourselves. As children enter the world, the world enters them. The process begins with fantasy, and fantasy keeps it going. Robert's love for trains, Papert's love for gears, spurred them on to want to find out more about real trains and real gears.

This is not to say that all our fantasies will necessarily have some obvious payoff. Papert's love of gears led him into the love of mathematics, which became his life's work. But it needn't always work that way. When I was four or five I loved to look at photographs of yachts, ships, and ocean liners and draw pictures of them. One yacht in particular had a shape that so pleased and fascinated me that I saved the photograph of it, and would look at it every so often just to give myself a treat. At age five or so I had no wish to own such a yacht, couldn't even imagine what that might mean. I just wanted to look at its picture. A few years later, the country's first streamlined trains, a yellow train of the Union Pacific and the stainless steel Burlington Zephyrs, caught my imagination.

Yet I never thought for a second about becoming a designer or builder of boats or trains. I had no interest at all in learning how or where they were made, or how they worked. All my fantasies did for me—no small thing—was to keep alive a feeling that the world is in many ways a fascinating and beautiful place. To this day I remain very interested in the shapes of things and can still be strongly moved by the sight or feel of a beautifully designed useful object.

Many people may not have even this faint a connection between the fantasies and passions of their childhood and their adult lives. No matter. These fantasies, if they are of things children love rather than hate and fear, will pull them into the world, and the world into them. If, on the other hand, they are fantasies of shame, pain, and terror, they will only drive children out of the big outside world and back into themselves, into a dream world of their own making.

As important as fantasizing may be for children, we can't make them do it on demand, and we risk doing them a serious injury when we try. I now understand more clearly why I have so long and so deeply disliked a scene that is very common in preschool and early elementary grades. While an adult plays a piano or guitar, the children are invited, i.e. told, to pretend that they are trees or birds or snowflakes or wildflowers or whatever. Children quickly learn that when someone says, "Be a snowflake," it is their cue to wave their arms and whirl and jump about the room. Since they get few enough chances to move in school, they are glad to seize this one. But we must not fool ourselves that they are really fantasizing. They are only doing what they know the adults want them to do, pretending to imagine what the adults want them to imagine, and pretending all the while that they are enjoying it. Whoever saw children, in their private lives and play, pretending to be snowflakes? What they pretend to be is grown-ups, kings and queens, or truck drivers and doctors, or mommys and daddys. If we try to make children fantasize, these fake fantasies, like the ready-made fantasies of TV, will in time drive out most of their true fantasies, the ones that come from their experience in the world and their need to make sense of it and become at home in it.

□THE MIND
AT WORK

One of the puzzles we had in my fifth-grade class was a geometrical puzzle called *Hako.* You began with a number of thin, flat, rectangular plastic pieces arranged a certain way in a shallow box. The aim was to slide them around, without turning them or lifting them out of the box, so as to finish with the largest piece, a square, at the opposite end of the box from which it started. Though I spent many hours on it, I was never able to do it. This exasperated me. What exasperated me even more was that I seemed to be able to prove that the puzzle was impossible—though I knew it was not. Like most people, I began by moving the pieces around in a kind of blind, haphazard way. Before long, and unwisely, I grew impatient with this. There were too many possible moves, this could go on forever. The thing to do was use the brain and figure it out. So, moving the pieces very carefully, and analyzing each move, I deduced that in order to get the large piece from the top to the bottom, certain other things had to happen along the way. There had to be a point at which certain of the pieces were going up past the big piece while it was going down. Then, still carefully analyzing, I showed that this could only happen if certain other pieces moved in certain ways. Finally, I proved that they could not be moved in those ways. Therefore the problem was impossible.

The trouble was, I knew it wasn't impossible. Companies don't sell impossible puzzles; they would be sued, or worse. Besides, the puzzle had been mentioned in *Scientific American*. Besides that, and worst of all, some students had done it. With all my heart I wanted to believe that they had lied or cheated, but I couldn't convince myself; they weren't the type. I remember thinking furiously, "I suppose anyone could do this puzzle if he were willing to sit in front of it like a nitwit, moving the pieces around blindly, until just by dumb luck he happened to get it. I haven't got time for that sort of thing." More to the point, I felt above that sort of thing.

I went back to the puzzle many times, hoping that I would find some fresh approach to it; but my mind kept moving back into the little groove it had made for itself. I tried to make myself forget my supposed proof that the problem was impossible. No use. Before long I would be back at the business of trying to find the flaw in my reasoning. I never found it. Like many other people, in many other situations, I had reasoned myself into a box. Looking back at the problem, and with the words of Professor Hawkins in my ears, I saw my great mistake. I had begun to reason too soon, before I had allowed myself enough "Messing About," before I had built a good enough mental model of the ways in which those pieces moved, before I had given myself enough time to explore all the possible ways in which they could move. The reason some of the children were able to do the puzzle was not that they did it blindly, but that they did not try to solve it by reason until they had found by experience what the pieces could do. Because their mental model of the puzzle was complete, it served them; because mine was incomplete, it failed me.

Soon after the Rubik cube first came on the market, someone sent me one. A few words of the blurb that came with it—"billions of possibilities"—were enough for me. I did not touch the cube but put it aside, out of sight. I was a little afraid of it. As if walking by a quicksand, I thought, "I don't want to get mixed up in that!" I doubted very much that any- one, except perhaps some mathematicians, could reason their way to a quick solution. If the puzzle had been that easy, it could not have been that popu- lar. Remembering the Hako puzzle, I suspected that I would have to spend quite a bit of time just messing about with the cube, randomly trying this and that, slowly getting to know its language, before I would know enough about how it worked to find a way to solve it. I didn't have that much time; there were oth- er things I needed or preferred to do. So I put it aside.

On a lecture trip to Australia I stayed for a few days at the home of a family in Honolulu. The par- ents were away, but the children, a boy of thirteen and a girl of nine, were there—another adult was taking care of both house and children. Both kids were working on the cube. The boy already could solve it. Whether he figured it out himself or some- one showed him, I don't know. I saw him do it one evening for a guest in a couple of minutes. Every so often I would see them working on it. Even though the boy "knew how" to solve the cube, he still liked to spend time just playing with it. It was nice to watch them. They were in that dreamlike state children get into when they are really absorbed in something. Time meant nothing. They sat in big chairs, comfy and relaxed, slowly turning the cube over and over in their hands, looking at it, every so often making a move, and then turning the cube around slowly a few more times to see what had turned up. I did not ask them what they were doing. I did not want to break their concentration or trance. I suspect if I had asked them, they would have said, "Nothing," or per- haps, "Just fooling around." Since they were old enough to think that you're not supposed to fool around, this might have made them a little ashamed or self-conscious. So I did not ask. Instead, I watched, out of the corner of my eye.

Time is money, we say, and never have enough of it. "But at my back I always hear, Time's winged chariot hurrying near." "It is later than you think." I envied these children their sense that time had stopped or did not exist or count. It was during summer vacation, when children have time. They seemed to be having a kind of conversation with the cube. They were not asking it probing questions, like lawyers cross-examining a witness. It was more as if they were letting the cube do the talking, and were listening to what it was saying. As scientists, they were more like naturalists, botanists walking slowly through a field to see what plants and flowers could be seen, or bird watchers watching and listening for birds, patient, not trying to make anything happen, just being alert to whatever did happen. For the time being, they had been able to set aside (as I wish I could!) anxiety, impatience, vanity. For all I know, they may have been enjoying the cube just as much as a shifting pattern of pretty colors as a puzzle to be solved.

By now several books have been written about how to do the cube. It does not surprise me that at least one has been written by a child. The other day, on the silent TV in the window of the corner drugstore, I saw a child, no older than twelve if even that, solving the cube before the TV camera in a minute or less. I felt a twinge of the usual feelings—admiration, envy, resentment, shame ("Why can't I do that?")—plus the usual wry amusement at those feelings.

But the Rubik cube is ordinarily the farthest thing in the world from my thoughts. So I was surprised a few days ago to find myself thinking about it, playing with a cube in my mind. The thought came to me that I could think of the cube in the middle of each side, i.e., the blue square in the center of the nine blue squares, the yellow square in the center of the nine yellows, etc., as being fixed, with the other eight blue squares all being free to move around it. Then I saw that these other eight blue squares could be divided into four corner squares and four squares that were not in the corners—call them side squares. Then I saw, still playing around with the cube in my mind, that a corner square, no matter what you did with it, could never become a side square, or vice versa. These were obviously very simple discoveries, but pleasant, like all discoveries, even the most simple.

About the same time, with the cube only in my mind, I realized that if someone began with a solved cube and then mixed it up before giving it to me to try to solve, and if I could make all the moves he had made, only backwards and in reverse order, I would solve the puzzle. In other words, if he made only fifteen moves in order to scramble the puzzle, fifteen correct moves could unscramble it. It's like a man stepping out of his house in a howling blizzard and getting lost. He knows the house is only twenty feet away, but every step he takes is more likely to be away from the house than toward it. In the same way, trying to solve an easy cube puzzle, every wrong move we make turns it into a harder one.

This morning the cube was in my mind again. After mentally looking at it a while I thought, "Suppose we start with the cube solved. Suppose we look at one face, say the blue face, and pick the blue piece in the upper right hand corner, and one move at a time, begin to move it away from its proper position. How many moves can we make before it is as far away as it can get?" Trying it in my mind, I guessed—wrongly, as I later found out—that it could not get more than four moves from its original position. Since no piece (I thought) could be more than four moves from its proper place, it seemed as if it might be possible to take one piece at a time, move it to its proper place, then do the same with another piece, and so until the puzzle is solved.

Then another question came to me. Suppose I began with a solved puzzle, and proceed to unsolve it by turning the blue face ninety degrees clockwise, then turning the red face ninety degrees clockwise, then the blue again, then the red, and so on, will the puzzle return itself to the solved position? At first I thought it would, then decided it wouldn't. Thinking about this made me decide to buy a cube and try it, keeping track of my moves so that by reversing them I could get back to the original solved cube. But somewhere along the line I made a wrong turn, and found myself with a puzzle to solve.

About that time a colleague answered another question I had been asking myself—if all the colors are right on one face, will they necessarily be right on all the others? The answer was no. Bad news. Even if I managed to complete the blue face, when I started work on the red, wouldn't it just mess up the blue again? So it seemed. Was it a good strategy to do one face completely, then another, then another, each face in turn, each time sneaking up a little closer to the solution? I had no idea.

I decided that instead of trying to get one face completely correct, I would set myself a simpler task, to get just the four side pieces of one face all in their correct positions. So far, I haven't been able to do even that. I could get three of the four in place, but the fourth would be far away, and any moves I made with it would move at least one and usually two of the others out of place. So the strategy of turning the hard puzzle into a series of simpler puzzles seems not to work. At least, not for me, not so far. But what other strategy could there be?

What is so frustrating and unsatisfying about the cube is that in my present ignorance I don't know how to find out from it whether a given move is taking me closer to or farther from the solution. I have no way to learn from my mistakes. I can't even tell when I'm making one. This is not at all like music, where if I make a mistake I have ways of knowing that I did, and what the mistake was, and how I can correct it. I don't like this stumbling around in circles in the dark. And I find the cube, unlike the Soma puzzle (see below), not much fun for my fingers to work on.

What I would have to do to solve the cube, if I could ever solve it at all, is imitate those children in Hawaii—step outside of time, just mess about with the cube, not trying to pry its secrets open, but waiting for the unconscious, silent, intuitive processes of my mind to tell me, gradually, what the language and laws of this cube are. But I'm not going to do this; I might find the patience, but I haven't the time, and as much as I hate admitting defeat (at least for now), there are many other things—the cello, for one—I'd rather do. So back goes the cube into its box. Perhaps someday I'll take it out and look at it again.

In one of the classes I previously shared with Bill Hull, we worked a good deal with a three-dimensional puzzle named *Soma*, also described and discussed in *Scientific American*. In this, twenty-seven cubes of wood were glued together to make six four-cube pieces and one three-cube piece. The aim was to use these seven pieces to make various other shapes, beginning with a cube and other simple shapes, and going on to more complicated and difficult shapes such as the Tunnel, the Bathtub, the Castle, etc. It was a splendid puzzle, one of the very best I have ever seen, among other reasons because children can work on it at many different degrees of difficulty.

My first meeting with this puzzle was embarrassing. A person familiar with it can make the cube in less than half a minute in any one of several different ways. By the time I started trying to make the cube, a number of the children were able to do it in about fifteen seconds. My first effort took me about fifty minutes. I tried to keep my struggles out of the sight of the children, but there were some pointed questions. Fortunately I was able to avoid falling into the trap of analyzing too soon, perhaps only because I could not see how to. Unable to think of any "sensible" way to proceed, I fiddled with the pieces, trying to fit them this way and that, making mistakes, working myself into dead ends, going back and starting again. One of the frustrating things about this particular puzzle is that if you have it almost right, you know you have it entirely wrong. When you find yourself saying, "If this piece just looked like that piece, I could do it," you have to start almost from the beginning. By many such trials and errors, retrials and corrections, I was finally able, like many of the children, to build up a good mental model of the way these pieces worked. With this model I could tell, without having to try it out, that a certain piece, or even combination of pieces, would not go in a certain spot, and could see several pieces in advance when I was going wrong. Before long I became one of the class experts.

Such experiences suggest a reason why so much that seems to me trivial, misleading, or downright false has been written about child psychology. The psychologists, on the whole, have not done enough of Professor Hawkins's "Messing About." They have not seen enough children in their native habitat—homes, schools, playgrounds, streets, stores, anywhere. They haven't talked or played with enough of them, or helped them, or comfort-

ed them, or coerced them, or made them pleased, or excited, or rebellious, or angry. Unless he is very fortunate, a
young psychologist is very likely to have his head stuffed
full of theories of children before he has had a chance to
look at any. When he does start looking at them, it is likely to be in very special laboratory or testing situations.
Like many teachers, he may not recognize the many ways
in which children betray anxiety, because he has never
seen them in a situation in which they were not anxious.
Also, like me trying to do the puzzle, he may be so much a
prisoner of his theories that he cannot see anything that
does not fit into them.

For such reasons I would like to stress again what I said
very early in this book. My aim in writing it is not primar-
ily to persuade educators and psychologists to swap new
doctrines for old, but to persuade them to *look* at children,
patiently, repeatedly, respectfully, and to hold off making
theories and judgments about them until they have in
their minds what most of them do not now have—a reasonably accurate model of what children are like.

I should add, too, that I am not trying to deny the importance of close, deductive, analytical, logical reasoning. In
its proper place, it is a useful, powerful, often essential
tool. I am only trying to say that out of its place it is likely
to be not only useless but harmful, and that its place is not
everywhere. It works when we have a very limited
amount of evidence, all we are going to get, and from it
have to reconstruct the past—find out who committed a
crime, or how and why an accident took place, or what is
ailing a particular man or machine. It works when we
can limit and isolate, one by one, the variables we have to
deal with. Thus the skilled repairman, trying to find out
why a machine is working badly, checks its various elements, one by one, until he finds the one that is causing
the trouble. Thus the scientist, meeting a new phenomenon in the lab, changes, one by one, the conditions of the
experiment until he finds the one that seems to affect the

phenomenon. And we use this kind of reasoning to check our hypotheses, our theories or hunches about why things work as they do. We say, "If this theory is true, then certain other things ought to happen," and then we find out whether in fact they do happen. If they do, the theory is confirmed, temporarily, at least. The story is told of Einstein that, after the observations of some astronomers seemed to have confirmed his theory of relativity, a woman congratulated him on his theory having been proved right. He said, "Madam, a thousand experiments can never prove me right; a single experiment can prove me wrong." Even when the facts seem to support our reasoning, we must, like Einstein, not assume that we have found the final truth.

But if there are times and places and conditions where this kind of reasoning is useful, there are others where it does not work at all. If the experience before us is completely new and strange; if there is much new material to be observed, material that doesn't seem to fall into any recognizable pattern or order; if we cannot tell what are the variables that influence the situation, much less isolate them, we would be unwise to try to think like a detective, or a scientist in a laboratory.

Some years ago, some sociologists were trying to draw analogies between the behavior of molecules in a gas and the behavior of human beings in society, and from there between the laws that describe or explain the behavior of gases and comparable laws that would supposedly describe and explain the behavior of human beings in society. This is a very good example of how not to use the scientific method. In such situations, we must use our minds very differently. We must clear them of preconceived notions, we must suspend judgment, we must open ourselves to the situation, take in as much data as we can, and wait patiently for some kind of order to appear out of the chaos. In short, we must think like a little child.

It may be useful to describe a few situations in which I

had to, and was able to, make myself think this way. One bright summer day some friends took me to the Haystack School of Arts and Crafts in Maine. There, for the first time, I saw a hand loom. One of the teachers had it out in the sunshine, on one of the many broad, wooden terraces that look down a hill and over the sea. She was setting it up for some weaving, and my hosts gathered around to talk about what she was doing and was planning to do.

After looking at the machine a while, and listening to this informed talk, I felt the faint beginnings of anxiety. A hand loom is a very open machine; all the parts of it can be clearly seen. It seemed to me that after some careful looking and reasoning I ought to be able to figure out how this machine worked. But I couldn't. It looked like nothing but a jumble and confusion of little parts, wires, and scraps of wood. None of it made any sense at all. Nor could I think how to make sense of it. Where to begin?

In such situations we tend to have a defensive reaction, which I began to sense in myself. Confronted with what it cannot grasp, the mind tends to turn away, to shut it out. We say to ourselves, "Oh, well, who cares about looms and weaving, anyway?" We seek the relief of thinking about something that we can grasp and understand. Having learned to recognize this protective and cowardly strategy, I would not allow myself to use it. I thought, "Come on, now, quit acting like a scared kid." I examined the loom more carefully, and began to ask myself intelligent questions. What's this for? Where does this lead? But no use. It remained as much a mystery as ever. The anxiety grew, with a little shame added. Some of this was caused by not being able to make sense of the loom. Some was caused by my feeling that as a supposedly fairly intelligent man I ought to be able to make sense out of it. Like children in school, I was worried by the fear of not being able to live up to my own concept of myself. Finally, I knew that everyone else around me knew how that loom worked, and knew that I didn't. I could almost hear them thinking,

"Funny about John, he's usually pretty smart about most things, yet that simple loom, that you would think anyone could understand, is too much for him." Then, to make matters worse, they began to try to help by giving explanations. They spoke with that infuriating mixture of indulgence and impatience with which the expert always explains things to the nonexpert. It is always gratifying to be able to understand what someone else cannot; and more gratifying yet to make yourself his benefactor by explaining it to him; and still more gratifying—unless you are required to make him understand—if in spite of your explanation he continues not to understand. In this spirit my friends began to say, "It's really very simple; this piece here . . ."

After a certain amount of this I said, rather sharply, "Please stop talking about it, and just let me look at it." I thought to myself, "Remember what you have learned about learning. Be like a child. Use your eyes. Gag that teacher's mouth inside your head, asking all those questions. Don't try to analyze this thing, look at it, take it in." And shutting out of mind the knowing conversation of the others, I did so. Now and then the voice inside would begin to ask questions. I silenced it, and for some time went on looking.

There were many other things to see: potters, print makers, and most exciting of all, glass blowers. After seeing them all, we started home. And as we drove, a most extraordinary thing began to happen. I was not thinking about the loom; as my host was a potter, we were talking mostly about the pottery. But as we talked, a loom began slowly to put itself together in my mind. There is no other way to describe it. Suddenly, for no reason, the image of a particular part would suddenly appear in my consciousness, but in such a way that I understood what that part was for. When I say "understood," I don't mean that some kind of verbal explanation went along with it. I mean that I could see what the part was for and what it did, I could almost see it doing its work. If I had been building a loom and had had that part in my hand, I would have known where to put it.

This loom-building process was very slow. It would be interesting to have a record of the order in which the parts of this loom appeared and assembled themselves, but I have none. Sensing that something important was happening in the nonverbal, nonconscious part of my mind, I did not want to look too hard at the process, lest I bring it to a stop. Also, I had no way of knowing, at any time, how much farther it would go. When the first part of the loom appeared in my surprised consciousness, I had no reason to believe that other parts would later appear in the same way. However, they did, some during our trip home, others during the rest of the day, some even the following day. By the end of that day, a loom had made itself in my mind. There was a working model of a loom in there. If I had had to build a loom, I would have known at least roughly what parts were needed and where they went. There was much about the loom that I didn't know, but I now knew where knowledge left off and ignorance began; knew the questions I needed to ask; knew enough to be able to make sense of the answers. Some of what people had told me, trying to explain the loom, came back to me, and now I could see what their words meant.

Explanations. We teachers—perhaps all human beings—are in the grip of an astonishing delusion. We think that we can take a picture, a structure, a working model of something, constructed in our minds out of long experience and familiarity, and by turning that model into a string of words, transplant it whole into the mind of someone else. Perhaps once in a thousand times, when the explanation is extraordinarily good, and the listener extraordinarily experienced and skillful at turning word strings into nonverbal reality, and when explainer and listener share in common many of the experiences being talked about, the process may work, and some real meaning may be communicated. Most of the time, explaining does not increase understanding, and may even lessen it.

A few years ago I spent an evening, at Bill Hull's house, in the company of a number of people who were all interested in teaching mathematics to children. For most of the evening we talked about things we had done in classes, or were thinking of doing. As the party began to break up one of the group, a most distinguished visitor from abroad, confessed that although most of the materials he had developed for children dealt with numbers and numerals, or with algebra, his own real love was geometry. Not the old-fashioned plane geometry that most people have met in school, but a much more advanced and exotic geometry. Memory tells me that he called it projective geometry, though it didn't sound like the only projective geometry I had ever read about. I asked him what he liked so much about this branch of mathematics. He replied that it was the beauty and simplicity of the theorems. "Such as what?" I asked. It was a mistake. His eyes flashed with enthusiasm. Such as the proof that the intersection of two quartics is a twisted cubic. Seeing a glazed look in my eyes, he began to sketch the proof. I held up a hand, laughing, and said, "Whoa, wait a minute, I've never even heard of these things. I don't know what a quartic or a cubic is, much less a twisted cubic." Too late. The teaching fit was on him. He began to "explain." As he saw that I still did not understand, he began to grow exasperated—like most teachers when their "explanations" are not being understood. "It's really very simple!" he said as his hands sketched complicated shapes in the air. I was amused, but appalled. Here was a really great teacher, who for years had been working with young children trying to find ways to have them experience and discover, with hands and eyes, the relationships of mathematics. Yet in spite of his long experience he believed so strongly in the magic power of explanations that he thought he could drop me into the middle of an advanced and complex branch of mathematics, in which I had absolutely no knowledge or experience, and with a few words and waves of the hand make the whole thing clear.

Jerome Bruner has said that one thing that happens in school is that children are led to believe they don't know or can't do something that they knew, or could do, before they got to school. I have seen this demonstrated many times, but never as vividly as in the following example, quoted from the prospectus of the Green Valley School, in which George von Hilsheimer writes:

> One of our art associates once conducted an experiment in her art resources classroom. As the children entered the classroom they found construction paper on the desks. The teacher held up a folded fan—like those you and I have made many times—"Know what this is?"
>
> "Oh, yes!"
>
> "Can you make one?"
>
> "Yes! Yes!"
>
> Every child quickly made the little fan. The teacher then read from the book the instructions on how to make the fan. She read slowly, with proper emphasis and phrasing. The instructions were well designed to be clear to the fifth-grade mind. After reading, the teacher asked the children to make the fans again. Not one child could make a fan. The teacher sat at each desk and tried to get the children to go back to the first way they had made the fan (with the fan still lying on the desk). They could not.
>
> There have been many such experiments in educational psychology. Unfortunately, few teachers and even fewer school systems take such evidence seriously. We do.

Such stories make many defenders of the system angry. They say, "But human knowledge is stored and transmit-

ted in symbols. We have to teach children to use them."
True enough. But the only way children can learn to get
meaning out of symbols, to turn other people's symbols
into a kind of reality or a mental model of reality, is by
learning first to turn their own reality into symbols. They
have to make the journey from reality to symbol many
times, before they are ready to go the other way. We must
begin with what children see, do, and know, and have
them talk and write about such things, before trying to
talk to them much about things they don't know. Thus,
given children who knew how to make a paper fan, it
might not be a bad idea at all to ask them to try to tell
someone else how to make one, without using any gestures, as if they were talking over a phone. I used to ask
fifth-graders how they would explain over the phone the
difference between right and left, to someone who could
speak English but did not happen to know those words.
Such games are exciting and useful. But when we do
what we do most of the time in school—begin with meaningless symbols and statements, and try to fill them with
meaning by way of explanations, we only convince most
children either that all symbols are meaningless or that
they are too stupid to get meaning from them.

Turning reality into symbols, and symbols back
into reality, is a tricky business. I've already mentioned the nice game of Gear that my four-year-old
friend Tommy invented and played with me in bed
early in the morning. At about that same time we invented or slowly developed another game, which we
called Machine. Tommy, sitting on my shoulders,
was the driver; I was the machine. The controls were
very simple. A pull on my right ear meant start turning to the right; on the left, turning to the left; a third
signal meant "Stop turning," or in the lovely words
of the sea, "Steady as you go." There was a signal for
go ahead, another for back up, another for stop. The

machine understood no words. Tommy's task was to use the controls to guide the machine through the house, going into various rooms, moving around the furniture, etc.

It was a hilarious game; it usually wasn't more than a few minutes before we were laughing so hard that we had to stop. Tommy kept assuming that I, the machine, was still really a person, with some common sense and judgment. I, on the other hand, understood a great truth: Machines Are Stupid. They can only do what they're told, and if told, they will do it, and keep on doing it, no matter what happens. So when Tommy, wanting me to go through a door, would give me a signal to start turning to the right, expecting me to understand what he wanted and do it, I would understand nothing; I would only do exactly what he told me to do. Unless he was careful to use his turn signals to get me pointed in exactly the right direction before giving me a go-ahead signal, I would not walk through the door, but into the wall beside it, and like some windup toy, would keep bumping into it. Tommy would then begin to laugh, and between laughs, would start saying "No! No! Not that way!" to me, and *telling* me what to do, which of course had no effect. Then he would begin giving me other signals, perhaps back up, perhaps make a left turn. But he would usually get excited and forget when to say "That's enough" or "Stop," would use too many controls, as pilots say of beginners, and soon I would be turning around in a circle or bumping backwards into some other wall. Except that it was playful and funny, with no danger of anyone getting hurt, it was much like someone just starting to learn to drive a car. And like more than a few novice drivers, if things got confused enough Tommy was likely to start shouting to his machine, "Stop! Stop!" (If he shouted loud enough, I would stop.)

I thought later that the game might have been more realistic if I had been blindfolded. But it might have been less funny, since one of the things that made it funny was that I *could,* after all, see perfectly well the things that I was bumping into. Later I thought that it might be interesting in school, say with fourth- or fifth-graders, to play a game of robot, in which one child tries to get another child, perhaps blindfolded, to do some task by giving it instructions. The difficulty would be that the "robot," being a real child, would find it hard not to think like a real child, that is, to use its intelligence to figure out what the task was and to do it, rather than to act like a real machine.

By now the art or science of giving complicated instructions to incredibly quick but still stupid machines has become the giant field of computer programming. Seymour Papert, in his book *Mindstorms* (see "Fantasy" chapter), shows us very convincingly, drawing on work that he and other computer experts have done with children, that a very good and perhaps the best way for children to become familiar with the truly basic ideas of mathematics (far more basic and important than the "basic facts" of addition, etc.) is to give them access to a certain kind of specially programmed computer (the program itself is called Logo, and at least two large computer companies are offering it), and let them use a very limited supply of instructions, much like the ones Tommy used in his game of Machine, to teach or program this computer to draw designs on its screen. They then see instantly whether their instructions, their program, has given them the results they want. If it has not, they learn to look for the bug in their program—the wrong step in their instructions—that caused the computer to do something other than what they wanted it to do.

As he describes children and the kinds of things they say, do, and learn while working with the computers—and there is no way to do justice to this fascinating story with a few quotes—Papert makes some very important observations about children and mathematics and learning in general, of which these quotes are a good sample:

> Children seem to be innately gifted learners, acquiring long before they go to school a vast quantity of knowledge by a process I call "Piagetian learning," or "learning without being taught.".... They have to *learn* to have trouble with learning in general and mathematics in particular....
>
> Our educational culture gives mathematics learners scarce resources for making sense of what they are learning. As a result our children are forced to follow the very worst model for learning mathematics. This is the model of rote learning, where material is treated as meaningless; it is a *dissociated* model.... The child's perception is fundamentally correct: The *kind of mathematics* foisted on children in school is not meaningful, fun, or even very useful....
>
> Already in the preschool years every child first constructs one or more preadult theorizations of the world and then moves toward more adultlike views.... Children do not follow a learning path that goes from one "true position" to another, more advanced "true position." Their natural learning paths include "false theories" that teach as much about theory building as true ones.

We see this process in children learning to talk, or, as Glenda Bissex has shown, in learning to write. Her son Paul did not keep repeating his wrong invented spellings but kept changing them as he kept revising and making more correct his general ideas about how English spelling worked. We could see it in children learning math, too, if we did not keep making the mistake of seeing all children's mistakes as stupid and careless, instead of the logical results of a misunderstood question or an imperfectly designed theory.

Perhaps the greatest danger of becoming too bound up with symbols, too symbol-minded, if I may be allowed the phrase, is that we don't know how to give them up, get them out of the way, when they are of no use to us. We become addicts. There are times when words, symbols, only get between us and reality. At such times, we must be ready to let them go, and use our minds in more appropriate ways—more childlike ways.

Such an experience took place not long ago when I was visiting A. S. Neill at Summerhill School in England. The weather was terrible, the public rooms of the school were deserted, the students were all in their rooms, so there was nothing much to see around the school. Neill himself was laid up in his room with a painful attack of sciatica, and was eager for company. So we had a long and very interesting talk. More than once, thinking I had taken enough of his time, I got up to go, but he waved me back in my chair, where I was more than glad to stay.

At about three o'clock his brother-in-law came in, and asked if he could use the TV to watch the England-Scotland rugby match. Neill asked me if I knew anything about rugby. I said I didn't; he said he didn't either. We decided to watch the game. Before it had gone on two minutes, I found myself in the same panicky confusion that had gripped me when I looked at the loom. Rugby is a hard game for a novice to understand. It is like a crazy combination of soccer and football, just enough like either one to be misleading. As I watched, the teacher-voice in my head began to ask, "Why did he do that? Why did he put the ball there? Why is he running that way?" And so on. But there were no answers.

After a few futile minutes of this, I saw that this was the loom situation again. I didn't know enough about the game to be able to reason about it. No use to ask questions. Neill couldn't answer them. His brother-in-law—a taciturn man—wouldn't. Anyway, I didn't know enough to know what questions to ask. The only thing to do was to turn off the questions and watch—like a child. Take it all in. See everything, worry about nothing. This is what I did. When the voice inside began to yammer, I silenced it. At half time I seemed to know no more than at the start. Everything that happened on that field surprised me. During the half the announcers, as in every land, talked learnedly about the play during the first half. Not a word they said made any sense. I listened, like a child listening to adult conversation, taking in the words without knowing or caring what they might mean. Soon the second half started, as puzzling as the first. Then, suddenly, about ten minutes into the period, the patterns of the game all fell into place. Like the loom, the game put itself together in my mind. I suddenly found that I knew what the players were doing, what they were trying to do, what they might do next, why the plays the announcer called good were in fact good, why the mistakes he pointed out were in fact mistakes. There was still much I didn't know, details of the game, rules, penalties. But I knew enough to ask about them, and to make some sense out of the answers.

Not long afterwards, I had another chance to think like a child. Going south from London on a train, I found myself in a compartment—a small, closed-in section seating eight passengers—with a Scandinavian couple. They were talking rapidly in their native language, of which I understood nothing. For a while I paid no attention, looking at England through the train window and thinking my own thoughts. Then, after a while, it occurred to me that this was an interesting opportunity to listen to lan-

guage as a baby listens to it. Still looking out the window,
I began to pay close attention to what they were saying. It
was very much like listening to a complicated piece of
modern music. I have discovered, after hearing many
concerts and records, that the best way to listen to strange
and unfamiliar music, to keep your attention focused
sharply on it, is to try to reproduce the music in your
mind—instant imitation. In the same way, I was trying to
reproduce in my mind, as soon as I heard them, the
sounds made by these people as they talked. I didn't get
them all, but I got many of them. Also, though I wasn't
looking for patterns—there wasn't time for that—I was
alert for them, so that when a sound or word came along
that I had heard before, it made an extra impression. It
was an interesting and absorbing exercise. By the time
forty minutes had passed, and I had reached my stop, I
had begun to feel, and almost recognize, a few of the
sounds and words in their talk. Perhaps this kind of raw
listening would be useful for students studying a foreign
language. We might have a record, or a tape, of a voice
reading a particular passage, first at rapid conversational
speed, then more slowly, finally so slowly that each word
could be heard separately. From listening to such tapes,
students might become sensitive to the relation between
the separate sounds of a language and the sound of the
flow of the whole language.

A few years later I was in Norway, visiting my
friend Mosse Jorgensen, for many years a pioneer in
alternative education. Thinking I might be interested in some of the groups she was involved in, she
took me to several meetings. Since they were business meetings, everyone spoke Norwegian. Now and
then people would pause while Mosse gave me a
quick summary of what had been said; then they
would go on with their work. It was a perfect opportunity to do again what I had done on that train—

think like a small child. As on the train, I just let the words flow in, listened to them as I might listen to music—all the more easy and pleasant to do because Norwegian is such a beautiful and musical language. And as on the train, I listened for sounds and patterns, above all those often repeated.

Some of the words and phrases, because of roots in Latin or French, soon became clear. *Skole demokratie* was obvious. *Eleve* sounded like and had to mean the same thing as the French word for "pupil." A puzzling word that came up often was *ikke*, which Mosse soon told me meant "no" or "not." Another frequent word was *barn*. Since this was a group of parents discussing their children's school, where Mosse taught, the thought came that *barn* might mean "child." The more I heard it, the more likely it seemed that this was so. When the Scottish word for child, *bairn*, popped up in my memory, I was sure it was so. At the next pause I asked Mosse if *barn* meant "child" and was as pleased as any child learning a new word to find out that it did.

As I listened to all the sounds and patterns and wondered about what they might mean, I did something else that little children do when they hear grownup talk. I asked myself, "What is happening here?" I wanted to know not just what certain words meant, but something larger and more important: "What is this meeting all about? What are these people here for? How do they feel about each other, and about Mosse and the school? How does she feel about them? Are they arguing, questioning, agreeing? Do they all like each other?" Like little children, I was trying to make as much meaning as I could, not just of the words but of the whole situation.

This must be the very first thing that tiny infants do when they hear our talk. They slowly intuit from what they see and hear that the sounds we make have something important to do with how we feel and what we do. They learn what we might call the emotional grammar of the language long before they begin to figure out its structural grammar, or later yet, the meaning of its words. This sense of the underlying content of talk, of what all this talk is *for,* what it is meant to make happen, is what infants learn first, and *must* learn first, about their language. It is the foundation on which all their later learning about that language will be built.

There are other ways to play the child game of "What's going on here?" In the window of the drugstore near our office are two TV sets, which are left on as long as the store is open. But the sound is off, or anyway can't be heard. Every now and then, as I go by, I stop for a moment or two, watch the pictures, and try to figure out what is going on. Often this is obvious—news, sports, quiz shows, commercials. At other times it is not so obvious. Who are those people on the screen, talking to each other? How do they relate to each other? Parent and child? Boss and employee? Friends? Rivals? How do they feel? What are they trying to do? In the short time I watch, I may get a hunch or two, or I may not.

Sometimes I play this game watching through my office window people down on Boylston Street, or looking through a bus window at people gathered outside at a stop. Who are they, what are they saying and doing? Of course, I never find out whether my hunches (when I get any) are right. No matter; the game is fun anyway.

People who need to have quick and certain answers to all their questions do not play such games. They tend to turn away from all questions for which they can't get such answers. But little children don't and can't do that. For most of their questions, they don't get any answers, certainly not right away. They live in perpetual uncertainty and wonder, and—unless adults are always asking them fool questions to test their knowledge—mostly thrive on it. This game without answers, this what-goes-on-here game that I play once in a while for my own amusement, is a very serious business for children. It is the game they play all the time, and the way in which they learn most about the world.

Let me sum up what I have been trying to say about the natural learning style of young children. The child is curious. He wants to make sense out of things, find out how things work, gain competence and control over himself and his environment, do what he can see other people doing. He is open, receptive, and perceptive. He does not shut himself off from the strange, confused, complicated world around him. He observes it closely and sharply, tries to take it all in. He is experimental. He does not merely observe the world around him, but tastes it, touches it, hefts it, bends it, breaks it. To find out how reality works, he works on it. He is bold. He is not afraid of making mistakes. And he is patient. He can tolerate an extraordinary amount of uncertainty, confusion, ignorance, and suspense. He does not have to have instant meaning in any new situation. He is willing and able to wait for meaning to come to him—even if it comes very slowly, which it usually does.

To this I would add something even more important. Children even as young as two want not just to learn about but *to be a part of* our adult world. They want to become skillful, careful, able to do things and make things as we do. They want to talk as we do, that is, communicate ideas and feelings, and in that sense they *do* talk—even before they know any "real" words, which they learn not so that when they have enough of them they can begin to talk, but so that they can talk even better *right now*. In the same way, when a little older, they often want to write to other people even before they know how to make letter shapes or spell words, and they learn real shapes and spellings not so that later they may begin to write but so that other people may *right now* be able to read their writing.

It is a serious mistake to say that, in order to learn, children must first be able to "delay gratification," i.e., must be willing to learn useless and meaningless things on the faint chance that later they may be able to make use of some of them. It is their desire and determination to do real things, not in the future but right now, that gives children the curiosity, energy, determination, and patience to learn all they learn.

Children also do much of their learning in great bursts of passion and enthusiasm. Except for those physical skills which can't be learned any other way, children rarely learn on the slow, steady schedules that schools make for them. They are more likely to be insatiably curious for a while about some particular interest, and to read, write, talk, and ask questions about it for hours a day and for days on end. Then suddenly they may drop that interest and turn to something completely different, or even for a while seem to have no interests at all. This usually means that for the time being they have all the information on that subject that they can digest, and need to explore the world in a different way, or perhaps simply get a firmer grip on what they already know.

In talking, reading, writing, and many other things they do, children are perfectly able, if not hurried or made ashamed or fearful, to notice and correct most of their own mistakes. At first they tend to see these mistakes not as things done wrongly or badly but only as things done differently. Like my six-year-old friend who right now writes her letters forwards but her numerals backwards, they may think that these differences don't make any difference—if you *know* that the sign 3 stands for "three," what difference does it make which way it faces? But just as she has already taught herself to write her letters our way, she will soon decide that she wants to make her numbers our way as well—and then, without fuss or uproar, she will do it.

Children's need to make sense of the world and to be skillful in it is as deep and strong as their need for food or rest or sleep. At times it may be even stronger. Millicent Shinn wrote that her niece Ruth, even when a tiny baby and "fretting with hunger," would often stop eating and ask to be held up so that she could see something that interested her. And we know how hard it is to get infants, even babies, no matter how tired, to go to sleep if they sense that there is anything interesting going on around them.

School is not a place that gives much time, or opportunity, or reward, for this kind of thinking and learning. Can we make it so? I think we can, and must. In this book I have tried to suggest, very briefly, how we might do it. To discuss this in any detail would take a book in itself.

In the next few years a number of such books were written, including George Dennison's *The Lives of Children*, James Herndon's *The Way It Spozed to Be* and *How to Survive in Your Native Land*, Herbert Kohl's *Thirty-six Children*, *Reading How To*, and others, Daniel Fader's *Hooked on Books* and *The Naked Children*, Joseph Featherstone's *Schools Where Children Learn* (mostly about British schools), Charles Silberman's *Crisis in the Classroom*, and several by myself. Such changes in schools as they may have helped to bring about did not spread very far or last very long. With respect to what I have said in this book about the learning of children, the schools are with few exceptions worse than they were when I wrote it.

What is essential is to realize that children learn independently, not in bunches; that they learn out of interest and curiosity, not to please or appease the adults in power; and that they ought to be in control of their own learning, deciding for themselves what they want to learn and how they want to learn it. To such ideas, people react in many ways, but two reactions appear so regularly that they seem worth discussing.

The first is often expressed like this: "Aren't you asking children to discover and re-create, all by themselves, the whole history of the human race?" It would be easy to dismiss the question as silly, except that so many sensible and serious people ask it. What trips them up is this word "discover." They act as if it meant "invent," that is, discover for the first time. But this is not what I mean, or any educators mean, when they talk about the importance of letting children discover things for themselves. We do not ask or expect a child to invent the wheel starting from scratch. He doesn't have to. The wheel has been invented. It is out there, in front of him. All I am saying is that a child does not need to be *told* what wheels are and what they are for, in order to know. He can figure it out for himself, in his own way, in his own good time. In the same way, he does not have to invent the electric light bulb, the airplane, the internal combustion engine—or law, government, art, or music. They, too, have been invented, and are out there. The whole culture is out there. What I urge is that a child be free to explore and make sense of that culture in his own way. This is as much discovery as I ask of him, a discovery that he is well able to make.

The second reaction is often expressed like this: "Aren't there certain things that everyone ought to know, and isn't it our job, therefore, to make sure that children know them?" This argument can be attacked on many fronts. With the possible exception of knowing how to read, which in any case is a skill, it cannot be proved that any piece of knowledge is essential for everyone. Useful and convenient, perhaps; essential, no. Moreover, the people who feel that certain knowledge is essential do not agree among themselves on what that knowledge is. The historians would vote for history; the linguists, for language; the mathematicians, for math; and so on. In the words of Jimmy Durante, "Everybody wants to get into the act." Moreover, the knowledge changes, becomes useless, out of date, or downright false. Believers in essential knowledge decreed that when I was in school I should study physics and chemistry. In physics we used a reputable and then up-to-date college text that announced on page 1 that "matter was not created nor destroyed." Of my chemistry, I remember only two or three formulas and a concept called "valence." I mentioned valence to a chemist the other day and he laughed. When I asked what was so funny, he said, "Nobody ever talks about valence anymore; it's an outmoded concept." And the rate of discovery being what it is, the likelihood that what children learn today will be out of date in twenty years is much *greater* than it was when I was a student.

My real reason, however, for believing that the learner, young or old, is the best judge of what he should learn next, is very different. I would be against trying to cram knowledge into the heads of children even if we could agree on what knowledge to cram and could be sure that it would not go out of date, even if we could be sure that, once crammed in, it would stay in. Even then, I would trust the child to direct his own learning. For it seems to me a fact that, in our struggle to make sense out of life, the things we most need to learn are the things we most want to learn. To put this another way, curiosity is hardly ever idle. What we want to know, we want to know for a reason. The reason is that there is a hole, a gap, an empty space in our understanding of things, our mental model of the world. We feel that gap like a hole in a tooth and want to fill it up. It makes us ask How? When? Why? While the gap is there, we are in tension, in suspense. Listen to the anxiety in a person's voice when he says, "This doesn't make sense!" When the gap in our understanding is filled, we feel pleasure, satisfaction, relief. Things make sense again—or at any rate, they make more sense than they did.

When we learn this way, for these reasons, we learn both rapidly and permanently. The person who really needs to know something does not need to be told many times, drilled, tested. Once is enough. The new piece of knowledge fits into the gap ready for it, like a missing piece in a jigsaw puzzle. Once in place, it is held in, it can't fall out. We don't forget the things that make the world a more reasonable or interesting place for us, that make our mental model more complete and accurate. Now, if it were possible for us to look into the minds of children and see what gaps in their mental models most needed filling, a good case could be made for giving them the information needed to fill them. But this is not possible. We cannot find out what children's mental models are like, where they are distorted, where incomplete. We cannot make direct contact with a child's understanding of the world. Why not? First, because to a very considerable extent he is unaware of much of his own understanding. Secondly, because he hasn't the skill to put his understanding into words, least of all words that he could be sure would mean to us what they meant to him. Thirdly, because we haven't time. Words are not only a clumsy and ambiguous means of communication, they are extraordinarily slow. To describe only a very small part of his understanding of the world, a man will write a book that takes us days to read.

I think of some good friends of mine. We know each other well, know each other's interests, speak each other's language. We may spend an entire evening talking, each of us intent on gaining a better understanding of the other's thought. At the end of the evening, with luck, we may each have a very slightly better idea about what the others think on a very particular subject. On the other hand, very often an evening of talk, however pleasant and interesting, may only lead us to realize how little we understand each other, how great are the gulfs and mysteries between us.

The human mind is a mystery. To a very large extent it will probably always be so. We will never get very far in education until we realize this and give up the delusion that we can know, measure, and control what goes on in children's minds. To know one's own mind is difficult enough. I am, to quite a high degree, an introspective person. For a long time I have been interested in my own thoughts, feelings, and motives, eager to know as much as I can of the truth about myself. After many years, I think that at most I may know something about a very small part of what goes on in my own head. How preposterous to imagine that I can know what goes on in someone else's.

In my mind's ear I can hear the anxious voices of a hundred teachers asking me, "How can you tell, how can you be sure what the children are learning, or even that they are learning anything?" The answer is simple. We can't tell. We can't be sure. What I am trying to say about education rests on a belief that, though there is much evidence to support it, I cannot prove, and that may never be proved. Call it a faith. This faith is that man is by nature a learning animal. Birds fly, fish swim; man thinks and learns. Therefore, we do not need to "motivate" children into learning, by wheedling, bribing, or bullying. We do not need to keep picking away at their minds to make sure they are learning. What we need to do, and all we need to do, is bring as much of the world as we can into the school and the classroom; give children as much help and guidance as they need and ask for; listen respectfully when they feel like talking; and then get out of the way. We can trust them to do the rest.

□LEARNING & LOVE

In the Foreword to the first edition of this book I said that if we looked carefully enough at young children (which does not mean hooking them up to exotic machinery) we might learn something important about them. In the fifteen years since then we have done a lot of both looking and learning. I myself have seen a great many small children in private and public places, have spent much time with many of them, and have come to know some of them well. Many hundreds of parents have written us at *Growing Without Schooling*, often more than once and at great length, telling about the thinking and learning of their babies and small children. What have I learned from all this? That children love learning and are extremely good at it. On this matter I have no more doubts.

This book did not change, as I had hoped it might, the way schools deal with children. I said, trust them to learn. The schools would not trust them, and even if they had wanted to, the great majority of the public would not have let them. Their reasons boil down to these: (1) Children are no good; they won't learn unless we make them. (2) The world is no good; children must be broken to it. (3) I had to put up with it; why shouldn't they? To people who think this way, I don't know what to say. Telling them about the real learning of real children only makes them cling to their theories about the badness and stupidity of children more stubbornly and angrily than ever. Why do they do this? Because it gives them a license to act like tyrants and to feel like saints. "Do what I tell you!" roars the tyrant. "It's for your own good, and one day you'll be grateful," says the saint. Few people, feeling themselves powerless in a world turned upside down, can or even wish to resist the temptation to play this benevolent despot.

On the other hand, the book does seem to have encouraged some people, parents and teachers, to take children more seriously, to observe them more closely, to think more carefully about the meaning of what they do, and to like, trust, respect, and enjoy them more. It may also have convinced some adults that the things they had already learned about children from their own experience with them were really true—that they were smart, eager to learn, eager to play a useful part in our world.

But I fear that at the same time the book may have done some harm. All over the United States and in many other countries people are designing techniques and organizing programs for the deliberate training of intelligence. The government of Venezuela has even established a ministry for that purpose, and I have been told that the man in charge felt that I had had some influence on his thinking. I am certainly sorry to hear that. This is not at all what I meant to happen.

Some will say, "But if we can make children smarter, why not do it?" Why not indeed? But almost all bad ideas start life as good ones, and I fear it will not be long before this seemingly good idea will turn into one of the worst, and ministries for the development of intelligence will be doing even more harm than ministries of education. We have already been trained to believe that knowledge, skill, and wisdom are the products of schooling, and that people should therefore be graded and ranked by the amount of schooling they have been able to consume. Soon we will be told that intelligence is the product of intelligence training and that people should be graded and ranked by how much of that process—like all manufactured processes, necessarily scarce and expensive—they have been able to buy for themselves. Indeed, *compulsory* intelligence training—by certified trainers, of course—may be only a step or two down the line.

Of course these people mean well ("Sir, the road to Hell is *paved* with good intentions!"—Samuel Johnson). One busy promoter in this field (Dr. Mary Meeker) writes:

Multi-stimulation must occur before school entry and more must be continued during the years spent in school.... Further development of human brain functions is a spiralling phenomenon and schools must address the teaching of figural, symbolic, and semantic intelligence equally in the curriculum.... We must proceed from Cognition to Memory to Evaluation to Divergent Thinking.... We first need to identify and nurture the general functions of the brain's thought processes.

Oh! Is that all?

Three things come to mind. First, the Chicago Board of Education's two hundred and eighty-three separate skills of reading, mentioned earlier. Are we soon to see three hundred separate skills of thinking? Second, Ivan Illich's remark about the modern world's belief in the infinite powers of process to create value. Finally, something that James Agee wrote in the 1930s in *Let Us Now Praise Famous Men*. Speaking of rural Alabama schools, and some of the

"advanced" ideas invented at various schools of education, that semiliterate rural schoolteachers were
then struggling to put into practice on the children,
he said that "if the guiding hand is ill qualified, an
instrument is murderous in proportion to its sharp-
ness." Are we going to give difficult tasks to the very
people in our schools who have so utterly failed to
accomplish simple ones?

Dr. Meeker goes on:

> When an infant ... does not receive a response to
> his only means of communication, a cry, the whole
> sensori-motor integration of vision, hearing, bal-
> ance, motor and tactile impulses is not developed
> in the vestibular and reticular formations in the
> brain—all of which are necessary foundations for
> developing the many pathways in the brain which
> connect the hemispheres and modes for mediating
> the external environment.

In Laing's words once more, this is the language of
hell, of intellect without heart. Is this then the reason for responding to a baby's cry, that it will help
develop the vestibular and reticular formations in
the brain? Can anyone be simpleminded enough to.
suppose that parents who will not respond to their
infants out of love and sympathy will be persuaded
to respond for this reason—*or that if they do, the effect on the infants will be the same?* Is a baby nothing more than a collection of neural pathways for us
to stimulate?

It is time to return once more to Millicent Shinn
and the final paragraph of her beautiful book, *The
Biography of a Baby,* which she ended with her
niece Ruth's first birthday and these words:

And so the story of the swift, beautiful year is ended, and our wee, soft, helpless baby had become this darling thing, beginning to toddle, beginning to talk, full of a wide-awake baby intelligence, and rejoicing in her mind and body; communicating with us in a vivid and sufficient dialect, and overflowing with the sweet selfishness of baby coaxings and baby gratitude. And at a year old, there is no shadow on the charm from the perception that its end is near. By the second birthday we say, "Ah, we shall be losing our baby soon!" But on the first, we are eager, as the little one herself is, to push on to new unfoldings; it is the high springtime of babyhood—perfect, satisfying, beautiful.

It is in this spirit and this alone that we can truly learn about children or help them to learn.

In *The New York Times* (April 18, 1981), Ben Barker, married five years and separated for five, wrote a beautiful short piece about his three-months-a-year life with his two small children. In it he quotes a note that his daughter wrote to him one morning before he woke up:

When are you going to get up. There is no milk and I am HUNGRY.

SO DO NOT STARVE ME, ME, ME, ME, ME . . . .
PLEASE, PLEASE, PLEASEPLEASE
   DO NOT STARVE ME.

      WIL YOU STARVE ME?

What is your ans.

   Sign Here on The Dots . . . .

      Love Cloud.

For days after I read it, that note haunted me, and a small voice kept saying in my ear, "So do not starve me, me, me. Will you starve me?" It made me want to both laugh and cry, made me want somehow to set those words to music, made me want to hug that small person and say "No, no, no, we will never, *never* starve you."

That note says so much about children. There is so much in it of love and need, of drama mixed with playfulness, of fantasy mixed with reality (Sign here on the dots). It reminds us by what odd paths, when we are young, we approach the world of the grown-ups. At one time in my childhood I too liked to write long strings of dots just so that I could sign my name on them. It looked so *official.* Magic in those dots!

What is lovely about children is that they can make such a production, such a big deal, out of everything, or nothing. From my office I see many families walking down Boylston Street with their little children. The adults plod along, the children twirl, leap, skip, run now to this side and now to that, look for things to step or jump over or walk along or around, climb on anything that can be climbed.

I never want to be where I cannot see it. All that energy and foolishness, all that curiosity, questions, talk, all those fierce passions, inconsolable sorrows, immoderate joys, seem to many a nuisance to be endured, if not a disease to be cured. To me they are a national asset, a treasure beyond price, more necessary to our health and our very survival than any oil or uranium or—name what you will.

One day in the Public Garden I see, on a small patch of grass under some trees, a father and a two-year-old girl. The father is lying down; the little girl runs everywhere. What joy to run! Suddenly she stops, looks intently at the ground, bends down, picks something up. A twig! A pebble! She stands up, runs again, sees a pigeon, chases it, suddenly stops and looks up into the sunlit trees, seeing what?—perhaps a squirrel, perhaps a bird, perhaps just the shape and colors of the leaves in the sun. Then she bends down, finds something else, picks it up, examines it. A leaf! Another miracle.

Gears, twigs, leaves, little children love the world. That is why they are so good at learning about it. For it is love, not tricks and techniques of thought, that lies at the heart of all true learning. Can we bring ourselves to let children learn and grow through that love?

"So do not starve me.
Wil you starve me?"

What is our answer?

ABOUT THE AUTHOR

John Holt (1923–1985), writer and leading figure in educational reform, wrote ten books, including *How Children Fail*, *How Children Learn*, *Never Too Late*, and *Learning All the Time*. His work has been translated into fourteen languages. *How Children Learn*, and its companion volume, *How Children Fail*, have together sold over two million copies in their many editions and influenced a generation of teachers and parents. His letters have recently been collected and published under the title, *A Life Worth Living*. John Holt's deep insights into the child's mind have become increasingly appreciated as we try to make both schools and homes better places for children to learn.

John Holt's work is being continued by Holt Associates, 2269 Massachusetts Avenue, Cambridge, MA 02140.

1187224R0

Printed in Great Britain by
Amazon.co.uk, Ltd.,
Marston Gate.